703

C215013126

CW00666057

= 6 APR 2011		
1 9 MAY 2011		
2 2 AUG 2011		
2 4 APR 2012		
2 8 NOV 2012		
2 4 JUL 2014		
= 6 AUG 2014		

~~24~~ Hour Renewal ~~Service~~

Phone ~~0845 330 4435~~

City Library
Department of Leisure and Community Services

The last date entered is the date by which
the book must be returned. You can renew
books by phoning or visiting the Library.

Nottingham
City Council

© The contributors

British Library Cataloguing in Publication Data
A catalogue record for this book is available from the British Library

ISBN 13: 978-1-906784-11-9

Published with the financial support of the Welsh Books Council.

Cover design: Annika Lundqvist
Cover image: Geoff Charles. By permission of Llyfrgell Genedlaethol
Cymru / The National Library of Wales

Printed and bound in Great Britain by
CPI Antony Rowe, Chippenham and Eastbourne

THE EDITORS

Leigh Verrill-Rhys was a lecturer in creative writing at San Francisco State University before moving to Wales. As a founding member of Honno, she served on the committee for many years before taking a break. She returned to the committee in 2007. Leigh was the editor of *On My Life* (Honno, 1989) which received second prize in the 1990 Raymond Williams Community Publishing Award and *Iancs, Conshis a Spam: Atgofion Menywod o'r Ail Ryfel Byd* (Honno, 2002) and the Welsh language counterpart to *Parachutes and Petticoats: Welsh women writing on the Second World War* (first edition, Honno, 1992; second edition, Honno, 2010). She has contributed widely to anthologies and essays, writing in Welsh and English. In 1987, she established a book distribution business which brought Welsh small press publications to the attention of booksellers in Canada, Australia, New Zealand and the US, as well as to bookshops and readers in France, Spain and Portugal, among other European countries. After many years as a marketing consultant, Leigh returned to her writing ambitions and completed her first novel in 2008. Her Welsh roots are in Pennsylvania where her grandmother, Rhobie Hewitt, was born to parents of Welsh descent. Leigh's dedication to and fascination for the Welsh language, culture and history find their expression in her writings about her adopted home. She is married to a Welsh musician and their three sons are now young men.

Deirdre Beddoe was born in Barry and educated at Barry County Grammar School for Girls and at UCW Aberystwyth, where she obtained a PhD in History. She is Emeritus Professor of Women's History at the University of Glamorgan, Pontypridd, President of Archif Menywod Cymru/ Women's Archive of Wales and received the Western Mail Val Feld Award for her services to the history of women in Wales.

She is committed to rescuing the lost history of women in Wales and to making their story available to a wide audience. She has researched and written extensively on both British and Welsh women's history and her books include *Welsh Convict Women* (Stewart Williams, 1979), the story of women who were transported from Wales to the Australian penal colonies; *Discovering Women's History: A Practical Guide* (first editon, Pandora, 1983; second edition, Pandora, 1993; third edition, Longman, 1998); *Back to Home and Duty: Women in Britain Between the Wars* (Pandora, 1989) and *Out of the Shadows: A History of Women in Twentieth-Century Wales* (University of Wales Press, 2000). She is editor of *Changing Times: Welsh Women Writing on the 1950s and 1960s* (first edition, Honno, 2003; second edition, Honno, 2010). She also works on television and radio. She is a frequent broadcaster and gives talks and lectures widely on her work.

CONTENTS

CHAPTER 3: **WAR WORK**

CHAPTER 4: **THE WOMEN'S AUXILIARY SERVICES**

CHAPTER 8: **HORRORS OF WAR**

CHAPTER 9: **MEDICAL WORK**

ACKNOWLEDGEMENTS

We would like to thank Ursula Masson, Fay Swain, Barbara Roberts and Lisa Dwerryhouse for their help, encouragement and support throughout the process of collecting and editing *Parachutes and Petticoats*. Most especially, we would like to thank all the women on Honno's executive committee for their enthusiasm, energy and unfailing support for this book: Rosanne Reeves, Luned Meredith, Liz Powell, Ronee, Susan Jenkins, Lis Woolley, Nest Lloyd, Althea Osmond, Eurwen Booth, Aeres Twigg. Liz Powell's help was greatly appreciated.

Also, for this new edition, we would particularly like to thank Honno Editor, Caroline Oakley, Lesley Rice and Helena Earnshaw, as well as members of Honno's current executive committee for their continuing commitment to this book.

INTRODUCTION

As editors, we wish to thank Honno for publishing this new edition of *Parachutes and Petticoats: Welsh women writing on the Second World War* thereby enabling a new generation of readers to enjoy this historically important and deeply moving anthology of wartime recollections written by women from all parts of Wales. The fact that we originally compiled this anthology in the early 1990s is its great strength: many of the women whose memoirs appear here are no longer with us and it may never again be possible to collect such a wide-ranging assortment of women's wartime memories, written by the women themselves. *Parachutes and Petticoats* is a unique historical, social and personal record of the experiences of women whose stories would otherwise have been lost.

This collection of Welsh women's experiences in the Second World War owes its origins to a number of book-length manuscripts submitted to Honno in the late 1980s and early 1990s. Whilst we immediately recognized the value of all of these to Welsh women's history, we could not undertake to publish them as individual books. Yet we were anxious to find a way of preserving these accounts and of making them widely available to readers. In the light of Honno's previous success in publishing anthologies, we decided to ask the authors to allow us to take extracts from their work. Among the writers who initiated Honno's commitment to this book were Eileen Jones, Beryl Mills, Irene Thomas, Johanna Wilkins, Mary Morris, G.M.M. McCarter, Stella Morgan and Emily Bond. We decided also to increase the range of contributors and to extend an open invitation to all Welsh women to submit shorter manuscripts. The result is *Parachutes and Petticoats: Welsh women writing on the Second World War*.

In gardens throughout Wales, the remains of Anderson shelters, corrugated tin huts, are buried beneath the lawn or the accumulated rubble of decades of neglect. After reading and working with these essays, poems and letters, it is not possible to look at these structures without thinking of the terror a night in one of them meant to so many women and their families. This collection will dispel many myths. Women did not merely wave goodbye to departing servicemen at the garden gate and then idly await their heroes' return. Many were in the Home Front lines, facing the same violence and destruction as their menfolk were on foreign soil. Women joined His Majesty's services too and others volunteered or were conscripted into the workforce to perform dangerous and arduous jobs. As posters and advertisements declared at the time, this was a woman's war.

Parachutes and Petticoats is a tribute to the courage and endurance of the women of Wales. There are but few war memorials to the women who lost their lives or sacrificed their loved ones in the fight against tyranny and fascism. It is easy for many of us to forget just what these women did: young people may simply never have been told. There is another purpose in publishing this collection. Over and over again, the contributors express the view that war is so appalling, so destructive, so crushing to the human spirit, that it must never be allowed to happen again. We whole heartedly endorse their plea.

The compilation of the first edition was well timed. Many of the contributors were already in their seventies and some were much older. They were asked to think back and to recall their personal experiences of over half a century ago. They travelled back into the past and revisited the scenes of their youth. Many told us that in doing so, they relived those years. For some, it was a painful and harrowing experience; for others it revived joyful memories of loved ones, old haunts and the camaraderie of war. But whether we evoked sad or happy memories, one thing is certain – what we have here, in this volume, is the authentic voice of Welsh women telling us exactly what life was like for them in the turbulent years of the Second World War.

In order to attract a wide range of responses, we appealed in the press and on radio for further contributions to this book from Welsh women, i.e., women who were born in Wales, women who lived in Wales, and women who had spent the war years in Wales. We asked for only *written* accounts – for women to write their own stories and to tell it as it was. We realized that by insisting on written contributions that we would be *de facto* omitting many women – those unaccustomed to writing, those whose educational background made them nervous of committing their thoughts to paper and those who lacked the confidence to submit a written account to a publisher. Nevertheless, since Honno is committed to encouraging and promoting women's *writing*, we held to our decision. We wanted women to write their own accounts so that they themselves could make their own selection of what to include. Oral history is a splendid tool for recovering the voice of the past but the answers it elicits are only as good as the questions the interviewer poses. We wanted to give women a free rein, and with only the minimum of editorial interference, to reproduce their own words here. We were, however, offered and chose to accept the typescript of Sally Davies's oral history, submitted on her behalf by Barbara Roberts.

At first we had only one concern. Would women respond? Would we receive enough accounts to justify a book and would these contributions cover the range of women's wartime experiences? We need not have worried.

The response to our appeal was overwhelming. Our letters to the Welsh press and our broadcasts on Radio Wales netted us well over one hundred enquiries and nearly as many contributions. The hardest task for the editors was selecting which to publish. There were many fascinating and eminently readable accounts which we were unable to include. But nobody was left out. The names of all those who submitted pieces which were not selected for publication are listed at the end of the book. Every single account sent to us, whether published here or not, has been deposited in the collections of the National Library of Wales, Aberystwyth, and the Imperial War Museum in London. The contributors have created a valuable archive.

Parachutes and Petticoats reflects the wide variety of literary experience of its contributors. For many of the women writing here this was the first 'essay' they had written since leaving school. Others are writers of international repute, literary prizewinners, academics or keen aspiring authors. We were happy to provide a platform for so many women to appear in print, especially those for whom this was their literary début.

The Second World War began on 1 September 1939 when Germany invaded Poland. British governments throughout the 1930s had pursued a policy of appeasement towards the fascist dictators, Hitler and Mussolini. This meant protesting and then concurring with each new territorial acquisition by Germany or Italy. In 1938 appeasement reached a climax when Prime Minister Neville Chamberlain returned from Munich, waving a piece of paper and declaring 'Peace in Our Time'. But it was a phoney peace and, whilst public opinion generally expressed relief that war had been averted this time, Britain used the period following Munich to prepare for war. In March 1939, Hitler took over Czechoslovakia. On 1 September, German troops marched into Poland. On 3 September, Britain and France declared war on Germany. Many of the writers in this book recall sitting around the wireless and listening at 11 a.m. to Chamberlain's dreaded announcement, 'I have to inform you, therefore, that we are now at war with Germany.'

The people steeled themselves for the horrors of total war. Gas masks had been issued; sandbags filled; air raids screamed out only minutes after Chamberlain had stopped speaking; children gathered at railway stations to be evacuated from London and other large English cities. But it was that strangest of phenomena – the Phoney War. The expected aerial bombardment did not materialize and the evacuees began drifting home. An expeditionary force was sent to France but was beaten into a hasty retreat from Dunkirk in May 1940. Barbara Buchanan, in 'Turning Glass into Diamonds,' tells of her job with the Army Records and Pay Office, where, wearing rubber gloves and a mask, she sifted through the blood-sodden pay books, diaries and snapshots belonging to British soldiers killed at Dunkirk. Now the war began in earnest and the threat of invasion was very real. In 1940, France fell and Germany prepared to invade Britain. The Royal Air Force in the summer of 1940 repelled the German Luftwaffe in the Battle of Britain. In the next five years the conflict became truly worldwide. Not only was there war in Europe and Russia but on 7 December 1941, the Japanese attacked the US fleet in Pearl Harbor, destroying much of it. There were theatres of war in Africa and in the East: Singapore and Burma fell to the Japanese. But, by 1943, the tide was turning. The Allies were victorious in North Africa and they began the invasion of Italy. In June 1944 the British and Americans landed in Normandy and in 1945, the Allies carried the offensive across the Rhine into Germany. Germany surrendered on 8 May 1945, Victory Europe or VE Day. The war in the East continued and it was feared that it might drag on with massive loss of Allied lives. On 6 August 1945, the first atomic bomb was dropped on Hiroshima: on 9 August, the second fell on Nagasaki. Japan surrendered and the Second World War officially ended.

Welsh women served with His Majesty's forces worldwide. Lisbeth David served in Sri Lanka (Ceylon) and Ruth Newmarch in Sri Lanka, Singapore and Hong Kong. Muriel Graham crossed the Atlantic in the *Queen Elizabeth*, dodging U-boat packs, thirty-six times. Emily Bond nursed patients in Egypt and France: she was then posted to the concentration camp at Belsen. Rona Price Davies ran a hospital in Bombay and Hilda M. Howells was in Tunisia in the crucial months of the North African campaign. Mary Morris landed on the Normandy beaches with the Second Front in June 1944 and nursed in the field hospitals behind the advancing lines.

The Second World War lasted six years. There was unrestrained rejoicing in May 1945 when the war in Europe was won. But there was still the war against Japan and no one knew how long it would take to defeat the enemy in that distant theatre of operations. We must not be surprised when we read several contributors to this book writing, 'and then, thank goodness, they dropped the atom bomb.' It is a strange sentiment to modern ears, knowing as we now do, the full horror of Hiroshima and Nagasaki. We have to understand their point of view and share their relief when, after six dreadful years, the Second World War ended. Weighed up against the potential Allied death toll and the possibility of the war against Japan continuing for years, contemporaries rejoiced that the atom bomb had ended the war. We now see what happened not as an end but as a beginning: we see it as the beginning of a horrific nuclear age, in which the shadow of holocaust has hung over us all. Although we wrote with hope in the previous edition of this book that, with moves towards world disarmament, the dark shadow of nuclear holocaust seemed to be lifting, the proliferation of weapons of mass destruction continues to threaten us.

The war had a profound impact on life in Wales. It finally jerked the country out of the economic depression which had paralysed its heavy industry and demoralized its workforce since the late 1920s. Young men were called up from every corner of urban and rural Wales to serve in the armed forces. Those left at home waited anxiously for news of fathers, sons, husbands and brothers: some never returned. Yet the effects of the war on Wales were far from even. The south Wales ports, notably Swansea and Cardiff, suffered devastating aerial bombardments particularly in 1941. In the countryside, life kept to a more even tenure. Even the shortages, suffered by town and city dwellers, were scarcely known there. Fresh vegetables, bacon, butter, eggs and cream continued to make life tolerable. As Olwen Hughes Jones, an engineering worker in Liverpool, who used to bring tea, butter and home-cured bacon back to her landlady after her visits home, wrote, 'there were never shortages on Anglesey'. There was one startling intrusion into country life. It came in the form of evacuees from the cities. Young girls and boys, with strange accents and speaking an alien language, were uprooted from their homes and relocated in Welsh country towns and villages. It was a culture shock for both sides.

But what about the Welsh women? How did the war affect their lives? In the years between the two World Wars, 1919–39, women in Britain were left in no doubt where they belonged. A woman's place is in the home. This notion, this domestic ideology, was brought into play once again with amazing rapidity as soon as the First World War ended. It had merely been put on ice for the duration of that first conflict. Women who had contributed so handsomely to the war effort of 1914–18 and had been feted in the press as 'Our Gallant Girls' and 'Our Amazons' were persuaded and coerced back into the home to resume their 'natural' roles as wives, mothers, daughters, sisters: those who wilfully persisted in seeking employment were widely condemned as 'flappers', 'hussies' and 'women who stole men's jobs'. One might say that women in Britain were told as loudly and clearly as women in Nazi Germany that their place was in the home. In Wales, there were very few job opportunities for women in any case. Young girls often had little choice but to leave home and take up positions as domestic servants in London or the Home Counties. By sending money home to depressed Wales, they were frequently the only family member contributing to its financial support. Once they returned to Wales and married, there really was no question of them taking up paid employment. In these years, Welsh women were amongst the least economically active in the whole of Britain. The Second World War was to change all that.

Women under forty years of age were categorized as 'mobile' or 'immobile': the latter included mothers of children under fourteen, those too old to work and those already in essential employment. But the government and employers were slow to avail themselves of women's labour and by early 1941, when Britain was fighting alone – without Russia or the USA – shortages of labour led to hold-ups in production. The British government took a decisive step. It mobilized women. In March 1941, all women aged nineteen to forty had to register at employment exchanges: this gave the Ministry of Labour a record of what they were all doing and enabled it to direct women into essential war work. The Essential Work Order (EWO) of the same date compelled reluctant employers to take women on and to keep them. All this meant that single women could be directed to work anywhere in Britain. By December 1941, the National Service (No 2) Act *conscripted* single women aged twenty to thirty: in practice they were sent to industry or the Auxiliary Territorial Service (ATS).

At first there was a reluctance to call on married women for war work: so sacred was the notion that a woman's place was in the home. Those without young children could already be directed to work locally but as labour shortages became more acute, many more married women were directed into work, full or part-time. The raising of the age of registration to fifty in 1944 also brought more of this group into the workforce.

By 1943, nearly eight million women in Britain were in paid work. If part-time and voluntary work are included, 90 per cent of single women and 80 per cent of married women were contributing to the war effort. In an area like Wales, where so few women had been in employment before the war, the profile of the labour force changed dramatically.

The contributors to our section on War Work show clearly the difficulties and dangers faced by women workers but they also reveal the range of skills women acquired and sometimes the fun they had in their new occupations. Dora Lemin was conscripted into industry and trained as a motor mechanic: she was lucky to be trained as many women were expected to learn on the job. In 'Give us the Tools', she recounts the initial resentment she encountered from her male colleagues and then her pleasure at being accepted by them: she even joined her workmates for cooked dinners at the Pleez-U café. Olwen Hughes Jones was called up and given the choice of industry or the ATS. Having to leave her home on rural Anglesey, she was directed to a training centre in Chester and then to an engineering factory in Liverpool. In 'At Chester Station I could have Sat Down and Cried', she writes movingly of the bewilderment and *hiraeth* of a young girl torn from her family, her home and her language. E.M. Mitchell's, 'Good Morning, Sister' is a lively account of a young woman's struggle against prejudice to take on the traditionally male job of gas tester with the Gas Board, after the call up of the man previously doing the job. With the help of the Municipal and General Workers' Union, she triumphed and was officially installed as gas tester at the full male rate for the job. Other women who wrote to us provide useful insights into attitudes towards women workers. We see women, who had trained and qualified, having to struggle to be allowed to do responsible tasks on their own: we see women earning just 80 per cent of the male rate for a job and we see the double burden on women workers – carrying out their jobs as well as their domestic duties. There was a huge demand for women in munitions production. Mair Davies worked in the stores at the colossal Bridgend Arsenal, which employed thousands of women from all over south Wales. She writes of the dangers to which women were exposed there. Ellen Duggan also worked in Bridgend: her wonderful, cheerful piece reminds us that there was time to laugh too. Edna Gorshkov's account of her work as an engineer in the Royal Ordnance Factory, Llanishen, brims with pride. She worked on a Cincinatti lathe 'as big as a house'. She was a 'bloody good engineer': she felt that, in making guns for the Navy, she had to be.

Gas masks, Anderson shelters and rationing brought the war very much into the home. Before the war, a woman's 'place' was in the home, but in wartime the word 'home' was given a broader definition. In the First World War, women had been admonished to 'keep the home fires burning' and in the Second World War their place was on the Home Front.

War affected every aspect of domestic life. Wilma Gravenor's smokescreens were a reminder to her mother 'that life was not "normal"... everything was different.' Rationing of basic food items such as meat and eggs at least ensured that everyone received the necessities and was intended to prevent an unequal distribution of food when shortages became severe. Food and clothing coupons were sold, exchanged and given as wedding gifts. Life became even more difficult with the loss of the breadwinner, the family home and the security of relationships, all of which Eva Pettifor's mother faced in the early years of the war. 'Our Little Family's War' describes the deprivation endured by three generations of women for whom the end of the war brought no relief.

Wartime shortages also created strong bonds of mutual suffering. For Joan Dickens, a lumpen mass of chocolate brought joy and 'the memory of a long-ago Christmas morning... when all the world is still'. A cookery class meant a bit of bread and jam – 'something to eat!' Nothing could be wasted. 'Manage, mend and make do' was one of the Home Front catchphrases. Old clothes were turned, cut down for children, patched, unpicked and reknitted. Welsh wool was in plentiful supply but had limited uses for garments since it was rough on the skin. Women had to be innovative – gravy browning became nylon stockings, potatoes became pastry flour. What we now call 'recyclable material' was called 'salvage' – everything from waste paper and rags to aluminium bottle tops was saved to contribute to the war effort. As short as the supply of fuel was, people were encouraged to be even more frugal in order to save fuel to build tanks. Decorative wrought iron fencing disappeared allegedly to build aeroplanes.

The 'green' lessons of the war years did not survive as well as those learned regarding children. Pregnant women received special attention during and after the war as Elaine Morgan points out in 'Lady Margaret Hall Potato Harvest', with the National Milk Scheme, orange juice and cod liver oil supplied to them as well as to new babies. Free clinical advice, free immunization and vitamin schemes all meant that the babies of the war years were healthier than their older siblings. Death from diphtheria showed a significant decline after the campaign of immunization of seven million children between 1940 and 1945. Many of these schemes were carried on after the war by successive governments.

M. Joan Morgan's life at Liverpool University was radically different from Elaine Morgan's idyllic times at Oxford. Although Joan struggled with punctures, she roamed far and wide on her bike between bombing raids. The effect of the war on her life is marked by her birthdays: on her eighteenth in 1939, she takes a walk to see friends; her nineteenth begins in an air raid; her twentieth is marked only by a gas mask inspection. For Marian Henry Jones, the war meant a leap from post-graduate research directly into the lecture hall as she was asked to take on the teaching loads of *two* male colleagues – for the price of one. After the war, it once again required two lecturers to fill her shoes – for the price of two.

Welsh women joined all three of the services. The Women's Royal Naval Service (WRNS) enjoyed a well-bred image: it did not conscript but was staffed by volunteers, from whom references were required. The Women's Auxiliary Air Force (WAAF) had a somewhat glamorous image, whereas the Auxiliary Territorial Service (ATS) was clearly the Cinderella service and dogged by the camp follower taint which had attached to the Women's Army Auxiliary Corps in the First World War. That the 'womens' army', the ATS, had such a peculiar name stems from the fact that it was set up in peacetime, in 1938, and modelled on the men's Territorial Army. Conscripted women were invariably sent to the ATS. The King astutely sent his elder daughter, the Princess Elizabeth, to serve in the ATS, thereby greatly raising its morale and its public image. The Women's Land Army, which we have chosen to include in our section on the Women's Auxiliary Services because it seems rightly to belong there, was not technically a service at all. Land Army girls were in fact employed directly by the farmers.

The contributors to the Women's Auxiliary Services section of *Parachutes and Petticoats* span the whole range of the services. Lisbeth David, an ex-Howell's School girl, trained as a wireless operator and cipher officer in the 'Wrens'. She writes affectionately of the great traditions of the Senior Service but astutely observed that one was recommended for a commission, 'at least as much because of the way one spoke as because of OLQ (Officer-like Qualities)'. In a beautiful piece, 'One Wren's War', she recounts her experiences in north Wales, Northern Ireland, Greenwich (the Navy's Holy of Holies) and Ceylon. The whole account is rendered all the more delightful by her sharp observations and her finely-honed language: 'only the willowy blondes of Mountbatten's staff', she tells us, really did a Wren's uniform justice. Muriel Graham from Barry joined the Wrens and saw the sea: she made eighteen double crossings of the Atlantic on the *Queen Elizabeth*. Pamela Barker, who had been persuaded to 'Join the Wrens and free a man for the fleet', did not get to see anything beyond the English countryside but at least her ambition was satisfied when, on her demobilization, her job was taken over by a sailor. The original idea in setting up the Women's Auxiliary Services was that women would act, as they had in the First World War, in an auxiliary capacity to the men. It was expected that they would be clerks, secretaries and canteen workers. In fact, they were often employed in highly technical tasks. Rhona Elias and Betty Howard were operators of that new-fangled and hush-hush thing, radar, in the WAAF and ATS respectively. Daphne Price performed the highly technical job of Kine Theodilite Operator, or 'Kine' for short, for which a thorough grounding in trigonometry was essential. These and other accounts also tell us what it was like to be a woman in HM's services. Eileen Gilmore's shocking account reveals a great deal about the sexual innocence of service women in those days and Barbara Buchanan's 'Turning Glass into Diamonds' shows us young, bewildered, trainees who were a long way from home. Ruth Newmarch was one of few women in 'Ack-Ack', assisting men to fire anti-aircraft guns. She was stationed on 'Doodlebug Alley' on the south coast of England, as the deadly V1's flew in. So thoroughly did she absorb army discipline, that even today she writes, 'I could still drill a squad'. Finally, Eileen Jones was called up to the Women's Land Army. In 'Down on the Farm', from her book *Teenager at War*, she shares her poignant and very funny memories of her days as a milkmaid, swineherd and rat-catcher. These accounts are a wonderful record of the courage, endurance and ingenuity of Welsh women.

Yet other Welsh women would have nothing to do with the war in any form. They were conscientious objectors. It is a measure of how much of women's past experiences are hidden from history that most people are surprised to learn even of the existence of women conscientious objectors. Women, as we know, were required to register for employment by the Register of Employment Order of March 1941 and they were conscripted into industry or the services by the National Service (No 2) Act of December 1941. These acts forced some women to confront their principles and to take a stand against what they firmly believed to be wrong, i.e., contributing in any way in furthering a war which was designed to take human life. Women who refused to be directed into industry or the services faced dire consequences. Iris Cooze, who as a Jehovah's Witness, considered herself to be a full-time worker of Christ, could not bring herself to break the commandment, 'Thou shalt not kill'. She appeared seven times before a reluctant magistrate, who finally sentenced her to a month's imprisonment in Cardiff gaol. Not only did she endure this, but, on her release, she suffered taunts of 'Conchie' and physical abuse. Hers was a brave stand in wartime Britain. Rosalind Rusbridge's experiences in Swansea are somewhat different. She presents us with a valuable account of the peace movement in Swansea, supported as it was by men and women disillusioned by the horrors of the First World War. Since she was employed as a grammar school teacher, neither registration nor conscription should have affected her. It was the emergence of the Swansea League of Loyalists, which influenced the City Council to issue a declaration of loyalty to be signed by all of its employees, which led to her suspension from her teaching post. 'A Woman Pacifist in Wartime' is a thoroughly intelligent article expressing the viewpoint of a pacifist, who was motivated by political, as well as Christian, convictions. If truth is the first casualty of war, then tolerance must surely not be far behind.

Although the heart is often wounded in wartime, love is rarely a casualty. It seems to take adversity, desire, disappointment, fear, separation and loss for its fuel, to put aside the ordinary considerations of a more settled time and leap as it will into the fray. As Kusha Petts says, love makes things 'right with the world'. But it does not always do this smoothly, sometimes meeting with parental disapproval and pronouncements that threaten the future: if Pamela F. Sanderson's mother had had her way, no more children would be born. Romantic interludes of the most innocent sort were experienced by nurses in the desert who, like Hilda Howells, received flowers from men they would never see again. Love could also mean desperate months of waiting for a loved one's return. For many, like Maureen Kouroupis, love in wartime led to early marriage and motherhood. For Stella Morgan, in the extract, 'All Leave Cancelled', from her unpublished novel *Goodbye is Not Forever*, it meant a Registry Office wedding and months of loneliness because she 'was young and very much in love and therefore in no mood to behave wisely'. Many of the other essays in *Parachutes and Petticoats* mention their loves – some like Mimi O. Hatton fell in love, waited to marry and lived on alone; some like Emily Bond, Rona Price Davies and Marian Henry Jones married but spent the war in separation; some married in haste and were widowed as quickly.

Many of the women who submitted contributions to *Parachutes and Petticoats* sent us childhood memoirs. That is not surprising given that greater numbers of 'younger' women are still around to tell their tales. It did, however, mean that the editors' task of making a selection to include in the section on childhood was extremely difficult. We have, from such a wide choice, come up with a superb selection of writings on Welsh wartime girlhood. Irene E. Thomas's 'War Child' (from her novel of the same title) tells of her 'exile' in heavily bombed Birmingham and Coventry, the traumatic event of the death of her father from a heart attack and her little family's forlorn journey home to Wales. Some things transcend war and peace. Elizabeth Wroe Jones's 'Up Penmaen' brings a sparkle to the gloom of war and Dorothy Thomas's 'Bombs and Beachcombing' moves from the horror of the Swansea Blitz to peaceful childhood days on Gower's beaches. Both Gabrielle Capus and Margaret Lloyd have written wide-ranging accounts of the whole war as seen through young girls' eyes. There are gas masks and air raids; half-time school and tinned Spam; knitting monitors and stirrup pumps; blackouts and sweet rationing; Hollywood films and American soldiers. We would be so indignant now if our children had to endure what they did. But they did and they survived.

Those children who stayed with at least one of their own parents were fortunate despite their deprivations. Evacuees and refugees, although possibly safe from bombings, were not always safe from others of life's dangers: not the least of which were unsuitable foster homes and disease. Evacuee children were sometimes treated as servants, little understood, distrusted and kept separate. Although there are many references to evacuees in this anthology, those we have chosen for this section were written by the evacuees themselves and some paint a dark picture of the treatment meted out to children separated from their parents at very early ages. In the rush to secure safe havens for children, no thought seems to have been given to who was suitable or what the needs of the child might have been. It was very much an 'Evacuee Roulette' (an extract from Beryl Mills's book, *Welsh Evacuee*) in which a vulnerable little girl could be dragged off by three unsympathetic unmarried sisters, tossed back to a hostel and passed on to a family who required a childminder. More fortunate children had the expert assistance of progressive and dedicated teachers like Mimi O. Hatton who could make the most of the 'Evacuee School'. Others faced abuse, violence and resentment. Sally Davies took in two evacuee boys in her home in Carmarthen, whilst she was able to love and provide for Morris, she had difficulty with Rodney and finally asked that he be removed from her home. 'Shadow Man' is Patricia Parris's moving fictionalized account of her own evacuee experience. Refugees as well as evacuees created lasting impressions, so much so for Mavis Machin Thomas that she spent years trying to locate three girls who arrived in her village with their leather boots and Continental ways. Danusia Trotman-Dickenson escaped with her mother from occupied Poland at the beginning of the war; they fled across Europe in a harrowing train journey and finally by fishing boat and Welsh coal steamer to England. Johanna Wilkins takes us back to Stettin, the city of her childhood, in extracts from her novel, *Going Home: Forty Years On*, where Vera (Johanna) relives the years before she and her mother (Mutti) were forced to flee before the triumphant Red Army. Johanna gives us a glimpse of the Second World War from the other side – through the eyes of a young German girl who, until Jewish friends were forced to flee from Nazi persecution, was convinced that Hitler was Germany's hope for the future. Before their flight, these friends left presents of clothing, some of which went to Vera's uncle Hermann, who soon joined the Nazi party because 'there [were] a few privileges involved...'

Johanna Wilkins's experience of bombings is echoed by the accounts of the contributors to Horrors of War, all of which are concerned with death. Menna Bassett lost her father and two uncles in a space of less than four months. The civilian casualties during the Blitz, which devastated many large cities, brought the reality of modern war into the lives of people on the Home Front in a way which had not occurred before. The war was not 'over there', it was next door, down the road and on top of everyone living anywhere near a town, landing strip or factory. For the people of Wales, the Second World War brought the massive destruction of the city centres of Swansea and Cardiff, which are graphically described by Kusha Petts in her poem, 'Figure in a Vestry' and by Violet Williams and Maud Prescott in their story, 'Cardiff Burning'. Betty Lucking lived through the bombing of Birmingham and came face to face with a German pilot who may have been responsible for her friend's death. Mary Evans, in 'Night of Terror', describes her own burial beneath her childhood home in the Rhondda and the deaths of evacuee children whose mother had brought them to safety, she thought, in a small Welsh village. Betty Howard dug people out of air raid shelters in London, lifted bodies from doorways and watched as firemen were blown up. And in Japan, Kusha Petts describes a father's horror at the loss of his little girls, '...grief...sounds the same...East and West.'

Medical personnel are used to the horrors of war, they steel themselves, harden their hearts and carry on with their work in the hospitals where war's victims are treated, comforted and laid to rest – but these veterans of suffering give us thoughtful and distressing accounts of their efforts. Welsh nurses and doctors were called to duty on every front in the global war – from the local hospital to the beaches of Normandy and coasts of North Africa to the field hospitals of the Far East. 'Finegan's Fair' is the story of Roberta Powell as a young trainee nurse in Llandough Hospital during 1942. Her daily routine in a wartime teaching hospital was 'something like being a maid-of-all-work in a convent'. She received a black eye from one of her oldest charges. Hilda M. Howells, in her own account of her tour-of-duty in Tunisia, gives us a detailed description of hospital trains in the North African desert which were used to transport casualties from the battles in Sicily and Italy in 1943. In the diary extracts included in 'A Wartime Nurse', from her book, *A Woman at War*, Mary Morris describes her experience on the Normandy beaches after the D-Day invasion and relates the stories of a few of the victims of those weeks in June and July, 1944. Her account is matter-of-fact but still full of her own reflections on what she sees. Elsie Hughes writes about escorting a young soldier to hospital from Normandy to Leeds, in her *second* war of nursing the wounded. Royal Army Medical Corps Captain, Rona

Price Davies, was stationed in the hospitals of India, giving medical aid to former prisoners of war returned from Burma as well as to the wives of Indian soldiers bringing babies into the world. In May 1945, Emily Bond celebrated with her Queen Alexandra Nursing colleagues but a major part of her work was still to come. She was transferred to the German concentration camp at Belsen and we print an extract from her book, written with Esyllt George. Here, she witnessed the Holocaust at first hand, as well as what she felt was the final death knell of Nazism. We close this book with the poem, 'Armistice', by Margaret Emlyn Jenkins.

What happened to women in Wales when the war ended? As the huge munitions factories closed and wartime production ended, many Welsh women were happy to return home and settle into domestic life after long years of separation from their husbands. Young women married their sweethearts, newly returned from the forces, and became the mothers of the new wave of post-war baby boomers. But those women who had experienced wartime work wanted more out of life than their mothers had had to settle for. Their experience of employment in wartime factories, despite the hours of travelling and long shifts, had been liberating: they had enjoyed the high wages, the camaraderie of the workplace and going out with their workmates in the evenings. They were no longer prepared to settle for the bleak and dreary existence of previous generations of Welsh mams.

While some women were happy to resume a domestic role, others wished to build on their wartime work experiences and continue working outside the home. These women came up against a wall of blind prejudice and fierce opposition to their desire to earn a living. The state (in the form of the newly elected Labour Government) once again promoted the notion that a woman's place was in the home. This was enshrined in the tenets of the new Welfare State: the benefits system, for example, shows clearly that women were seen as dependent on men. Those who wielded power in Wales – an exclusively male group of politicians, trade union leaders and a strongly unionized male workforce – sought a return to the pre-war social order with a male breadwinner and dependent stay-at-home wife. Politicians and public figures railed against working women, accusing them of destroying the very fabric of Welsh society and local newspapers were full of letters demanding that men should be given priority over women in the labour market. These forces of patriarchy made life hard for women but there were other forces at work, which pulled in the opposite direction and would in the long run prevail. Indeed, the most powerful agents of long-term change were economic and social.

Economists and the government were agreed that the post-war Welsh economy needed to diversify and not just rely on heavy industry. The solution was to attract new manufacturing industries. Wales had two great advantages here – the availability of many large empty wartime factories, depots and warehouses, and even more significantly, a large reservoir of female labour, including many trained factory workers. In fact, in wartime Wales, factory work was seen primarily as women's work and disparaged by men as not 'proper' work. Across Wales, former munitions works were turned into trading estates. By the early 1950s, almost a third of Welsh women workers were engaged in manufacturing everything from clothing, textiles and footwear to washing machines, toys, lipsticks and zips. Women, many of them married and part-time workers, went out to work for the money but being in the workplace brought a new dimension, which many of them craved, to their lives. However, women's work was valued at far less than men's and rewarded with wage packets of just over half the male rate in the late 1940s. The outlook improved too for women in the professions and administrative jobs. Marriage bars, i.e., the dismissal of women in the professions from their posts as soon as they married, were seen as outdated and were widely abandoned although in south Wales it was very difficult for a married woman to secure a teaching post, despite the fact that the 1944 Education Act had abolished the marriage bar in the teaching profession. A whole range of administrative and secretarial positions opened up for women in government departments and the new National Health Service quickly became a huge employer of women. In short, the immediate post-war period was to set the broad pattern of female employment in Wales for much of the rest of the twentieth century.

Six years of war had a profound effect on the lives of Welsh women. Women bore the brunt of life on the Home Front: they worked in the factories; served in the forces, the police and the fire service; they tended the wounded and stared the horrors of war in the face. The war gave them a new confidence and, if circumstances prevented them ever again displaying that new-found confidence in the public sphere of work, then that new sense of self-worth operated in the private sphere of the home. Welsh women of the war generation transmitted their confidence and their ambition to their daughters. It is no accident that they were the mothers of a new wave of Welsh feminists.

We dedicate this book to our mothers – to our mams.

Leigh Verrill-Rhys
Deirdre Beddoe July 2009

Suggestions for further reading.
For a Welsh language anthology of women at war see Leigh Verrill-Rhys, (ed.), *Iancs, Conshis a Spam: Atgofion Menywod o'r Ail Ryfel Byd* (Honno, 2002). Deirdre Beddoe, *Out of the Shadows: A History of Women in Twentieth-Century Wales* (University of Wales Press, 2000) examines the impact of the war on women's lives and Mari Williams provides a detailed study of women munitions workers in *A Forgotten Army: Female Munitions Workers in South Wales*, 1939–1945 (University of Wales Press, 2002). See also Deirdre Beddoe, (ed.), *Changing Times: Welsh Women Writing on the 1950s and 1960s* (Honno, 2003).

CHAPTER 1

CHILDHOOD

Air raids, night bombings, the loss of loved ones, food shortages and half-time school disrupted the normal life of Welsh girls and boys in the war years. And yet the everyday preoccupations and concerns of childhood remained – fitting in at school, playing with friends, passing the scholarship, feeling securely loved by one's parents, summer holidays – and learning to tap dance...

War Child

~

Irene E. Thomas

I was regarded as an alien by the other children, partly because of my Welsh accent which was unacceptable to them and partly because I was unable to tap dance, a vital ability, if one was to be included in their games. It seemed to me that all the girls went to lessons and they practised steps and turned cartwheels in the yard while I looked on. I begged my mother to let me have lessons but I knew the answer would be, 'We can't afford it,' before I asked.

However, I did find favour in one direction.

'You're from Wales,' said Mrs Brown one afternoon in the hall, where we had been doing some gymnastic exercises.

'Get up there on the stage, and sing.' She assumed that all Welsh people had singing voices and because I was able to produce a reasonable soprano, her assumption was reinforced. I only knew two songs, 'Rose of Trallee' and 'There'll always be an England' and these I churned out frequently, while the other children joined in the choruses. When the sirens blew and we filed into the school shelter and settled down, I had to sing. I belted out 'There'll always be an England' over the noise of anti-aircraft guns, bombs and the intermittent throb of German bomber engines.

'Don't you know any other songs?' Mrs Brown asked.

'Only Sosban Fach' I said.

'What's that?' she enquired.

'A Welsh football song,' I said.

'We'd better not have that then,' she said apprehensively.

There were other lessons to learn, more vital than arithmetic and English. They were based on survival.

I often stopped on my way to school, to watch dog-fights between our planes and the Germans. Vapour from their exhausts drew deadly patterns in the sky, as the enemy planes tried to escape our anti-aircraft guns. In daylight, it looked as if the guns were puffing harmless balls of black smoke which spread out and burst as if someone had shaken ink from a full fountain pen on to the white parchment of clouds. These deadly blots spread over the planes and made them explode into flames and dive downwards, tails streaming with black smoke. In the night, if the moon was out, we could follow the course the raiders took, by watching grey trails of condensation coming from their exhausts.

When German planes were looking for targets to strafe, women and children were not excluded. With the help of diagrams on the blackboard, we were instructed never to run away from a plane, but to run towards the machine guns, so that the bullets would fly over our heads. As an alternative, which I must say I preferred, we were to fling ourselves into the nearest ditch, if there was one available, and lie down with our hands placed over the back of our necks. Mrs Brown carefully explained that hands should be placed over the back of the neck, because it was a vulnerable part of the body and that we were to practice this feat if we were caught in a shower of shrapnel.

Shrapnel consisted of very nasty jagged pieces of iron from shell casings, which fell every night on our shelters and our houses. It rattled on the roofs and sounded as if we were in some gigantic metallic hailstorm. It whistled as it fell and thudded into the ground. One night, we ignored the howling dogs and left it rather late to run up the garden path in single file to get to the shelter. We heard shrapnel screaming down and suddenly I flung myself onto the garden, flattening the haulmes of some potatoes Dad was encouraging to grow, and lay face down in the earth, hands over my neck.

'What's happened? Where's she gone?' shouted my mother. 'Is she all right?'

'I'm over here.' I said in a muffled voice, trying to cope

with a mouthful of soil I had taken in after my sudden leap.

'Have you been hit?' Mam shouted.

'No,' I said.

'We will be,' said Dad, 'if you don't get into the shelter quick.'

Mam shook me as I climbed down through the doorway.

'What the dickens were you doing, flinging yourself down like that? I thought you'd been shot or something. Don't you ever do that again,' she said, and I heard her breathe hard in the darkness of the shelter.

'But Mam, they told us to do it, in school.'

'I'll give you school,' she said.

Dad came home one evening in November, at half past five. He looked grey and tired and after he had hung his bicycle up on the two nails punched into the wall on the outside of the house, he flung himself into the armchair at the side of the fire.

'Thank goodness that's over,' he said. 'Let's have tea. It's hard work getting around in the mess the air raids leave. There's water and muck and rubble all over the roads. How can you ask people for money to pay their bills when half their homes are gone or their windows blown out? It's not an easy job.'

Mam poured him a cup of tea from the brown teapot that she had covered with a green knitted cover, made with scraps left over from my sister's cardigan. She gave us cheese sandwiches, cutting the cheese as thinly as possible to make it last. My father bit into his sandwich and then put his hands to his head.

'Oh!' he said, in a surprised voice, 'My eyes feel funny.'

Then he jerked violently. Foam bubbled on his lips as he choked. Mam thumped him on the back, thinking the bread had gone down the wrong way, but he went suddenly still.

'Oh my God,' she said. 'Oh my God. We'll have to get a doctor.'

She rubbed his hand and loosened his tie. We were still not 'under the doctor', as we had been at home. 'I don't know where we'll get one,' she said 'especially at this time of night.'

'I know where there's one,' I offered.

'Go and get him quick,' said Mam, not thinking to ask me where I was going.

It was pouring with rain and my wellingtons were underneath Dad's chair, so I had to get them out from between his feet. His arm dipped down over me and swung backwards and forwards until it was still. It was a long way to the doctor's house, through the dark wet streets, and I went Scouts pace for speed, but my wellingtons slowed me up a bit. On any other occasion I would have been afraid to be out in the dark, but thoughts of devils and *bwgi* men did not cross my mind as I ran through the streets to the house with the brass plate. The blackout made speed difficult and I almost fell a number of times as my feet caught in kerbs. Luckily, that night there was no air raid, because the weather was too bad. It was further than I thought and I was wet through and weary when I arrived at the doctor's house. His wife opened the door.

'Can the doctor come quick,' I said breathlessly. 'My father is dead.'

I just knew that he was. I had seen people killed in gangster films and knew they were dead when their arms hung down.

'Oh, your poor mother,' she said, and took me in to sit by the kitchen fire and dry my socks.

'The doctor is out,' she explained, 'but as soon as he comes in I'll send him.'

I gave her our address, but did not wait for my socks to dry, and hurried back through the dark streets to my mother.

The way back seemed much longer and I did not run. My fear of the dark increased as I went along and the rain soaking through my dress and cardigan made me miserable. I swallowed hard and tried to fight down my rising fear. A few cars passed and honked their horns, but I walked on, bending under the lashing rain.

When I arrived, the doctor was leaving by the front door. There was a great deal of activity going on in our room, so I sat in Mr Evans's front room to keep out of the way. Someone wanted bandages and two pennies and I wondered what they wanted them for. I went down the passage to find out, but Mrs Evans stopped me.

'Go back to my room,' she said. 'Your father is dead.'

'I know,' I answered and went back to steam in my wet coat in front of her fire.

That night I shared the big bed with Mam and my sister, who slept soundly. We waited for the dogs to bark, but they were silent. We were being left alone that night. There was nothing to be heard, only the incessant rain beating on the window and the voice of my mother saying over and over, 'This is terrible. This is terrible.'

I was more frightened of this situation than I had been in any of the air raids, but managed to say, 'What shall we do, Mam?'

'Go back home,' she said.

Financially all we owned were the remnants of my father's weekly pay which was in my mother's purse. We did not even have our fare home, but some of the neighbours, whom we did not know, called in and gave my mother a few half-crowns, which was just enough to pay for our train fare.

On the day before we left, I went to a shop a few miles away to pick up a *Schoolgirl's Annual* which Mam and Dad had been paying for each week. It was to be my Christmas present and we still owed one-and-sixpence. Mam gave me the money and I put the book, wrapped in tissue, into a brown paper carrier, and I promised not to look at it until Christmas.

The next day, Saturday, was the day of the funeral. We were going home, but would not arrive in time for the funeral. Dad had been taken in the hearse to be buried at Cwm Cemetery in Ebbw Vale in the afternoon and we were to take the 1.30 train from Birmingham Station. Mam had been expecting some money from Mr Evans, who had made a collection in the Journey's End, a nearby pub, where Dad had gone for an occasional drink. As we left, Mr Evans said that he had not finished making the collection and would send the money on to us.

'We'll be lucky if we see any of it,' Mam said quietly to

me. She was right.

Mam held the large suitcase in one hand and my sister on her other arm, who was dressed in a fawn coat and a faded pink lock-knit dress with a teddy bear motif on the front. I carried the smaller cardboard suitcase and a wreath which a neighbour had brought in just as we were about to leave, thinking that we would be home in time for the funeral. We had to take it with us, not to cause offence, and I had to carry it.

'Leave the book then,' Mam said, as my hands were full.

'No fear. I'll manage it,' I said and held on tightly to the string handles of the carrier.

We took the bus to Birmingham, but before catching the train, we found S & U's, which fortunately had not been bombed. A kind assistant helped Mam to try on some black dresses. I held on to my sister, who opened her large brown eyes wide and stared in fascination at the electric lights. Undecided, Mam asked me which dress I liked. It was a gift from the store where Dad had worked.

'The one with the diamond brooch,' I said. It was a large, round gold brooch, like a flower with a centre of sparkling stones. I thought it was really beautiful and had quite a film-star effect.

When we arrived at the station, the platform was crowded with soldiers and we discovered that our train did not go to Abergavenny, but only to the Junction some miles away.

'We will have to walk to the bus stop in Abergavenny,' Mam said.

'Is it far?' asked anxiously.

'It's a tidy step,' she answered and added, 'One good thing out of all this though, if there is any good thing about it at all, is that we'll be out of the bombing.'

Then we heard the news that Coventry Cathedral had been hit and knew I would never see it or my father again and I fought back tears, not wishing to shame Mam in front of all the people. We had to stand in the corridor and I wanted to sit on the case, but Mam wouldn't let me because she thought that the cardboard would collapse. The train windows were painted with wide black borders and there were blue bulbs in the carriages to keep the light to a minimum. A soldier standing next to us was sick out of the window. He lay on the floor afterwards trying to sleep.

'Poor dab,' Mam said, 'he's only a kid, but we all have our troubles I suppose.'

The train pulled into the station. 'Abergavenny Junction!' called the porter, and we stumbled out, over sleeping soldiers, while one who was awake handed out our bags and the wreath.

We walked from the shelter of the station into sheets of driving rain.

'Which way, Mam?' I asked, looking both ways down a country lane.

'This way,' she said, without much conviction. We battled down the road for miles, Mam stopping now and then to put my sister on her other arm.

'She's killing me,' she said, 'She's heavier than the case.'

The cardboard case I was carrying became increasingly soggy and Mam kept looking at it anxiously, hoping it wouldn't split. Every few minutes a jeep full of soldiers trundled past us and we had to get into the side of the lane where branches picked at our clothes and mud splashed on us from the churning wheels. The wreath became soggy and grew heavier and the wires at the back bit into my hands and made cuts. Wind tore at the flowers and some of the petals blew away. I became very tired and my legs felt like lead.

'Let me hitch a ride from the soldiers, Mam?' I begged.

'Don't you dare,' she said, 'We'll keep our independence.'

A vicious gust of wind picked up the wreath, twisted it in my hand and tore it from my grasp, together with the brown carrier. It fell on its side into a pool and water flowed into the bag, soaking the tissue paper and the book. The sodden carrier broke in two as I picked it up and the book fell again into the water.

'Leave it,' said Mam, 'It's no good now, the pages will stick together.'

More army lorries came by and we stood aside and one of the wheels ground my book into the mud. Red dye was already flowing over the pages from the crushed spine, but it was my Christmas present and I was going to keep it.

I rescued the pages which were left and held them together under my arm and we walked on. At last we came to the bus station where a bus was waiting. It was crowded, but a man gave his seat up to Mam while I remained standing, still clutching the remnants of my book and the battered wreath, conscious that I was the object of a few curious glances. We were soaked through and shivered as we climbed down from the bus at Libanus Corner, but in spite of everything, my spirits rose as we walked up Bridge Street, past the Post Office and came once again into Colliers Row. It was still grey and scabby, but it was home. We opened the front door to anxious questions and cries of welcome from Gran, Grancher, Mrs Tiley, Uncle Jim, Auntie Ada and the two boys. They had come home on a special free train pass for the funeral. I put my arms around Gran's handspan waist and buried my face in her flannel blouse, and knew I was home as I smelled the carbolic and wintergreen.

We sat by the fire in bare feet while our stockings dried on the brass rod, and told them something of the horror of the air raids and the bombing and strafing, the searchlights and the incendiaries and how my father had died. It was the first time I saw my mother cry. After more tears and cups of tea, we told the story over again to Mrs Tiley, who kept wiping her eyes with her home-made apron. After my sixth Welsh cake I said, 'I'm glad to be back home, Gran, to peace and quiet.'

'Well, we have had some excitement 'ere mind, as well,' she said. 'Guess what, we have had a whole family of evacuees come to live in the old shop-house opposite the Post Office, and every one of them except the mother is black as the Ace of Spades.' Her eyes opened wide. Then she added, 'And we've had our share of the bombing mind.'

I was all ears.

'Yes,' she said, 'Since you've been away we've had two bombs on the top of the Domen mountain, but they didn't go orf.'

'Two!' I shouted, 'only two?' and I started to laugh and couldn't stop, until laughter came to crying.

Parachute-silk Ribbon for my Hair

~

Gloria Evans Davies

During an air raid my father,
an engineer, at Filton airport
ran to an air raid shelter
only to be blocked by someone
at the entrance saying it was full.
Dashing pell mell to another,
the one he had just left had
a direct hit with no survivors.
We moved a few years previously
from Wales to Bristol, and returned
from a heap of rubble. Like so many
families we were separated throughout
the war, mine consisted of my older
brother John (named after father),
and younger sisters Jill, Alathea
and Diana, except for a few occasions
when Blodwen, my mother, managed to
keep us under the same roof. I
flowered, taking up once more
interrupted, ill-afforded piano lessons.
Mother loved music. Her source

in childhood was from her much older
sister Mabel who served in the Queen
Mary's Army Auxiliary Corps., in the
First World War, 5th Army, Nobecourt,
Northern France. Enrolled Birmingham
5.11.1917, discharged London 20.11.1919,
at the end of the war. She missed
the freedom and comradeship, and wished
she could have stayed in the army.
When home on leave in the village
of Llanfihangel-Talyllyn taught Blodwen
all the songs of the trenches,
and Blodwen in turn taught me.

When the Yanks hit town, the women
sparkled. To be switched off
when their husbands came home
on leave. The teachers never
mentioned them although the
windows shook as they passed by
in their tanks. The first time
I looked up without fear, except
to my golden mother, for the sweets
they rained upon us from their
tanks. They were the only sweets
I had during the war.

Mother coming out of the blue,
bringing a parachute-silk ribbon
for my hair, filling my gloves
with her breath to keep my fingers

warm on my way to school,
trailing my gas mask through
the corn, the smell of fresh wood
from the woodcutters blowing into
the classroom. Bobby,
a London evacuee, working as
a baker's boy, taking my sisters
and I for spins around the block
in the bread basket on the front
of his bike. He was as merry
as a Yank. Siani waves goodbye
to her son in uniform
with a hen tucked
under her arm.

A spring with Elsteg. The
right of way to the kissing-gate
ambled through the bottom of her
cherry orchard much to her annoyance.
There was no end to the Yanks
and their girl-friends lingering
as if her place was on show.
Her garden path composed of old,
discarded mill stones as much
an attraction as the blossom.
Wmffre, her sheep-dog, overweight
from the tit-bits they gave,
bounded to greet them with
welcoming barks alerting swans
to the footbridge waiting
for their share, and waking

the road sweeper, covered
in blossom like the hedge crab,
from one of his siestas on the
primrose bank.
She put up discouraging notices
like 'Beware of Flying Bees'
and 'Vipers' but they only
squealed with excitement,
and daring, having the time
of their lives. She took
the notices down. There was
more noise with them up.

She shivered at the thought of
what would happen if they knew
she had orphaned twin black lambs
in the airing cupboard to keep them
alive, wearing newly knitted
jumpers gift-wrapped for her
nieces. The unwrapping made
the lambs bleat thinking it
was the wind coming down
the chimney to cover them
with snow. She had given
her old jumpers to Llew
for his flock. He was apt
to wear one.

Not many knew if you turned right
by the kissing-gate the sheep trail
led to the Cursing Well. She took me

with her to curse the Gods,
after Gwawr's unfulfilled request
if anyone was going to Brecon
for the day, to bring her back
a bucket of Brecon's beautiful
red earth she longed to see again
before she went completely blind.

If only Heulwen, her old mare,
had been up to it, she could
have gone over the mountain ranges
in half the time. Twigs slide off
her sheer slate roof from a jackdaw
trying to make a nest.
We collect the twigs for the fire,
helped rapturously by Wmffre.

At twelve I saw my first lighted
street, as amazing to see
as getting to know my brother
and sisters. On Victory day
at a street party fleeing
the balloons fearing they would
burst, sounding like the bombs.

Up Penmaen

~

Elizabeth Wroe (Jones)

My mother's favourite expression – meant to put us off continually asking for money for sweets or something not exactly essential was, 'Good Heavens! Have it and we'll all be *up Penmaen!*'

'Penmaen' was, and still is, a particularly lovely, spacious building, on a perfect site overlooking Three Cliffs Bay, Tor and Oxwich Point. At that time it was still known as 'The Workhouse', although we children didn't know the meaning of the name. We went there from time to time with our Girl Guide Company to give concerts for the old people. I don't know who enjoyed them most – the inmates who had someone to fuss over, or us, loving the limelight and concert clothes, not to mention the splendid tea afterwards (in wartime too!). The Master and Matron Thomas were like friends of the family and Penmaen was on our regular visiting list.

One morning, after a particularly heavy bombing raid on Swansea the previous night, we went out of our house to find a large and very deep hole in the lawn. At first we thought our fox terrier 'Astra' had burrowed for something. But this was not an ordinary hole, it was very very deep and went down and down.

Everyone was excited – everyone of school age that is – and wondered if there was a time-bomb ticking away down there. All the adults looked worried or terrified or both, and went to see the Authorities. These consisted only of our village policeman, PC Fry, who came and inspected the hole and issued the order to evacuate.

This was adventure indeed for us children. The war was at last beginning to mean something. Apart from those of us who had a father on the Front, the war had made very little difference to our lives. Not for us the worry of food rationing and clothing coupons – those things were for grown-ups. It meant little to us at that time that half Swansea was in ruins, and that the great black cloud in the sky wasn't a rain cloud, but the smoke from High Street Station which was by now but a cinder.

Evacuate – but where? The orders were for us to come as we were, no luggage, everything to be left. The occupants of perhaps fifty houses around Pennard Drive made a motley procession. All the mothers came with as much as they could cram into a handbag. My own mother's handbag normally weighed about a hundredweight and now must have weighed a ton.

Where were we going? The answer came – 'Up Penmaen!' Dormitories were cleared and tables were laid, relatives were telephoned and letters were written. We stayed for about four days, while bomb disposal soldiers dug and dug and dug. There was never any sign of a bomb. When we returned, our homes were exactly as we had left them. It had never occurred to us that we might never see our own things again.

So when anyone tells you they just can't manage

another treat or they'll be 'up Penmaen', tell them to try it – we found it great!

Bombs and Beachcombing

~

Dorothy Thomas

I was thirteen years old when war was declared and about to start my second year at grammar school in Swansea. I was excited, and my greatest concern was whether we would have a longer holiday. I don't think we did.

We were issued with gas masks and identity cards, and an Anderson shelter for the garden. At school we had our air raid drill. It was a real anticlimax. Rationing, and what was going on overseas, didn't mean much to me. People were called up, and every street had a team of men who practised dealing with incendiary bombs. Nothing much happened for some time. There was the occasional air raid, but I got used to getting up at night and going to sit in the shelter.

The war really began for us with the 'Three Nights' Blitz' of Swansea in February 1941. The sirens sounded at 7.45 p.m. on the first night. First came the flares which lit up the town like daylight. We felt very vulnerable, sure we could be seen cowering in our shelter. Then came the incendiaries, like Christmas lights. Then the bombs. They continued for hours.

I never listened to Lord Haw-Haw's broadcasts from Germany, but news got around that he'd promised another raid for Swansea on the following night. I felt uneasy. When the siren sounded again at 7.45 p.m. exactly I began to panic. It was just like the night before. The following night Lord Haw-Haw announced that they would be back again – he even forecast which districts would receive special attention. I lived in one of them. It was the worst of the three nights. In the early light of morning I saw houses that had collapsed like packs of cards. Some had their roofs intact, but lying on the ground. People I knew lay buried beneath. I saw half an Anderson shelter balanced on top of a chimney. Where were the occupants? I grew up quickly during those three nights.

Everyone who had anywhere to go left Swansea the next day, including my mother, my brother and myself. My father was in the police so he stayed behind. We walked to High Street Station through the ruins of a prosperous town. Craters lined the road full of smoke, water or unexploded bombs, with a little notice advising pedestrians not to fall in the hole. Our train stayed until no more people could squeeze aboard then pulled away from what was left of Swansea.

A month or so later we moved to a remote house on the Gower peninsula, just a stone's throw from the sea. My father would visit us on his day off. We shared our house with a lady who had lived in Canada and told me about the Red Indians who looked at her through slits in her log cabin. The house was haunted. We fetched our water from a stream and we had no electricity or telephone. Our only lavatory was at the end of a kind of garden maze, much frequented by adders. It was a two-seater earth closet, and if the wind was blowing the wrong way the toilet-paper you put in one hole blew up and flew away out of the other. As we had no newspapers and only a battery radio, the war seemed very distant. Even the postman found it too far to walk down the sheep track to our door, so we collected our mail in the village.

I spent most of my time on the beach seeing what the tide brought in. Sometimes I found emergency rations from a plane or ship. What luck! Plenty of chocolates and raisins. Once a mangled bit of an aeroplane was washed up on the shore. I seized hold of it, and found a little mouse nestling on board. I caught him in some wet sand and put him in a box. However he had gone by morning, so perhaps he was a German mouse determined to escape.

I was often worried by the threat of invasion. Our long beach was such a suitable place for an enemy landing. Once the army came and stuck lines of stakes like pit-props in the sand. They were to prevent boats coming ashore, but they were washed away after a few days. A pill-box was built on the dunes as well, but I never saw any soldiers defending it. I used it as a shelter when it rained. If we were invaded the church bell was to be rung, but we lived so far from the church we didn't think we'd hear it. A friend promised to let us know if the bell rang. Early one morning it did. There was a rope from the vicarage to the belfry so the vicar could toll the bell without having to run across his churchyard. After a stormy night the rope had slackened and it lassoed an unlucky farmworker on his way to the morning milking.

The more he struggled to free himself the louder the bell rang. We heard it all right, but our friend never came to tell us it was a false alarm.

Aeroplanes practised shooting on part of the beach. One trailed a target for others to attack. We weren't supposed to be there: the entrance to the dunes was closed off with barbed wire, and behind the wire were mines. I went there just the same. I must have been crazy. I was ready to run like hell if the shooting began.

Mines often floated in with the tide. The coastguard shot them and they exploded with a terrific bang. One evening I watched a mine come in that seemed to be heading straight for our house. I told the coastguard, but he said it wouldn't go off unless it hit a pebble. The next morning my mother, very anxious, looked for it out of the bedroom window, and as she couldn't see the mine she assumed it had been washed out to sea. I went to the beach and saw the mine close inshore, hidden from the house by a bank of sand. I went round it on tip-toe. The points were pearly pink. Later the bomb disposal men came and blew it up.

An enemy was washed up once. There was much discussion as to whether he should be buried in the churchyard. Most people were against. His body was carted away and I never discovered what happened.

In the spring I had to collect gull's eggs. I didn't like it. The gulls didn't either, and swooped down at me. The eggs were large. They weren't very nice boiled or fried, but were good for cakes if a bit fishy. They were a useful addition to our rations along with the salmon bass my father used to catch.

I ran wild for about six months and then I was sent to a commercial school in Swansea. When I came home on winter nights the walk along the side of the hill was long, and very dark. I only had a small torch because of the blackout. Every morning I left my wellington boots in a farm shed. When I put them on in the evening to go home the evacuees from the farm had often dropped half a dozen little potatoes into each boot.

In about 1944 the ghost that haunted the house made my mother decide to return to Swansea. She preferred to take her chance with the hazards of war than with the supernatural.

I still walk on the same beach whenever I can. The track from the beach to the house can hardly be seen any more. My mother, my father and my brother are all dead. My love of the sea, particularly just here, and our old home, is as strong as ever. Had it not been for the war perhaps my life would have been in some ways the poorer.

Never Tell

~

Alison Bielski

when she walked briskly home
one drunk soldier tumbled
from walltop crushed her to ground

she struggled escaping bruised
clutching torn dress broken beads
opened the house door trembling

ran upstairs to her room
sobbed in panic changed clothes
unable to say goodnight

in soothing darkness she
clutched her torch for sudden
reassurance of hands limbs

afraid her explanation
would provoke disbelief's harsh
attack on ragged senses

loneliness overwhelmed
as daylight seeped through cracks
brought routine with nothing told

Don't you Know There's a War On?

~

Gabrielle Capus

It didn't take long for things to change. Suddenly the
iron railings in the streets were gone, taken away from
the house fronts to be used for more warlike weapons.

Signposts and street lights vanished, leaving us at night in an unending darkness. Even more devastating for an eight-year-old, never again would I save for a halfpenny-worth of mint imperials or a penny bag of Palm toffees. Instead, we had blackout curtains, gas masks, gummed paper strips on the windows to protect us from blast damage, barrage balloons, sandbags, barbed wire on beaches, identity cards, ration books, searchlights and horror of horrors, the air raid shelter.

Before the war was declared I can remember us being issued with gas masks, which we collected from the chapel down the road. My sister had a Mickey Mouse one in blue and red and I was very jealous. Mum made us covers in Rexine to fit the gas mask cardboard boxes we took with us everywhere. In anticipation of war, we had gas mask drill in school. The drill was to breathe in and pick up a piece of paper with our gas mask trunk.

At first, air raid practices in school time were considered very exciting but rapidly lost their charm when they were for real. No sooner had we settled back into the classroom to do some work, but the air raid siren would go again, and back into the shelter we would trip. The school shelters in the orchard next door were dug low into the ground, and gave off a very cold earthy odour. They had a tendency to fill up with water when it rained, so were constantly damp.

I don't think I have ever been more frightened than I was in the very first air raid of the war. Mum had decided that the safest place for us was under the stairs, so she put down an old mattress for us to sleep on. Dad was out on duty with the Civil Defence, making sure that no lights were visible through the blackout curtains we were all compelled to use. I remember still, hearing the siren in the middle of the night for the very first time, and the sudden stabbing fear in the pit of my stomach. We dashed downstairs in our pyjamas and dressing gowns and huddled together waiting for the bombs to drop. The deafening noise of gunfire from the 'Big Bertha' at Belmont punctuated only by the dismal drone of bomber planes sounding directly overhead, kept us continuously from our slumbers. We heard the bombs whistling down and exploding, and felt the blast shake the whole house, as it resounded through the streets. This ear-splitting terror made us cling together and pray as we had never prayed before, as we waited for the next earth-shattering onslaught to engulf us.

As we had no proper air raid shelter of our own, it was later arranged for us to share with the elderly couple next door. Every time we trotted out in the depths of the night, I could smell that earthy damp smell. After a few frantic nights trying to dress three children and get them into the shelter when the air raid warning wailed, Mum made us lovely warm 'siren' suits which we could slip on quickly and zip up over our pyjamas rather like cat-suits. My sister and I had scarlet ones and my brother's was black. Such suits were very popular at the time and worn even by Winston Churchill.

I was in the second year of the junior school when war was declared and it was announced that we would all attend school part-time. We secretly cheered. Soldiers were to be billeted on the upper floor of the school so we had to share the downstairs classrooms with the infants.

My parents owned a grocery business and when rationing started, I can remember recording in alphabetical order the names and addresses of the 'registered customers' from their ration-book counterfoils. It meant that a person could only buy rationed goods at the shop where they were registered. They could apply to transfer to another shop if they were dissatisfied but it was a lengthy business and meant queuing for hours at the Food Office. Queuing was a new word in our vocabulary, and how I remember the hours I queued. Someone would poke their head around the shop doorway and announce: 'Fish in Harpers' and off I would be sent for the next hour or so with Mum's wicker basket, to stand in line with the exhausted housewives. I didn't like it; the language was quite strong as the assistants bantered with the waiting crowd, cracking jokes I couldn't understand. One phrase I did not want to hear as my turn came nearer, was: 'Sorry, dear, we're sold out.'

When customers had registered with their chosen grocer, they collected their weekly rations and had their books marked or stamped to make sure that they did not return for a second helping later on in the week. At the beginning of the week, we children would help to make up the bags of rations, packed according to size of family. The butter, margarine and lard were sliced with a wire cheese-cutter and wrapped in greaseproof paper. We became experts at judging the right size for 1/2lbs, 1/4lbs and ounces, and if a small morsel were left at the end of packing, a treat might be some butter on a cream cracker for us.

About this time, Merchant Navy ships were being

attacked by torpedoes and mines in the Channel and food was becoming increasingly scarce. Bringing food into the docks became more difficult and the points' system was introduced. It entitled each person to so many points to spend a month on tinned goods, biscuits, fruit, etc. These points were often saved for special occasions like Christmas, birthdays and weddings. Another chore we children were drafted into was counting the points coupons to be sent to the Food Office.

We saved everything we could. The most ordinary simple things became unobtainable and I would be sent out to scour the town, when we needed something urgently. Frequently outside shops one would see a large blackboard chalked with the words 'We have no...', and then a great long list of what was not in stock. It was the same in our shop. Some irate customers would accuse us of keeping things 'under the counter'. To a certain extent it was true: if there was not sufficient to go round, our registered customers were given first choice.

Once America entered the war, we began to see a few changes in our lives. Tinned Spam, jam and sausages were a welcome addition to our meagre rations. The arrival of the 'Yanks' caused great excitement on our road. Because it was a main road into Newport, convoys of GIs in army trucks would be stuck there for some considerable time and all the local folk would be out to greet them. The stock excuse for turning up late for school had now become, 'Please, Miss, the bus was stuck in a convoy.' As for our playtimes, gone were the skipping ropes and balls, now we jitterbugged everywhere we could find space, schoolyard, landing and cloakroom. Some experts among our classmates had obviously learned the steps first hand. They seemed to have a fair amount of candy and chewing gum and were not averse to shouting at the Yanks as they passed, 'Any gum, chum?' It was about this time too, that nylons first made their appearance. Quite different from those worn today, they had the look of sheer glass with a dark seam up the back of the stocking. Many a young girl would cover her legs with gravy browning and draw a dark eyebrow pencil line down the back of her legs, imitating the much-prized nylons.

When the war eventually ended we celebrated VE day with parties and Victory teas, the streets decorated with flags. Our shop window displayed an iced Victory cake and framed sketches of Winston Churchill and Monty, which my mother had drawn herself. For six long years we had waited for the moment when we could banish that pathetic cry: 'Don't you know there's a war on?' The anticipated bonfire of ration books did not take place; coupons and points were still to be counted and sent to the Food Office and more shortages were to come. The darkness of the blackout had not faded and seemed to linger on as the days grew more grey and gloomy. Inevitably improvements were slow and if life never did return to the dazzling pre-war days, at least all that awful bombing was finally over; a ghastly chapter had finished but the child that had been – was no more.

The Day War Broke Out

~

Margaret Lloyd

'The day war broke out' was a catchphrase first coined by an old radio comedian, Rob Wilson, to imply that it was the day that life began. For many people, certainly, it was the beginning of a lifestyle hitherto undreamt of.

When war broke out on 3 September 1939 I was being hurried along a country road by my aunt. I spent every school holiday with her and my cousins on their farm six miles outside Builth Wells, Powys, and I was being taken to catch the local bus and begin my three-hour journey back to my home town of Merthyr Tydfil. As we arrived at the village a telegram boy in his smart, short, navy jacket and pillbox hat, came tearing up to us on his bright red bicycle. He took a telegram out of the leather pouch on his belt and handed Aunt an ominous yellow envelope. Telegrams meant trouble in those days before private telephones, usually a death in the family. My aunt tore open the envelope. It was from my parents instructing her to keep me with her until they could collect me. The adult conversation of 'troop movements and the uncertainties of public transport' meant nothing to me, a diminutive nine-year-old. All that concerned me was that I was to have an extended holiday on my beloved farm.

Some weeks later my parents persuaded the local baker to come and fetch me. The interior of his small van had been swept clean of its crunchy crumbs. My mother and I took our seats on the two deckchairs that had been placed in the back. As we bounced and swayed our way over the winding road of the Brecon Beacons I knew life would never be the same again.

School had still not started as the building was being used as a distribution centre for gas masks. When it did re-open I was one of the 'honoured' girls chosen to knit khaki socks and gloves for our soldiers fighting in the war. I became quite skilful at knitting socks on three needles, turning heels with aplomb and completing the complicated procedure of knitting glove fingers. We chosen few were expected to carry out these tasks during storytelling sessions, assembly and playtimes. The less able were conscripted to wind wool into balls from the prickly drab-coloured skeins of which our teacher seemed to have an endless supply.

At this time, I noticed that all the insignificant little men in the neighbourhood acquired navy uniforms and wore black tin hats with ARP written on them. They developed voices that boomed in the darkness 'Mind that light'. They seemed to have gained a mysterious power over the neighbourhood and what was described by my granny as the 'goings-on in the blackout'.

War, to many of my schoolmates, meant fathers going to work after years of squatting at street corners and being on the dole. It meant better food as regular wages came in and rationing made it compulsory that everyone had the correct number of calories to keep healthy –

something not considered essential to survival during the Depression. I was lucky, my father had always worked. Before the outbreak of war he had joined the Auxiliary Fire Service, which was formed to release the police force from fire duties. When war was declared he and his fellow firemen were employed full-time and were later to become the National Fire Service. My father was issued with a stirrup pump to keep at home in case any incendiary bombs fell in our neighbourhood. He would insist my mother and I practise fire drill. My poor mother, who was rather large, would puff up and down the garden steps with buckets of water, refilling the water bucket in which the stirrup pump stood. I had the task of pumping it up and down to get the pressure going, no mean task as the pump was nearly as tall as me. My father would direct the thin erratic stream of water onto an imaginary fire. On certain days he would insist we wore our gas masks, but as the visor misted over with condensation from our sweat, I never did see the point. He called these gas mask drills at such odd times as when we were laying the table for supper or listening to the wireless. My father was very conscientious.

When the siren sounded, usually at night, never mind how often, we had to get up from bed and sit huddled on small stools, under the stairs. The flickering light from an old miner's lamp threw up shadows more frightening to me than any war. I wouldn't be allowed back to bed until the 'all clear' siren sounded some hours later. Next day, it was school as usual; tiredness was no excuse for 'mitching'. Only once do I remember any semblance of a raid. I was awakened one night by the violent shaking of the windows. Next day it was rumoured that a bomb had been dropped in a local quarry and the vibrations had travelled a great distance. That was the night we weren't sitting under the stairs.

When my father was at home, I was allowed to view the bombing of Cardiff docks, twenty-four miles away. Standing in the back doorway I'd watch the searchlights sweep the night sky and cheer when an enemy plane got caught in the beam like a hypnotized moth. The exploding shells from the ack-ack guns added to the spectacle.

Sometimes my father was away for days when the local brigade were sent to help out in badly hit areas like Coventry or Bristol. He rarely spoke about it in front of me. Only once did I hear him tell my mother that it had been so cold that their saturated jackets had frozen on them as they fought fires throughout the night.

The arrival of the American soldiers in the town was quite a cultural shock. These brash, noisy young men in their smart uniforms of fine wool, stood on the pavements outside their billets and catcalled and whistled after any female between the age of sixteen and sixty. To me – a young girl approaching puberty with trepidation (the word teenager hadn't been invented then) – they were both embarrassing and intriguing. My intense shyness caused uncontrollable blushing as I stalked passed, eyes front, head held high. The more outgoing of my friends seemed to take delight in making frequent detours so as to pass through the barrage of invitations. Later, during visits to an aunt who kept a hotel, I was often commandeered to play their piano for many young

GIs. The homesick, frightened young men sang about Broadway, Dixie, Texas and every state in the union. I'm afraid I wasn't impressed – I was still a prudish fourteen-year-old who defended her virtue by insisting that all American men drank too much, swore a lot and cried a great deal.

War to me was the horror seen on Pathé News in the cinema or the news on the wireless that had to be listened to in silence several times a day. It was women wearing scarves around their heads, smoking, working in factories, smelling of oil. Things I hadn't experienced before. Saturday afternoons meant strolling up and down the High Street. The factory girls always appeared to have extra-large heads as their scarves covered curler-wound hair. I couldn't fathom how they expected the 'boys' to forget this afternoon image when they met again at the dance that evening – hair exposed in either corrugated waves or 'victory rolls'.

War was bedroom walls plastered with posters calling for 'Aid to Russia', glamorous Generals, newspaper cuttings on plane recognition and uniforms. Uniforms... everywhere uniforms. Men in uniform, women in uniform. Soldiers, sailors, airmen, wardens, firemen, Home Guards. To belong one had to be in uniform. I joined the St John Ambulance Brigade. I don't remember learning much first aid but I do remember receiving a parcel from America sent by schoolchildren. Mine came from a 'Barbara Babitt'. It contained a bar of scented toilet soap which was too precious ever to use and, amongst other forgotten things, a pair of hair-clips with bows of red ribbon and white stars. They were kept for that special occasion which never came. I would take them out of the drawer in my bedroom and look at them and wonder about the little girl who had sent them to me.

'The day war finished' I was to be found at the same farm where my story began. As the news of peace came over the wireless the church bells echoed across the fields. We all gathered at the church hall, precious food was brought and a grand tea put on. Young wounded servicemen from a local convalescent home arrived in their bright blue suits, red ties and white shirts, accompanied by pretty Red Cross nurses. During the evening I was asked if I would play some dance music. My father had never approved of my playing such rubbish, so I had kept secret my daily stint of piano playing during school dinner times. I think I was forgiven my frivolity that evening as the dancers swirled to the foxtrot, dipped to the tango and whooped to the hokey-cokey and the conga. I may not have made much contribution to the war effort but I think I made a contribution to the beginning of peace.

The Woman in her Fifties

~

Alathea Thomas

The woman in her fifties
hurriedly swept the cobwebs
        from her face,

even something so light
brought back the suffocating
effect of her Mickey Mouse
        gas mask.

CHAPTER 2

HOME LIFE

For many women, 'normal' home life ceased during the war. Their place was now the Home Front, facing danger at every turn as well as coping with the 'Manage, Make Do and Mend' of everyday life. Their sacrifices, deprivations and losses were harrowing but their will to survive was paramount. Manage, make do and mend were what one did. In spite of the deprivations, war babies were healthier than their older siblings.

Our Little Family's War

~

Eva Pettifor

Much has been written of the bravery and sacrifice of those caught up in the main events of the Second World War. Some returned after the war with medals, scars, public recognition of their service on film and in print, at the very least with their lives. For those who returned, and those whose consciences allowed them to forget the war, there was a new start. For the widows of those who did not return, of whom my mother was one, their lives were shattered, their struggles only just beginning. For them, the war did not end in 1945.

My mother was born in 1915 during the First World War, in which her only brother was killed. She was the youngest member of an artistic, well read and enterprising family. Her childhood on the Isle of Man she remembered with affection as being happy, countrified and idyllic. In 1935, she met and married my father who was a merchant seaman from South Africa. I was born in 1936 and my sister Osa in 1938. My mother rarely spoke of her life before the war but when she did it was of having her own home, being able to buy whatever she wanted, and having her parents 'just down the road', if she needed them.

The outbreak of war in 1939 brought this ordinary, comfortable family life to an abrupt end. My father's ship was adapted for use as a hospital ship and was to be caught up in many actions. The bombing in 1940 and 1941 saw our house and many houses around it reduced to rubble by a landmine. I remember the green and yellow patterned tiles on the walls of somewhere underground where we sheltered from the bombs. My grandfather was blown down the stairs of the hospital where he was a patient, and critically injured.

My mother, who was only twenty-five, had to find accommodation away from the bombing, for her parents and her children, having lost her home and virtually all of her possessions. Somehow she managed to rent a house on Anglesey in north Wales. After what seemed an endless train journey to a five-year-old, we eventually arrived at a rambling run-down farmhouse, situated in fields between the villages of Rhydwyn and Llanfairynghonwy. My grandfather was brought by ambulance from Liverpool and died there a few months later. He seemed very old to me, but was only sixty-three.

The people at the next farm were very kind to us, and looked after us on the day of the funeral. The farmer gave us a sheepdog puppy, and I remember that it nipped our heels and herded us about. They also had a tame sheep that had been brought into the farmhouse as an orphaned lamb, and ever after behaved more like a dog, lying on the front doorstep and racing across the fields to greet visitors.

The farmhouse was rat-infested and was dubbed 'rat-villa' by my mother. All water had to be carried from a well or trough a field away from the house, from which the sheep drank and in which frogs swam, to my mother's disgust. The furnishings of the house were spartan, lacking even cups. My mother was visited by the parents of a young man from Holyhead who was serving on my father's ship. They brought cups and saucers and a large cake, which was a great kindness.

Evacuees had not yet arrived in any numbers in this corner of Anglesey, and my mother was not always received with kindness and understanding. The door of a nearby farmhouse was slammed in her face when she spoke English in an effort to buy potatoes, and a village shopkeeper complained about evacuees 'coming to eat our food'. My mother considered that people so far removed from the realities of war could not be expected to understand what was happening to others' lives.

At the local school, as the first representative of the evacuees (as I was perceived to be) I was given my school dinner at my desk, away from the other children. Whether this was because I did not speak Welsh, or because I was an evacuee, I do not know. I flatly refused to go to school after that. Some months later a Miss Buckingham arrived with a number of 'real' evacuees, and a school was set up in the village hall. My mother insisted that I go to join them. All I remember of my schooling at this time was being whacked across the knuckles for not attending. It was a harsh justice for a five-year-old and I was not too willing to go to the village hall schoolroom, or to struggle to learn 'Nymphs and Shepherds' with Miss Buckingham hammering out the tune and singing shrilly.

All was not lost on the education front. My mother had by some means acquired various books and annuals for me and I soon learned to read. I remember a story about a greedy boy who ate oyster patties and a 'gingerbread, gingerbread, gingerbread brown, that rose in the tin with a golden crown...' I can still see that particular page in my mind's eye, and must have been impressed by the large illustration of a cake.

In the early hours of one morning, at the beginning of 1942, a taxi pulled up unexpectedly. My father had arrived on a brief leave bringing with him oranges, tins of sweets and rolls of dress materials for my mother. Great was the joy and excitement. I can still see my mother and father standing together with their backs to the fireplace. He so tall, over six foot. three inches, and my mother so tiny, only five foot nothing. The difference in their heights struck me then. I cannot remember his face.

On the 29 October 1942 my father was lost at sea. The dreaded telegram brought the news. My grandmother, still grieving after her own loss, took charge of us. We realized that something terrible had happened, and sensed my mother's misery and loss.

Early in 1943 we left Anglesey and stayed for the best part of the year with my mother's eldest sister on the Isle of Man. Our sheepdog Prince had been sent to be trained as an aerodrome guard-dog, and ever afterwards would walk to heel and jump over obstacles and walls at our command, which was to give us the edge on what other children's dogs could do.

At the end of the year we went back to Liverpool, and stayed near our other aunt who had remained there during the bombing to be near her husband who worked on the docks. My mother and grandmother decided to return to the safety of the country, after my sister became ill, and they received replies to their advertisement for a house to rent from Shrewsbury and from north Wales. My mother chose north Wales.

I remember arriving at Caernarfon and seeing the massive walls of the castle for the first time. We travelled the nine miles to Rhyd-Ddu on a utility bus with slatted wooden seats which were very hard, and arrived at our rented house and the village that was to be our home. My sister and I were enrolled at the village school and brought the complement to nine. Soon we were speaking Welsh as naturally as children do when left to their own devices and when they need to do something for their own reasons.

Our primary school years were very happy at this

homely little school. I remember the big coal-fire that heated the one large room, and all the usual activities that kept us occupied, of which art and craft was my favourite. Mrs Williams, the school cook, looked after all of us as if we were her own children. She made wonderful puddings in cloths, and stood over us if we showed reluctance to eat. We used to help her with the washing-up on wet days when we all had to stay in the big hall that served as a dining room.

During the celebrations of the Victory in Europe in 1945, and the later celebration of the Victory in Japan, we had great bonfires on the top of a hill, and parties in the chapel vestry. The welcome home celebrations must have been poignant and distressing for my mother. She was the only war widow in the village. A concert and tea-party were held for the returning servicemen and all were given a utility radio complete with an acid battery. My mother was given one too, to her great pleasure, and such kindness and sensitivity on the part of the village was never forgotten.

At eleven, I tried and passed the scholarship entrance examination to the grammar school, as did my sister a few years later. My mother received a small war pension and cleaned the schoolhouse to earn extra money. We were tolerably comfortable by comparison with the hard times that were to come. My mother still had a gold watch, rings, and some ornaments and mementoes of her so different life before the war. During the summer months she worked as a waitress, walking the six miles there and back to the next village where the big hotels were. Eventually she arranged a lift with the milk lorry which wended its way through the villages early in the morning. Her life was unrelentingly hard, the hours long, and the work exhausting. She was, however, doggedly determined to keep her family together and to ensure an education for us. A photograph taken on the chapel Sunday school trip to Rhyl, shows her thin, worn face and body, and illustrates without the need for any words the harrowing experiences the war had inflicted on her, so unprepared for such hardship at so young an age.

Somehow we survived by dint of her efforts and sacrifice. In later years we never spoke of this awful period in our lives, deeming that it was too personal and hurtful. In consequence we do not know enough about our father or our family. Now that my mother is dead, we wish in some ways that we had asked her. She appeared to have closed the door on the past, and to be interested only in the present. We realize that we should have created opportunities for her to speak about our father, and that perhaps she really wanted to do so. Perhaps she in turn was afraid of hurting us.

My mother's sense of duty, triumph over disaster, her integrity and steadfastness, and her will to overcome the trials brought her by the war deserves to be placed on record, as do the experiences of so many war widows, who received so little support from a nation grateful in word but not in deed, and who were relegated to the side-lines of the history of post-war Britain.

This brief account of the way in which the Second World War changed the course of our family's lives is written with deep regret that war caused my mother such anguish and hardship, and with pride that she bravely overcame every obstacle, was able to retain such a sense of perspective, and emerge without bitterness or self-pity from the difficulties of those years. Our parents, Eva and Ben Wilkinson, are a hard act to follow.

Smokescreens

~

Wilma J. Gravenor

I was born in Guthrie Street in Barry, south Wales, a small Welsh seaport that took its fair share of battering during the war. I was unaware at the time that ships were not always grey and camouflaged and that they should not normally 'appear' and then 'disappear' from our docks so quickly and so silently. I was totally ignorant of the fact that somewhere along the South Glamorgan coast was a secret ammunition supply depot. The Germans knew that much, but its exact location remained a secret. So, like Cardiff, Swansea and Milford Haven, we were often bombarded by the enemy planes as they searched for that vital depot.

Consequently, a sharp night sky with a glowing moon and twinkling stars was not greeted with joy by the inhabitants of Barry. The sparkling ribbon of the Bristol Channel was a clearly defined line to lead the enemy planes to the coastal towns and enabled them to drop their bombs with maximum damage. To counteract this lethal night-time danger, we had smokescreens.

As a small child I was not often out after dark, but occasionally my mother and I would visit relations nearby, and together we would make the half-hour walk home after tea. In the winter, this meant 'in the dark'! – an exciting journey (for me) as there was complete blackout: no street lights, no traffic lights, no cosy windows glowing out across the pavements – just dark, silent roads. The route we used was little more than a lane edged by rickety fences and chicken sheds, where pigs, goats and geese were kept. In the velvety blackness, we would hear the scratching sounds of restless creatures. Although my mother always carried a torch, it was seldom used – after all, muggings and confrontations were almost unheard of in those days. There was such mystery in the dense darkness – but I felt no fear.

On moonlit nights, the journey home was the best of all because of the eerie drifting emissions from the smokescreens. Sitting silently on the pavements, these machines lazily released a steady blanket of artificial fog. I always thought that they were like giant stovepipe hats as they loomed over me, belching out their protective fumes. They created an artificial blanket of cloud that would hang over the town, deadening the sharp lines of the houses and roads so that densely populated areas would be less visible to the pilots of German planes. Therefore, the clearer the night the more 'smoke' belched out of these gross and frightening contraptions. As far as the German pilots were concerned, our town had disappeared like Brigadoon!

The smoke added to the rare sense of Halloween

excitement that only a child can feel – that tinge of happy fear, that anticipation of the unknown. To my mother, it must have been an added reminder to her that life was not 'normal' in those days – everything was different. . . but, that was the way it was, during the war.

From the Home Front – 1942

~

Joan Dickens

It's strange how certain phrases can bring to mind a whole era: Don't you know there's a war on? Is your journey really necessary? Waste not, want not. Dig for Victory. Walls have ears. EWS means Emergency Water Supply.

Each corner of the Rhosddu district of my home town of Wrexham, holds memories: the familiar streets of childhood, the school. The formative years of our lives, the war years with their shortages (especially of food) bonded us together. Although some children were better clothed, we invariably wore navy-blue serge gymslips and jerseys that showed the straight lean lines of our bodies. There was a perpetual pang of hunger and we would crowd around anyone who arrived at school with some delicacy. A girl called Edna brought to school (in a paper bag – that in itself was rare) a huge lump of chocolate. It wasn't a bar: it was as if a whole batch of chocolate had been over-heated and had solidified into a marbled block.

We gathered around her in the school playground, unable to believe our own eyes. We could smell the chocolate as she showed it around but did not let it leave her hands. Her brother had come home on leave and brought it for her. She eventually broke, chipped and knocked pieces from this treasure and gave them to her special friends. She gave me a small piece and, into this frugal and sparse childhood, it brought back to me the memory of a long-ago Christmas morning: the crackle of a Christmas stocking and the deliciousness of crisp, dark chocolate at an unearthly hour when, to a child, all the world is still.

Cold and hunger brought with them a share of childhood misery. We frequently suffered with chilblains. Fingers and toes would swell up, red and shiny, and then the most excruciating pain and irritation occurred when our bodies slowly warmed in the spartan heat of the classroom. In severe cases, the skin broke open in long cracks and we often cried and bandaged them with pieces of rag. The cold penetrated our shoes: they seemed to be made of compressed cardboard.

We dreaded the first frost of winter that brought patterns on the windowpanes, icicles on roofs, frozen ponds and frozen pipes everywhere. The winters were cruel. To me, there was no beauty in winter. The biting winds and the thinness of our clothing is etched in my mind for ever.

We were bonded together by shared experience. We played together (for sometimes the schools were closed for weeks at a time) at rounders, cricket with makeshift bats and skipping all in unison with rhymes that generations of children had sung, and the new ones of war: 'We'll beat the Hun, We'll make them run.' As many as possible joined in the games – even afflicted children from the special school, for they knew more games than we did. Huge circles of hands joined together: 'The big ship sails on the ally, ally-o... on the last day of September.'

We knew the names of the regiments of the British Army better than we knew any geography or history: the Royal Welch Fusiliers with the three black flashes of ribbon down the back of the collar. We were familiar with the Barrack Square of Wrexham Barracks, the shouts of sergeant majors and the parades of raw recruits through the town, spurred on by a brass band. We knew the badges of the regiments: the gun carriage badge of Woolwich Arsenal ('The Gunners'), the Royal Artillery, the pick-and-shovel badge of the Pioneers ('first onto the battlefield') who dug the trenches and were based at Eaton Hall (the country house of the dukes of Westminster between Wrexham and Chester), with its grand long drives and acres of land. We joined in the rush to touch a sailor's collar 'for good luck'. We were a cohesive band of aeroplane-spotters and collectors of regimental ribbons and badges, although warned repeatedly never to pick up anything off the road in case it had been dropped by enemy planes and was an incendiary device disguised as a butterfly.

At school our cookery lessons were held in a room with a roaring coal-fire and a cold pantry. There was also a parlour with leather furniture, dining table and chairs, and a special corner with a large doll, cot, bath, enamel bucket and towels for the lessons on home-nursing, invalid cookery and general housewifery.

Every lesson, Miss Hughes, the cookery teacher, began with assembly and the reading from the First Book of Corinthians. I can see her now, dressed in a crisp white coat, expounding on this chapter, always ending on the last verse with great emphasis: 'And now abideth faith, hope and charity. But the greatest of these is charity' (explaining charity meant love).

Before work, our uniform of white apron and cap was duly inspected. The cap was to keep the hair back from the face and food. 'It's not on your head as a decoration,' Miss Hughes would say, 'It has a purpose.' She would then proceed to examine our hands for any dirt or grime and (even worse!) nail varnish, clear or coloured. Then the class would explode into activity, gathering together bowls, measuring jugs and spoons, and weighing scales. There was a reason for this mad scramble, as the ones who were last to the cupboards had to make use of chipped bowls, bent forks, broken wooden spoons, or baking-tins that looked as if someone had stamped on them in a temper. And all this jostle, hustle and bustle went on with the strict admonition that we must always 'Keep to the right!' – a rule to prevent anyone bumping into another girl carrying a hot saucepan or iron.

The temperature of the room would begin to warm up with all the activity of beating and stirring, and the fire glowed as it was prepared to prove the dough for the bread. In bread-making, everything had to be warm – bowls, utensils and cloths – and this warmth was even more inviting when it was cold outside. We pounded the dough until our arms ached, put it to prove by the glowing fire, and covered it with clean white damp cloths. Then we waited for the transformation, to see if the dough had doubled up in size. Back again to the breadboard for the final preparations, before the dough, plaited or shaped into cottage loaves, was placed in well greased bread-tins which disappeared into the hot oven, like pots into a kiln. Soon from the oven would waft a delicious aroma. The slightest hint of this smell brings back the memory of the fresh, red faces of the girls glowing in the light of the fire.

The loaves were inspected by Miss Hughes who tapped her knuckles on the bottom of each loaf to hear the hollow sound of bread well baked. Next came the cutting of the loaf with a bread saw to see whether the bread was of a uniform texture and whether crumbs would fall onto the breadboard and, last but not least, the tasting of a crust of warm new bread with rationed butter, or, on a really special day, butter and home-made strawberry jam, generously spread on a thick slice.

With sleeves rolled up well past the elbow, basin and utensils were washed up in zinc baths full of hot water. The tables had to be scrubbed with a hard-bristle scrubbing brush and a piece of tallow soap that had been cut from a long block. Finally, the zinc baths were polished to a silver sheen with the aid of wire wool and lots of elbow grease, ready to be lined up on the long draining boards like a regiment of soldiers.

In my years in school, I loved the cookery classes better than anything. It was a whole world of warmth and delectable smells – something to show for the day's effort, and something to eat!

Lady Margaret Hall Potato Harvest

~

Elaine Morgan

When war was declared there was a short period of confusion during which many people expected instant Armageddon. We were ordered to carry gas masks at all times, while mothers of young babies were issued with gas-proof boxes the size of small coffins. Hospitals were alerted to prepare for massive casualties by encouraging patients who were not very ill, or past saving, to go home. My father was in the Royal Infirmary suffering from heart disease, and my mother was told to expect him home within twenty-four hours. She had to race around Pontypridd in the blackout knocking up doctors, begging for the oxygen cylinder she had been advised to 'try to get hold of' for him. He died just before Christmas.

I only learned later just how tough things had been because I had won an exhibition to Oxford and had already moved into a kind of dream world. Oxford's famous bells were silent: if ever they rang, it would mean that Germany had invaded. Otherwise it had changed little in 1939 from the image of it I had formed from reading novels and poems and memoirs. The great trees in the University parks were turning gold outside my window. I had a room to myself bigger than the one five of us had always lived in. I acquired a bicycle and a mortarboard-shaped hat and an undergraduate's gown – obligatory for attending lectures. I hoped I looked like a bona fide undergraduate though it was months before I stopped feeling like some kind of stowaway. Every evening there was a three-course dinner in Hall served by uniformed maids, and at night, instead of GWR coal trucks hurtling past and rattling the bedroom windows, I heard nothing but deep silence and the occasional owl.

All I had to do in exchange for all that luxury was what I liked doing best – reading and writing. Sometimes I felt pangs of guilt at having so much more than a reasonable share of good luck. I had been awarded a Miners' Welfare grant to eke out the money from the exhibition, and I used to tell myself that was a sign that the community back home, as well as my immediate family, thought it was OK for me to be there. And for month after month the 'phoney war' continued. There were no air raids, no lists of casualties, and the gas masks were stowed away in attics and forgotten.

Oxford's short academic terms meant that I still spent more than half the year in Pontypridd. Wales was a reception area for evacuees, and later for a dispersed workforce. Oxford, too, saw an influx of people. It was a magnet for academic refugees from the continent; a number of government departments commandeered buildings; the Slade School of Art moved in for the duration. As time went by the influx was not always so élite. One day, after heavy bombing, a couple of train-loads of Londoners arrived unheralded, mostly mothers with young children, and the elderly. A cinema was requisitioned, and they all lived and slept among the tip-up seats for a couple of weeks while welfare organizations searched for accommodation for them. I wondered why no college asked its students to double up and offer them more civilized living space.

In the men's colleges, many of the undergraduates enlisted in the Officers' Training Units and faced the prospect of being called up after two years instead of completing their courses. Some went on to Sandhurst for further training, so it was only towards the end of my time that I began to hear names of some of the brightest and best who would never come back. In the meantime, the call-up meant that the women's role in the University became slightly more important.

There were still die-hard professors around like A.L. Rowse who, while they could not exclude women from attending their lectures, enjoyed raising a titter from the lads by an elaborate pretence that we were invisible to them. Institutions like the Oxford Union were all-male, but I attended – in the gallery – one session of that debating club in which the Committee graciously allowed Iris Murdoch to make a strong case for the admission of women. (It would be a long time before the suggestion was acted on.) When I became Chair of the Oxford University Democratic Socialist Club I invited a woman speaker. Susan Lawrence was a tall white-haired woman, not only an executive member of the Labour Party but, as it turned out, a veteran of the 'Votes for Women' campaign. She brought some stirring echoes of that earlier feminist solidarity to a generation that had virtually forgotten all about it.

Lady Margaret Hall was then, of course, an all-women college. Even inside it things were changing fast. The maids became fewer and older as the young ones moved to better paid work in the munitions factories. Some of the lawns were sacrificed to the 'Dig for Victory' campaign. I remember one year when we were invited to volunteer to help bring in the LMH potato harvest. By and large the students did not come from the horny-handed classes, and the response was poor. They were gently prodded in the right direction by two successive dinners featuring boiled rice as a vegetable followed by rice pudding as a dessert. Next day there was a rush of volunteers to wield the garden forks.

In the long vacations, I used to take jobs to help the home budget; the one thing not in short supply during wartime was employment. One summer I worked in a sparking-plug factory on the Treforest Trading Estate. The job was described as 'progress chaser' and it entailed, among other things, keeping up to date the chart in the office recording the factory's output of plugs. The workforce was almost entirely female and I never heard any of them discussing the progress of the war, but all the same, whenever there was news of an Allied victory, morale went up and the graph showed that production went up, too.

I graduated in 1942, but I didn't go up to Oxford for the ceremony. People were discouraged from travelling by large hoardings demanding 'Is your journey really necessary?' The mainline trains were usually crowded, with standing room only, and journeys were made more difficult by a thick mesh glued onto the insides of the windows to prevent flying glass in the case of an air raid. The top corner of this was inevitably peeled back by travellers, and the official admonition: 'I trust you'll pardon my correction – that stuff is there for your protection' was liable to invite a scribbled retort: 'I thank you for your information – I want to see the bloody station.' When the station name was called out we had to get out promptly, and one night I alighted in Pontypridd when the blackout was compounded with fog. I stepped confidently out of the wrong door of the train and landed on the tracks.

Most of the Oxford women I knew went on to jobs in education, or in the higher echelons of the Civil Service. I don't remember any of my college friends being fired with the ambition to become a nurse and serve overseas, as Vera Brittain was in the First World War. It was a different war, and anyone with the urge to tend the maimed and wounded needed to go no further than London.

I was married just about a month before the war in Europe ended, and I remember the crowds in Pontypridd Market Square on VE night. There was not exactly dancing in the street, but that was partly because there was no room to shake a leg anyway. We felt there was a new world around the corner:

Bliss was it in that dawn to be alive,
But to be young was very heaven.

So peace returned, but plenty was a long time coming.

Britain was economically flat on her back after putting everything into the war effort, and for many months the shortages got worse instead of better. I learned my trade as a housewife in the era of snoek and Spam and whale meat and dried egg. Rationing was stringent and the queues were long, but nobody doubted that if distribution had then been left to market forces, most of the people would never have seen a fresh egg or a few weekly ounces of butter and meat. I gratefully collected the green ration book which allowed a pregnant mother to go to the head of any food queue, and the free milk and orange juice and cod liver oil. The British babies born at that time of the greatest scarcity were the healthiest that the country had ever produced.

On my Bike: Extracts from a Wartime Diary

~

M. Joan Morgan

1939

Friday 17 March. Neville Chamberlain speaking on radio from Birmingham, 8.15 – practically anti-Hitler.
Saturday 18 March. Finished reading *South Riding* – good but disappointed somehow – rather sordid and unnecessarily so – prefer the picture. Prime Minister seventy today.

Saturday radio programmes are deteriorating, esp. after 9.30 p.m. News goes on so long and then sports and German news bulletin. Read in paper that after April dance music not starting until 11 p.m.

Thursday 23 March. III's and LIV's Open Day. M. went. R. had large quantities of needlework on show. Letter from University Hall to say I'm accepted on receipt of £1 deposit and medical certificate.

Monday 28 August. Mr Wilkinson and other ARP personnel occupying dining room all evening for practice. Tried on gas mask – have to take it to Liverpool.

Friday 1 September. Germany started bombing Poland 5.30 a.m. I went to Electric and saw *Son of Frankenstein* and *Exposed* – both good. Making black curtains most of evening. Ernest came at night looking most miserable because called up.

Saturday 2 September. Sewing and putting up black curtains. D. working most of day including evening. Hitler says 'No war on Poland'!

Sunday 3 September. Didn't go to church at all. Britain declared war on Germany 11 a.m. and France at 5 p.m. Ernest came at night wearing new khaki uniform – looking rather sweet and self-conscious.

Monday 25 September. Birthday – eighteen. D. gave me 10s. and R. gave me Coty talcum powder. Took Rudge for walk. Walked to Halifax after dinner. Went to Mr Dodd's and had a top tooth filled – also to have a bottom one done.

Wednesday 4 October. Packing all a.m. Went to Liverpool. Got 1.37 train, there 3.30. Family came to station. Only seven freshers and sleeping in one room at 45 Ullet Road but may be moved to 42 later. Had tea 4.30, dinner 6.30 and hot milk 9.30. Went to see Buller 5.30 for a few minutes only. Wrote to family.

Thursday 5 October. Breakfast 8.30. Got 9 a.m. tram to 'Varsity. Registered and saw Dean about subjects. Dinner at cafeteria. With Christine Wright and Joyce most of day. I had no lectures. Went to town and bought white overall. Had coffee with Buller after dinner. Wrote to family for S.C. and £2 fee for exemption from Matric certif. Wrote D.M.S. for certificate of good character for Dean.

Thursday 21 December. Went to Hx. to get Christmas presents. R. and I bought fountain pen for M. – 7s.6d. between us, then parted. Bought *Through the Looking Glass* and *Swiss Family Robinson* 2s. and 2s. for R. Bought Coty talc and shaving stick for D. and Dubarry bath cubes for Mabel 1s. M. and D. feathering geese at night – one for us.

1940

Sunday 28 April. Went to the Cathedral a.m. Hundreds of French-Canadians billeted in Warwick Street, off Princes Road.

Wednesday 1 May. Parcel from home and letter which seems to suggest that I shall have a bike in the near future.

Friday 3 May. Posted letter home – enthusiastic about bike! Discussed Buttery with Peggy F.

Thursday 16 May. Letter from D. to say that bike sent off Wednesday.

Friday 17 May. Bike arrived but the pump was missing.

Alison and I had a ride round Sexton Park and the bike seems very good – quite thrilled.

Saturday 15 June. Zoo. exam 10–12.30. Very nice paper and I think I've got a 2 all right. Got another puncture when riding down so had to walk all the way back to Hall with it. Olga and Alison and I went to the Phil. to see *The Birth of a Baby* – quite a good show but very short – only 1¾hrs. Spent most of the evening mending the puncture but fear that there is still another hole somewhere.

Monday 17 June. p.c. from the railway to say I'd to go to Exchange Lost Property Office about my pump so went and got it although it may not be mine – seems all right. Bought a puncture repair set at Woolworth's. Buller told us in supper that there would be no Hall dance and we must go home immediately we finished exams. The French wanting to stop fighting.

Tuesday 27 August. Slight air raid at night – nothing happened though. Bennetts there plus five children and Mrs B. proceeded to feed baby quite brazenly and publicly which surprised me,

Saturday 21 September. Got 1.38 train to Liverpool. Had four air raids and spent half the night in the cellar.

Monday 23 September. Freshers arriving all p.m. and helped to look after them – forty of them! Air raids at night – back in bed 4.15 a.m.

Wednesday 25 September. Short notes from all the family including 5s. from D. for birthday. Got letter and handkerchief from Linnie. Walked right down to town with fresher. Saw shop windows broken in Church Street.

Thursday 17 October. Worked hard all day. Heard bomb drop nearby.

Saturday 19 October. Went and did Zoo, prac. a.m. Bomb in Princes Road so had to make detour on way to 'Varsity by way of back streets. Siren from 7–12. Couldn't do much work in the cellar due to fearful row. Finished first sleeve of jumper.

Sunday 20 October. No.40 had house-warming p.m., quite amusing but lasted all afternoon and air raid all evening and next morning as well, so got very little work done.

Monday 21 October. Choir practice 6.45 and sirens and guns went soon after seven so had to stop in no.44. Buller made a great commotion and wouldn't let us come across until nearly nine – with cushions on our heads! Again I got no work done. Raid finished 2.45 a.m. and lights went out soon after as I was eating an orange, so undressed in Stygian darkness.

Monday 18 November. Auntie Enid sent me three boxes of Black Magic – quite stunned! Choir practice after supper, prolonged until nearly 9 p.m. because of raids. Five incendiary bombs fell on the premises, one on the front doorstep of 42, gallantly extinguished by Miss Black and soldier from next door.

Thursday 28 November. Should have had a choir practice with Dr Wallace but ill, so didn't. Bad raid from 7.30 to 4 a.m. Bomb dropped by traffic lights in Croxteth Road – Lodge Lane junction on bank. Lots of windows in Hall blown out – not ours though.

Friday 20 December. Went to see *Dr Ehrlich's Magic Bullets* (Edward G. Robinson) and *The Lone Wolf* (Warren Williams). Both quite good. Unfortunately a siren went at seven and Mabel insisted on going but I stayed until nine to see the performance through. All the family in the cellar when I got home. Had supper there, though no 'all-clear' till after eleven.

Wednesday 25 December. Had a lazy day – mainly eating and reading. Got some quite decent presents. Yardley April Violets from R., Romany calendar from D., Grannie's gold bracelet from M. (who also gave R. a watch), knitting book and sponge bag from Auntie Midge, hanky from Mills's, silk stockings from Auntie Phyllis and also two pairs from Auntie Cis, really meant for M. but too thin for her. Wrote letters of thanks at night.

Tuesday 31 December. It seems a terrifically long time since I finished off my diary at the end of last year; then I was sitting in front of a dying fire in the sitting room, tonight (not having any kind of fire in the sitting room!) I'm huddled up in bed with my feet getting colder and colder. Probably by the time I write up at the end of next year there'll hardy be a presentable male left in the place!

1941

[*After 1940 I no longer kept a journal but only an ordinary diary, mostly with details of academic timetables, letters written and brief references to other activities. At the top of the page starting January 1941 is a note*: '✓ = no siren between dinner and breakfast'. *I returned to Liverpool on 8 January. Frequent air raids continued.*]

Thursday 9 January. Got a 1 for Zoo. and a 2 for Botany.
Friday 10 January. Joyce Sargent killed last night.
Friday 21 February. Went to mass meeting on Conscription in Union.

Thursday 27 February. Puncture.

Monday 3 March. Talk on gas and first aid by Dr Cronan Lowe.

Thursday 6 March. Got new tyre for bike.

Sunday 23 March. Church 3 p.m. National Day of Prayer.

Thursday 1 May. Large parcel of food from M.

Friday 2 May. 1st team for firewatching – long raid. The sirens went at 10.15 before we were properly ready and we didn't get any work done all night to my great annoyance. We had to sit in the office and then when things got rather hot sat under the stairs, so we sat under the stairs most of the time. It was about the worst raid we've had and things were dropping all round. Buller's room got covered with soot and her window blew out. We ate dry bread and black coffee to keep awake as the raid didn't finish until nearly 3 a.m. Lots of Hall windows were broken but to our relief we found our room was completely all right. Joan looked a bit shaken towards the end, but quite honestly I never turned a hair. I don't know why, but I've absolutely no dread of being hit at all, in fact I feel quite convinced that I shan't die yet. I shouldn't be afraid to die, what does it matter anyway? – but I enjoy life and I know deep in me that it isn't my fate to die like this. Perhaps that is why I am not afraid. In some ways I'm such an awful coward as I can't bear physical pain, such as going to the dentist, but yet I've no dread of bombs which surely might cause one the most agonizing of physical pains. I'm glad I haven't got parents who get frightfully agitated about whether I'm all right after every raid. I wonder if in their hearts they're afraid for me – I hope they're not. Anyway I'm glad they let me come here because I'm happier than I've been before in my life, and even if I were killed I hope they wouldn't regret it because I'd rather die being happy than go on living in a sort of vegetative state.

Saturday 3 May. With great difficulty I arose at 8 a.m. longing to stay in bed another six hours at least. Alison and I went down to do the Zoo. prac we'd missed yesterday and took twice as long as usual to get there due to the large numbers of bombs about and the number of impassable roads. After lunch I mended a puncture and adjusted the carrier of my bike. Then I washed and wrote to M. and R. Joan went to the Sports at Wyncote as Ken was running. I didn't go. Had another bad raid at night and we didn't get much sleep due to the noise of guns and bombs until early morning. We came up to our room at 4.30 but no one else heard the all-clear. Miss Black made us go down to the cellar two hours later (where we stayed for ½hr) because a lot of time bombs were going off. Craddock Thomas was killed.

Friday 16 May. Letter from home – Bernard missing.
Wednesday 28 May. Irene Hilton spoke on jobs we could go into.
Tuesday 3 June. Got new inner tube for back tyre.
Thursday 25 September. Gas mask inspection.

1942

Monday 23 February. Broke 3-speed and had it mended.
Monday 2 March. Had a puncture – front wheel.
Monday 9 March. Terrific puncture in back tyre.

Friday 13 March. Got a new tyre and inner tube on my back wheel.
Tuesday 21 April. Wrote home – got 2nd in terminal. Cyclometer 1,375.
Monday 14 September. Back to Liverpool. Cyclometer 1,757.

Keep Calm and Carry On

~

Marian Henry Jones

The outbreak of war signalled the end of my life as a student. For the previous two years I had been studying the history of Austria in London and Vienna, but the dark shadow of approaching war had already fallen across my path. After the annexation of Austria by the Nazis in March 1938, obstacles were raised to my further studies in the Vienna State Archives, probably because the eminent professor in the University of London who supervised my research, a great friend of President Masaryk and an outspoken critic of all illiberal regimes, was regarded with suspicion by the new masters in Vienna. I remained in London, working on material there all through the tragic Munich crisis and the subsequent annexation of Czechoslovakia. But much of my time was spent looking for work in this country for Jewish friends from Vienna and then helping them to settle down. For the women, it meant almost invariably domestic work; all were anxious and heartsick while trying to be grateful.

I returned home to the village of Cwmtwrch in the upper Swansea valley in late August 1939, followed by two German-Jewish refugee children, to share what their parents in London considered would be the greater safety of our remote valley. They settled down happily and were everywhere well-received by classmates and grown-ups.

I listened to Neville Chamberlain's speech that first Sunday morning in September at a friend's house, on my way from chapel. I was shocked to find that I felt relieved that the real situation had at last been faced by this Prime Minister who had betrayed Czechoslovakia, crying 'Peace, Peace,' where there was no peace. But I knew that I alone in that small parlour felt that way. A young woman, just recently engaged to be married, sobbed hysterically. Her elderly mother consoled her silently and later spoke of men she remembered leaving for other wars, on the African veldt and the fields of France.

My parents shared my own mixed feelings. They too had been forced by Hitler's evildoing to abandon their traditional, unquestioning Christian pacifism for a reluctant, troubled acceptance of the necessity to resist his pagan ideology and programme for the expansion of Germany. Our despair at the failure of the League of Nations was relieved, now and then, by the decent sentiments of President Roosevelt, soon to become our only hope in the coming months of 'blood, toil, tears and sweat'.

Side by side with my international connections went the love of my own country, Wales. Indeed my interest in the problems of the multinational Habsburg empire arose in no small measure from my understanding of the natural tensions felt by a subject population. I was very keenly aware of the perils Welsh culture faced when the emphasis was first and foremost on the British aspect of our nationality. Rather than return to London for employment in a government agency as my professor suggested, I decided I would teach in Wales. I was invited to join the staff of the History Department of University College, Swansea, in place of a lecturer who had already left for a post in the new Ministry of Supply. My duties would be to lecture mainly on Welsh history. Joy was soon followed by an oppressive responsibility, turning to panic when I heard that I would give my first lecture only four days later to a class of over a hundred students. For the rest of that first term I worked feverishly to keep at least one lecture ahead of each class, giving nine lectures a week, excluding seminars. The remuneration was £300 a year, a good salary for a young person then. However, when the second lecturer departed a year and a half later to the Offices of the War Cabinet and all his work was added to mine without further pay, I did feel somewhat aggrieved. Nevertheless, as the additional work was in my own field of European history, I accepted it as valuable experience. The slogan 'There's a war on' soothed many feelings of indignation at that time. It was with rueful satisfaction that I heard on my departure that two new lecturers were appointed to take my place.

Looking back on my first hectic year, with its unremitting preparation of lectures, and the annoyance of repeated changes to the timetable as we lost lecture rooms to accommodate the University of London's School of Mines, I see how greatly I was helped by the students' cheerful acceptance of me. The classes were quite large then, about seventy in each of the second and third year courses, fourteen Honours candidates, and as I took the first and second year students together for alternating courses of Welsh history, they numbered 120 in my first year. My appearance in the larger classes was at first greeted by the chorus: 'Why was she born so beautiful, Why was she born at all?' sung to a well-known hymn-tune and repeated with *hwyl* several times. The smaller classes amused themselves in quieter ways by removing my gas mask when my back was turned, passing it to the back of the class or onto the window ledge outside. It would have been fatal to show annoyance. The attendance sheets I sent round the larger classes carried the names of the illustrious and the infamous, from Garbo to Goebbels. These and other antics became trivial as I wondered how many of the men now just marking time before call-up, would eventually survive what I knew would surely become a long-drawn-out and devastating struggle.

In 1939, there were seven women lecturers in University College Swansea, two of them professors and heads of their departments. They were not wartime appointments, but had been there since the college was first established. The Librarian was also a woman, as well as her deputy and an assistant, so there were ten of us sharing the Women's Staff Common Room – a small, dark cupboard of a room in a narrow passage. The male staff never entered our portals, nor did we think of going into their large, sunny common room. It never struck any of us at that time that we were underprivileged. The two very imposing women professors, Dr Mary Williams and Dr Florence Mockeridge, and the equally formidable Librarian, Miss Olive Busby, seemed to our generation living proof that there were no barriers to a woman's academic advancement provided she had the qualifications, ambition and dedication. One of the professors was married, and eventually two of the lecturers, so even that did not present barriers to us in Swansea.

One afternoon in mid-May 1940, the magnolias and camellias of Singleton were well past their best but the weather was glorious, as if trying to make up for the dire news from the Low Countries. I called to see if anything in my pigeonhole needed attention before I left for my digs, when the head porter came in and apologetically pinned a red poster to the noticeboard. In large white capitals it read 'Keep Calm and Carry On!' My heart sank. The news had been bad enough, but if the time had come when the academic Amazons of Singleton needed such instruction, the plight of the country was desperate indeed!

By the end of that first session my friendship with a colleague in the Classics Department was assuming a more romantic aspect, and at Christmas 1940 our engagement was announced. We had no plans for an early marriage until the raising of the age of reserved occupations the following Easter posed the prospect of a long separation. In the moral climate of that time, and our own convictions, it would have been impossible for us, unmarried, to spend much time together once he had left the college. The heavy bombing of Swansea and the constant air raid alarms deepened the sense of insecurity and heightened our determination to belong fully to each other and make the most of our newfound happiness. Our wedding early in September 1941 was no quiet, hurried wartime event, but thanks to my parents, as resplendent an occasion as could be managed. The service was at Bethesda Welsh Baptist Chapel, Swansea, four ministers officiating. I wore an ivory lace gown and the wax orange blossoms on my veil had adorned my mother-in-law's wedding hat in 1908. The three-tiered wedding cake was made and iced by a family acquaintance, from ingredients gladly contributed from the rations of many relatives and friends, and the reception at the Langland Bay Hotel for sixty people was a happy occasion, timed so that everyone could be safely out of Swansea before blackout. We little thought the peace of Lampeter, where we had arranged to spend the weekend, would be broken that evening by an air raid warning, sounded after the dropping of two landmines some miles away.

In term time at home in Cwmtwrch, I was lucky to share fire-watching duty with two cynical, witty colliers. Our skill with stirrup pump and sand buckets was never once put to the test. The coming of evacuees from Liverpool in 1940 had been seen by some as a great threat to the Welsh language and way of life, but in my experience a fear not justified by events. In our village the children were warmly received, and if the warmth was dimmed a little by constant bed-wetting and importunate visiting parents, that helped to give us Welsh people a better opinion of ourselves in comparison! On the whole the children who came to Cwmtwrch were soon turned for the duration into God-fearing chapel-goers, singing hymns and reciting verses in Welsh. Some of them brought joy to childless homes, and a lifelong connection was often formed. My parents had been scrupulous not to expose our Jewish evacuees to direct Christian instruction, but doubtless they hoped that the lives of some Christians they now met would speak for the faith and offset some of the harm done to their people in the name of Christianity.

Clothes rationing presented me with no great problems. My bed-ridden grandmother had given me all her margarine coupons for my trousseau. My mother had laid by several lengths of dress material at the beginning of the war, along with other household goods, all of which proved invaluable later. Most villages could boast of a seamstress or two in those days, women well used to turning garments inside out and cutting them down to fit younger children, so we were not shy of asking them 'to alter' for us. The availability of coupon-free Welsh wool led me, after a WVS apprenticeship in making gloves and socks for the forces, to venture into pullovers, even graduating to cable stitch. I embroidered cardigans with flowers for my young sister, which pleased her and reminded me of Tyrolean jackets in happier days in Austria. But coupon-free or not, there was a limit to the uses of itchy Welsh wool!

In the centre of Swansea it was discouraging to find the bombed out shops, reopened in their new locations, so limited in choice and quite stripped of former glamour. Fortunately the Plaza was spared, to offer us tea as well as a film. I seem to have spent much time in the cinema during wartime: away from home, in winter, 'flicks' and café-crawling were the most agreeable ways of gaining some privacy and keeping warm at the same time. Thus Charles Boyer, Clark Gable, Katherine Hepburn and Ginger Rogers seemed like personal acquaintances. At home, on the radio, 'Much Binding in the Marsh' and 'Itma' delighted my younger siblings and the evacuees, but exasperated my mother, who peremptorily hushed us up when it was time to listen to 'Mr Churchill' or the postscripts to the News. My father endlessly twiddled the knobs of the wireless set, as he had done throughout the war in Spain, in a quest for more and 'different' news, but usually getting only Lord Haw-Haw for his pains. The amount of Welsh then broadcast was minimal, but we noted the time of every programme, from school broadcasts to religious services, not forgetting 'Adar Tregaron' and its like, so that my monoglot grandmother should not miss one precious word.

I have said little about the main turning points of the war although I followed its course so carefully, day by day, atlas open, hardly a news bulletin missed. I can only conclude that faced with the huge uncertainty of life itself, the small certainties of personal life, the ties of family, friends, career and faith, became all the more important and therefore memorable. It is my good fortune that they remain in the memory as blessings, with the same power to help me 'Keep calm and carry on'.

From March 1941 all women aged between nineteen and forty (raised to fifty in 1944) had to register at

CHAPTER 3

WAR WORK

employment exchanges. Once registered, women could be compulsorily directed into war work. Welsh women worked in engineering, in munitions and in aircraft factories: they took over civilian jobs vacated by men on the trains and on the buses, in the gasworks, in the police force and anywhere else they were needed.

Give us the Tools

~

Dora Lemin

I presented myself at the requisitioned Central School of Arts and Crafts in London with a Ministry of Labour pass, an identity card, a gas mask and a sinking heart. I was a conscripted woman. I had been allowed to finish my course at drama school, and had been offered the choice of nursing, the forces or industry. I had chosen industry, which seemed to offer the best chance of staying in the

United Kingdom, and perhaps be near home. Motor mechanics seemed to be the most interesting, and I chose that. The course lasted for three months after which, pass or fail one supposed, one could be sent anywhere in the United Kingdom for the duration.

My fellow conscripts were a strange mixture. They were a flashily smart hairdresser from the East End of London, a nurse recovering from a nervous breakdown, a dressmaker, a girl from Woolworths, an artist, a middle-aged lady who was not a conscript but wanted 'to do her bit', and two silent women in their early thirties who were not communicative about their previous occupations. They were obviously above call-up age at that time, and they remained a mystery to the end. There were horrifying speculations as to what they might have done before joining us.

Our instructors accepted us with resignation. They did their best to teach the basics of mechanics to a group of women with no previous experience and little natural aptitude. It was hard going. We made files, screwdrivers, spanners and tweezers, filed metal and cut screws with taps and dies, and made nails in the breathtaking heat of the forge. We took engines to pieces and struggled to reassemble them.

Our metalwork instructor was a silversmith by trade who had helped to design and make the beautiful Sword of Stalingrad. The electrician was a rugby player who had been invalided out of the army having broken his leg in a forces rugby match and not, as he told us, in mortal combat with the enemy. When he was late he shaved with razor in one hand and wrote on the board with the other. He soon gave up the struggle with us, and in end-of-week tests gave us the answers in the same breath as the questions. We had to pass, so he said that this was less trouble than cheating with the marking. Workshop routine was taught by a mid-European refugee, a gentle, white-haired craftsman in a carpenter's apron. With his thick, drooping moustache, he looked just like Albert Schweitzer. His work was exquisite, but his English was appalling. With him we neither knew what we were doing nor why – but we loved him.

I remember the feeling of utter hopelessness, when surrounded with dozens of little greasy wheels and a forest of tangled coloured wires, wondering how this could possibly help to win the war. Eventually things became clearer. At the end of our three months we felt we might manage with a bit of help and a lot of luck. The hairdresser still could not be persuaded that the tweezers she had made were not for plucking eyebrows, a service she performed for anyone who wanted it. The file was more often in her handbag for her nails than in her toolbox.

On our last day our instructor, bidding us goodbye, said, 'It isn't "Give us the tools and we'll finish the job" as far as you lot are concerned. I don't know about the job, but you'll certainly finish the tools.' He had despaired of instilling into us the love these craftsmen had for their precious tool kit.

There was much anxiety as we waited to know where we were to be sent. Ford's at Dagenham was the place that everyone dreaded would be her destination, having heard awful stories of what happened if one did not keep up with assembly lines and piecework. In the event only the hairdresser was sent there and we all felt that she would be able to stand up for herself anywhere.

I was sent to the garage of a large firm of builders now on government contract to build airfields. I found I was the only woman in the whole place. Another had been allocated but she had been ill and sent to a lighter job. They had never had a woman there before and obviously there had been certain instructions given to the men on how they were to treat me. They tried not to swear and, if they did, they apologized. When Jim, the mechanic with whom I first worked, sucked petrol from the carburettor, he walked, lips pursed, holding his breath to spit it outside. This conduct did not last beyond the first hour, and soon I was accepted as inevitable.

Young men had been called up, so the mechanics were mostly old, unfit or from neutral countries. Among these were some young Irishmen whose boisterous horseplay was quite frightening. They were basically kind, but resented a woman doing 'a man's work'. Two I remember especially were brothers, Mick and Paddy, both brake testers. They were big and strong with bright auburn hair, red faces and thick, hairy tattooed arms with leather straps round their wrists. They would never trust my work. I would pull the nuts as tight as I could, sure this time they could not be shifted. Mick would saunter up, put a spanner on the nuts and effortlessly turn it round two or three times. Then Paddy would jump in the cab and drive as fast as he could at a brick wall, and when within inches of it, slam on the brakes, squealing to a shuddering halt.

The only amenities were a cold water tap in the yard,

and a gas ring and kettle in a lean-to shed. There was no cloakroom. In theory I was allowed to hang my coat in the manager's office, but in my greasy boiler suit the carpeted floor and white woodwork forbade me, so I hung my old raincoat on a nail in the wall like the men.

My job was to help service the huge lorries as they came in from the construction sites. We hauled the engines out on a chain pulley and stripped them down, replacing the worn parts and cleaning the re-usable ones in a bath of paraffin. This was often down to sludge at the bottom as the foreman pondered how to spell paraffin on the requisition papers. Why he bothered I do not know, as a spelling mistake would not have been noticed on that greasy form.

Oil saturated through to the skin. In this condition I felt I could not go to a restaurant for lunch. To take sandwiches meant sitting on the concrete floor inside the garage or, in fine weather, outside on the ground leaning against a rough brick wall. When I finally left the oil oozed out of me for weeks.

Eventually, Percy, one of the fitters, took me to the Pleez-U café where he went for lunch – a hot, steamy little shop just off the main road, a pull up for lorry drivers. The filthy boiler suit was not objected to there. One had beautifully cooked meat and two veg., a boiled pudding with creamy custard, and a huge mug of really hot tea, all for 1s.6d. We sat on a bench at a long oilcloth-covered table. The set meal was ready promptly at twelve o'clock, and had to be ordered and paid for a week in advance. It. was served by the woman who cooked it. She scuffed along in bedroom slippers and wore a wrap-round overall, her damp wispy hair hanging untidily round her face. Her teeth were few and far between, but she was kind and took a motherly interest in her customers. After working from half past seven in the morning I was awfully hungry by twelve o'clock. One day when Percy did not appear I went on my own, but by then I was one of them.

I remember lying under a lorry just in from the construction site trying to take off the sump. The nuts were encrusted with mud and rust. After a terrific effort I managed to move them and carefully lowered the sump – then blackness. I had forgotten to empty the oil out and slopping over me was a stream of filthy engine oil. I felt like crying. I had nothing to change into and nowhere to change if I had. They gave me wads of cotton waste to take off the worst, but my ultimate shame was to travel home at night in a crowded bus. No one would stand near me. I must have smelled and looked horrible.

Eventually, another woman, Elli, arrived. She was a Hungarian refugee, a doctor, who had escaped to England with only the clothes she wore, a ring, a watch and a diamond bracelet. She wore her beautiful fur coat over her overalls as she had no other. She had applied to work in a hospital but for some reason she had been sent to us until she had been cleared for security. She was engaged to a 'free' Polish sailor and there were unpleasant rumours at the garage about spies. I found myself becoming a protective wall between her and them. I was darkly warned not to have anything to do with her – in case…

Soon we had another two women. Joan, a model, tall and slim with shining red-gold hair, arrived in a dazzling white boiler suit in which on her first day she walked, swaying, the length of the garage. Before she had reached the other end there was a large, black handmark on the seat of the trousers. She had been accepted – joyfully.

Our number grew to ten and occasionally I had company to the Pleez-U but Joan still went to a nearby restaurant where with poise and complete self-assurance she had gone on her first day in the handmarked boilersuit. She said with a charming smile that no one had complained.

I had now become a kind of liaison/welfare/mechanic, in charge of training apprentices. When the time came I actually felt sorry to leave. I still have the piece of paper which wrapped my leaving present. It is creased and filthy and smells of oil. Some of the signatures, written with the blunt stub of a pencil, are hardly decipherable, but I will not throw it away. It is part of a period of my life I shall never forget.

At Chester Station I could have Sat Down and Cried

~

Olwen Hughes Jones

I was called up fifty years ago, when I was a girl of eighteen. They gave me a choice – the ATS or industry. I chose industry and I was issued with a rail warrant to

Chester, where I was to report to the training centre on Foregate Street.

My home was Anglesey and, apart from the odd Sunday school trip to Rhyl, I had never left the island. When I arrived at Chester I did not know a soul; at home I knew everyone and they all knew me. At Chester station, I could have sat down on my case and cried. But I thought, 'No, girl, carry on.'

There were lots of girls at the training centre but none from my part of Wales. The next problem was digs. They gave an address to me and we set off. The landlady asked, 'Trainees?' and when we said 'yes' she halfheartedly took us in. The rent was twenty-seven shillings a week and we were only earning thirty-nine shillings. We had just twelve shillings a week to manage on and out of that we had to pay our bus fares, buy our teas in the canteen and stamps to write home. The landlady was not a nice person. She was able to get hold of plenty of cheese so we had cheese sandwiches everyday for four months. We got to look like a pair of mice. When at last, our training completed, we officially passed out, we were both sent to Liverpool – to Napiers on the East Lancs Road. I worked on grinding and Gladys on a lathe. I lived with Gladys's mother and she was very kind. But I still felt a stranger. Not a word of Welsh did I hear and *hiraeth* would come over me. I got used to the huge factory with the hundreds of workers. I was given free passes home, and used one at Christmas and the other for our one-week annual holiday. I used to bring back tea, farm butter and always a piece of home-cured bacon. Food was very scarce in Liverpool but on Anglesey there was never any shortage.

I had no regrets about going to Liverpool. The Scouse people are very friendly and have a wonderful sense of humour: you have to live there to appreciate it. Despite the bombs and the fog, I settled down. I lost my homesickness and I was happy. I made friends, not acquaintances, and when I came home to Wales I missed the company of the girls very much. I married in 1947 – a local boy, who had been in the army in Italy. We are now both OAPs and lucky enough to still go about and have my friends of fifty years ago come and visit.

'Good Morning, Sister'

~

E.M. Mitchell

At seventeen, my first job as junior clerk was in the Gas Office for the princely wage of £1.7*s*.4*d* per week. My main task was to call the rebates for the head clerk: he would call out the meter reading from the ledgers and from my card I would call back the due rebate. The job was utterly boring, and after a couple of weeks I knew all the rebates off by heart; the only ones which threw me were the odd madly extravagant consumer or the penny-pinching skinflint.

Every morning when I rode by bicycle into the yard, the storekeeper, a short, stocky man of five foot two in a greasy flat cap would call, 'Good morning, sister.' I later learned that he was a union official, but all I knew about unions then was that a couple of pence was taken from my wages for something called NALGO. Each morning I would brace myself to reply, 'Good morning, brother,' but bravado fled at the last moment.

Our office was on the top yard opposite the stores but it was down the steps in the bottom office where the enchantment lay – in the various workshops run by men all over fifty. The retiring age of sixty-five had been dropped due to the war and military call-up. Three of the men were well into their seventies. It was the laboratory which drew me like a magnet, a large building with double Bunsen burners and charts all around the walls, intricate instruments and domes set on the shelf-like desks. The gas tester's military call-up had been deferred because his work was of national importance. It was so important that this man, in his early thirties, spent most of his day reading and studying form.

By law, the gas calorific value must never drop below a certain figure, and four tests a day had to be made to ensure this was maintained. He had become blasé and would look at the flame from the Bunsen and guess. Mind, he had an experienced eye. That worked fine as long as the gas examiner didn't call. The examiner was from an independent board and came on no set day. With his own instruments he made a test that was perfect and precise down to the last nth. Gas testers were allowed to be 2 per cent either side of this test – a larger difference and they had some explaining to do! With an eye to the future (and my continual badgering) he taught me to test. Each test took four minutes on an instrument called a calorimeter and the result was worked out in logarithms. I loved it. Then I did a specific gravity test to see how much impurity was in the gas due to tar. There was no natural gas in those days; it came from coal, fed through pipes, then through large oxide boxes for purification and finally into the holder. When the massive oxide boxes were open, for checking purposes, mothers brought children suffering from whooping cough to breathe the fumes which were reputed to have healing powers. True or not I never knew, but mothers and children came during all the years I worked there.

Every lunchtime was sacrificed (very willingly) to testing. The gas tester would use my four tests for the day, adjusting them only by a point or two according to which way the flame flickered. I resented going back up to the office and secretly eating my sandwiches. How I coveted that tester's job. I didn't wish him to fall down the yard steps, or have a little accident in his Austin Ruby, but why oh why wasn't he fired with ambition and aiming for greater heights? Not he. His salary was £5 per week, one of the top paid men; labourers earned £3.15s., gas collectors £4, fitters and other skilled workers £4.15s. The head clerk and foreman were also in the £5 bracket. I helped with the wages so I knew. On this salary he ran a car and sent his two young sons to private schools, *and* was deferred from call-up. It looked hopeless.

One morning word buzzed around the yard that the gas tester had been called up. Sympathetically I asked him if it was true. On confirmation my face and words were truly sorry but my heart and hopes surged with joy.

The following week the laboratory position appeared in

the local paper: 'Experienced man required, familiar with all aspects of gas testing, good wage.' That was me. The only thing the tester had not let me do was to climb the holder. This had to be done to check the holder plates for pressure. No problem. I could climb the highest tree in our wood. Heights held no fear for me. I sent my letter and signed it M. Evans. The gas engineer and manager Mr Muir, who was my boss, was unaware that I had learned this job while he was at lunch.

On Tuesday evening I stood nervously outside the Council Chambers in the municipal building, waiting to be interviewed. I was called into a large room, where Councillors and members of the Gas Committee sat around a huge table, and at the top sat the boss. I drew myself up to my full height of four-foot eleven and smiled, avoiding the boss's eyes. 'We were not expecting a young lady,' said the spokesman, and although I gave a detailed explanation of my knowledge, while the boss's steel-grey eyes glared at me from beneath lowered brows, they just didn't want to know. As though talking to a six-year-old, the spokesman announced that this was definitely a man's job; it was unheard of for a woman to contemplate gas testing, climbing holders and so on. I replied that women were doing very unusual things these days, like driving trucks. Politely, but firmly, I was shown the door.

The gas tester left at the end of the week and the boss locked the lab. But by law gas had to be tested every day. Who would the replacement be? I knew next morning.

'Into my office,' ordered the boss. Then, 'We're going down the lab. Let me see you do all those things you laid claim to in the Council Chamber.'

Great, I'd do headstands on the holder if needs be.

'Quite good,' he said. 'And what about climbing the holder?' he said, staring at my dress.

'I'll show you tomorrow.' I replied quickly.

When the vacancy appeared in the local press I applied again. I sailed into the Council Chamber and beamed at all present, including the boss. Once more the spokesman explained this was a man's job; once more I protested that I was doing the job.

'Yes,' he said, 'Mr Muir has mentioned how good you are at filling the gap, but it is a man's job.'

I looked at Mr Muir, but he was looking elsewhere… Once more I found myself outside the door.

Next morning I rode into the yard.

'Good morning, sister.'

'Good morning, Mr Waite.'

'Heard they turned you down for the job again.'

I'm only a fill-in,' I answered.

'I'll get you that job, sister,' he said. 'First resign from NALGO. Fill in this form to join my union, the Municipal and General Workers.'

That completed, he pinned a small, button-size, navy blue badge with gold writing onto me. 'Wear it with pride, sister,' he said, 'and when you apply for the job this week I'll be with you in the Chamber.'

Once more I stood outside the Chamber door, but not alone. In a slightly cleaner check cap was my five-foot-two knight.

'Ah it's you again,' the spokesman wearily said as I beamed all around.

'Well I'm afraid what I told you previously still applies.'

'One moment, brother,' said my mouthpiece. 'My member here is carrying out the work to the Manager's satisfaction.' He stared pointedly at Mr Muir, who nodded briefly.

'It's not a woman's job,' snarled the by now very irritated spokesman.

'And she's a member of NALGO anyway.'

While Mr Waite tapped the badge on my lapel, I quickly diverted my eyes from the boss's. My champion was still speaking, '...and furthermore the lab is a closed shop to all my members, and unless given the job she will never put a foot inside again.' There was some muttering around the table, then the spokesman asked us to leave as they wished to discuss the matter. 'You'll have that job, sister, you'll see,' said Mr Waite when we were outside again.

Next day, wearing a dress, I arrived at work.

'Into my office,' said the boss. 'I want you to start testing early today.'

I was glad he was sitting at his desk. At least half of his eighteen-stone presence was hidden, as I mustered the courage to reply, 'No. Mr Waite said I was to stay in the office.'

'Who manages this works?' he asked.

'You do, Sir.'

'Well?'

'Mr Waite said I mustn't go into the lab.' Fearfully I glanced up at him.

His mouth was twitching at the corner; it looked like the start of a smile, on the other hand it might be a nervous tic. I fled to my office. The next three days he repeatedly asked me to test and somehow I found the strength to refuse. Thankfully a letter arrived to say I had the job and the wages would be £3.17s.6d. – a rise of £2.10s.2d. What wealth! 'Buy me a boiler suit, Mum,' I said, donning my trousers. I stuck a yellow pendant into the front of my bike. I timed my arrival in the yard to when all the men would be queuing up to sign the time clock. I did two victory circles around the yard and they shouted, 'You got it.'

Triumphantly, I handed the letter to Mr Waite.

'Refuse it, sister.'

Refuse it? Oh brother! 'But why, Mr Waite? I don't want any other job and I have a rise of £2.10s.2d.'

'Sister, for three interviews in that Chamber they've been telling you it's a man's job.'

'Yes but...'

'Well now, sister, you want a man's wage to go with it, the same as the tester.'

'I don't, Mr Waite.'

'Oh yes you do, sister. Go in the office to work now.'

Deflated and wearing trousers I went inside.

One whole dreary week dragged by. Once more I was fluent on rebates and then the letter arrived: 'On further consideration and discussion' they had increased my wages to £5, as they realized I would need industrial clothes, etc.

Thank you, brother.

Edna 1939

~

Alison Bielski

glaring at the red stove
she ruled her kitchen domain
each evening not subject
but monarch our fawning cat
blanketing her black lap
she had polished washed dusted
in our classtime absence

now threw off this role slammed
the kitchen door against us
as we wrestled with late
homework in the dull study
her afternoons off left
gloom permeating cleaned rooms
that dark prowling spirit
followed by silkensoft paws

when war shattered routine
she suddenly announced her
imminent departure
for shiftwork in munitions
tackling allotted jobs
we missed her orderliness

the damped stove smirked greenly
before her deserted chair

under night cover boxed
bombs filled camouflaged lorries
passed checkpoints to aircraft
with hold flaps soon to open
above distant targets
one error killed families
in blazing dust-choked homes

The Royal Ordnance Factory, Bridgend

~

Mair Davies

At eighteen I went to work at the Royal Ordnance Factory (ROF) at Bridgend. My job was in the stores office, keeping account of goods received and booked out, charging them to the Army or the Navy. We worked three shifts – the red, blue and green. To arrive by 7 a.m. for the morning shift we had to leave home very early. We would catch the 5.10 bus up to Nantymoel station to catch the 5.30 train. Although it was only a journey of ten miles from there to Waterton station we would not get there till seven. We had to wait about on a siding, to let the mainline trains from Swansea through. We wouldn't get home till about 4.30 p.m. When I was on afternoons it meant leaving home at about one o'clock and not getting back till eleven at night. When we were going to the station for the night shift we would see people going out to the pictures or the dance halls.

We had passes to get into the factory. There were searches too. People would be picked out at random and checked to see if they had matches or cigarettes. It was an explosives factory and these things could have caused a blow up. We left our outer clothes and shoes in the shifting house. Those of us working in the office did not have to wear overalls but we had to wear special shoes. The clearways where we walked were very slippery; it was like walking on an ice rink. It was extremely dangerous for those carrying the dets (detonators) to the transit stores ready to ship out on the railway.

I never worked in the shops, as the workshops were called, but I did see people running out of them after an explosion. The Dets Section was the most dangerous. Some were killed and others had hands or fingers blown off. There were lots of accidents in the High Explosives Section too. The Pellets Section was not dangerous but nobody wanted to go there because the powder turned the skin and hair yellow. I remember one person – a lady in her sixties – being sent there for stealing money from the pocket of a workmate.

We would take our break in the canteen and sometimes there would be a dance band and people would dance in the small space available. We would have concerts too. There were some marvellous singers, some played musical instruments and others tap-danced.

Sometimes, during the night, German bombers would fly over the factory. Then the sirens would go off and we would have to run to the air raid shelter – I don't know what good they were as they were above ground in concrete buildings situated amongst the workshops. The German bombers did not once hit the factory in six years. People used to say it had been built in an area where there was a great deal of mist so it could not be located by the fliers.

As we looked out of our window we could see the place where rejects were exploded. There would be a loud, loud bang and thick black smoke would rise into the sky. A girl from the Rhondda, who worked in the outer office, lost her father there. He was one of those getting rid of the reject explosives when he was killed. Quite a few lost their lives like that.

My wages were under £3 a week when I worked day shifts but I got over £3 when I was on nights.

I remember the excitement when VE day and then VJ day were announced. It came over the loudspeakers and everyone was so happy. When the war ended the factory closed. Then people who wanted to open new factories on the site used to come to the ROF to buy tables, chairs and filing cabinets. I stayed on to book these out to people. I was one of the last to go.

War Wounded

~

Ellen Duggan

I worked in the ROF, Bridgend – in the laundry for about five years. It was hard work and it was hot work too. When we worked at night, in the blackout, we were not able to open a door or a window: we used to sweat streams.

One thing happened to me that I will never forget. It was about half past six in the morning. I was waiting for the bus to go to work and it was cold standing there. A woman behind me in the bus queue sneezed. As she sneezed, her false teeth shot out and bit me on the leg. I couldn't see, owing to the blackout, but when I got to work my foot was awash with blood. I had to have a plaster on it. They were happy times, even though there was a war on. Everyone was more friendly and more caring then.

The Forgotten Army

~

Edna Gorshkov

At eighteen, I married a Russian sailor. He was on the Murmansk run and sometimes on the North Sea and Atlantic. He was torpedoed several times and he was reported missing. Times were hard and we had to live from day to day.

I was an engineer at the ROF, Llanishen. I was trained and I was good. We worked eleven-hour shifts – day or night. I was a 'blue girl', wearing blue overalls, a helmet and goggles. I worked in P shop making breach blocks for 85mm naval guns. There were only a few elderly men so we women did everything. I worked on a Cincinatti lathe as big as a house and, overhead, women worked on cranes. The crane women lifted the guns and the breach blocks off our machines. We had to produce eight breach blocks a shift. There were six bays in my part of P shop – six cranes and a number of lathes. If we reached our target and *providing the breach blocks were perfect,* we got a bonus. We made sure the breach blocks *were* perfect and if the machines broke down we repaired them. The blocks and guns had to be absolutely spot-on for our boys in the Navy.

The wages were good at the ROF and they looked after

us. We were privileged because of our training. Doctors examined us regularly. If our husbands came home on leave we got a few days off, but we were warned, 'Try not to get pregnant.' You see, it took time to train an engineer.

Welsh women engineers had no medals but bloody well deserved them. We gave our all to the war effort. We kept the boys supplied. We had to – there was no one else. We are the forgotten army. We are the mams and grandmothers who did our bit for King and Country.

It is the old men who make wars – old men who should know better. I hope this book is read by a lot of people from all over the world and I pray to God for peace for all peoples.

The Women's Auxiliary Police Corps

~

V. Harvey

In 1939 I was interviewed for a post of civilian clerk/typist in the Glamorgan Constabulary and I commenced work in the Air Raid Precautions Department – there were four of us girls. Things were quite spartan for the Police in those days. To everyone's great amusement, the women introduced coffee breaks, but the men soon joined us and looked forward to their 'cuppas'.

As more male members of the Constabulary were being

called up for war service, two of us were transferred to the Aliens and Firearms Department. Things were very hectic there at that time as all aliens had to complete the Aliens Protected Area 1 form which had to be checked individually. A distance of eight miles around the coast of Britain was designated a 'Protected Area' and if any 'enemy' aliens wished to come into this area for any reason, they had to apply for a permit. This was an important job for the sergeant in the department at that time.

Some German and Italian males under the age of sixty-five were deported to Canada to be detained for the duration. We learned that a ship called the *Arandora Star* was torpedoed in the Atlantic and many of these men lost their lives.

We were now becoming valued members of staff. To prevent us being called up it was decided that we should become part of the Women's Auxiliary Police Corps and we were to be measured for uniforms. The police tailor was a bachelor who, it later transpired, had no idea how to measure women and was a bit shy of us. When some of the well-endowed ladies received their jackets there were red faces as they could not button them up.

At that time some young children from Europe came to stay at Llandough Castle in the Vale of Glamorgan. They were termed 'Refugees from Nazi Oppression'. They were probably Jewish and they all had to complete the APA1 form and be registered as aliens. It was quite a task and we clerks were sent to help complete the forms with the aid of interpreters.

The Glamorgan Police Headquarters were in a

small, old building opposite the Coliseum Cinema in Cowbridge Road, Canton, Cardiff. We were working in extremely cramped conditions but were a happy crowd and had some memorable times together. Bombs dropped on Cardiff caused quite a bit of damage in nearby Neville Street. I well remember that in the offices we had notices pinned on the walls with the words printed in red, 'Keep Calm and Carry On'. When we heard air raid warnings or if the war news was bad, I would take a look at these words and feel a bit reassured. In fact, to this day, if the going gets tough I visualize this notice!

The Women's Auxiliary Police Corps in Glamorgan was disbanded in March, 1946, but women continued to be employed in a civilian capacity and I was, in fact, employed by the Authority until 1951. I remember my time with the Police with pride and affection.

CHAPTER 4

THE WOMEN'S AUXILIARY SERVICES

Until 1941 women, up to the age of forty-five, volunteered to join the Women's Auxiliary Services – the Women's Royal Naval Service (WRNS), Women's Auxiliary Air Force (WAAF) or the Auxiliary Territorial Service (ATS). After April of that year women were conscripted into the services or industry. Welsh women joined all three of the services – the well-bred Wrens, the glamorous Waafs and the humble ATS. Others donned corduroy breeches, picked up their pitchforks and joined the Women's Land Army.

One Wren's War

~

Lisbeth David

It would have been an awful anticlimax (though even at school one did not admit it) if war had *not* been declared. It was such an immense, new happening and there had been such a build-up. It was exciting for the young. To our parents, only twenty-one years away from the nightmare of the Somme, it was a very different matter. But it came. On Sunday 2 September 1939 Dean Jones brought a wireless set into Llandaff Cathedral at the eleven o'clock service, and we all heard Prime Minister Neville Chamberlain declare, sorrowfully enough, that Britain was at war with Germany.

What then? Life went on as usual at Howell's School. Could I hope to get into Oxford? After the phoney war was swallowed up in the Battle of Britain and real hostilities, I spent the time at a crammer in north Oxford, working unsuccessfully for college entrance and living on the fringe of the university in its strange wartime half-life. The Air Ministry, as I remember, was in New College, the War Office in Keble; St Hugh's (my ultimate destination) a hospital for head injuries, and at Woodstock, a few miles to the north, was a brainy beehive disentangling the enemy's intentions.

Once it was clear that I wasn't going to get into Oxford that round, I volunteered for the Wrens. My call-up came in March, 1942. I was to join as a trainee wireless telegraphy operator, reporting to Dundee. We trained in a civilian wireless college which had been taken over, with its instructors, for the duration. These hapless men had to adapt from teaching bright young Merchant Service recruits with aptitude and at least a basic knowledge of radio, to communicating something to young ladies straight from school.

'Well, you all know what a cell is?' asked one, starting at the beginning. 'No,' we chorused.

Baffled, he finally gave up trying to teach us what actually happened inside the sets we would be using. We just learnt to use them.

At the same time we assimilated the naval way of life, learnt to call our bedrooms 'cabins', reported to the 'bridge', sat around in the 'fo'castle' – all this in Mathers Temperance Hotel, which was strangely ship-shaped in construction and lent itself to the convention. At divisions every forenoon we heard our own naval prayer:

O eternal Lord God, who alone spreadest out the heavens and rulest the raging of the sea, who hast compassed the waters with bounds until day and night come to an end, we beseech Thee to receive into Thy Almighty and most gracious protection all who go down to the sea in ships and occupy their business in great waters; preserve them both in body and soul, prosper their labours with good success, in all time of danger be their defence, and bring than to the haven where they would be.

We got quite handy at squad drill, and (once we had our uniforms – ugh, those pudding-basin hats!) marched proudly through the streets of Dundee amongst the trams to college and back in the evening. We spent six months getting up speed transmitting and receiving morse. We dreamed morse, we breathed morse, our heads sang with morse. At the final exam we were reading at twenty words a minute (code, plain language, Polish, anything) and transmitting at about eighteen. Almost everyone passed, and those who won their blue category badge, a winged streak of lightning, sewed it on their right sleeve with enormous pride. It had been hard earned. The first batch of Wren telegraphists, chief petty officers, sailed for Gibraltar in SS *Aguila* in August 1941. They were all lost when she was torpedoed by U-boats attacking the convoy. Subsequent drafts were rated as Wren telegraphists only, but they were still sent anywhere they were needed to release men for sea.

I was posted to Holyhead – and many a night thereafter was spent on Crewe station after home-leave, waiting for the mail train from London. Crewe at 02.00, all canteens closed, was pretty bleak, but one could count on kindness from any matelot in the same predicament. My immediate boss at Holyhead was a stout old 'Chiefie Tel' dug out from Naval Reserve, experienced, tolerant, not terribly good at explaining to a novice. I learnt more from my first watch actually on the air than from six months training. As with any skill, doing it for real is the best way to learn.

The wireless cabinet occupied a tiny pantry in the naval base, a large isolated house close to the shore. There was just room for a single operator to sit at a desk in front of banked transmitter and receiver, and I was glad it was small because we had to scrub the floor before going off watch in the morning. Most of the time we worked in four watches, two of us doing the night in four-hour spells – I can still hear the voice of my 'oppo' trying to dig me out of deep sleep at 4 a.m. to go back on watch. We lived in digs, and cycled down the long lonely road to the base in all weathers and the dark without a qualm. The last two male telegraphists went off to sea soon after we arrived. Women were quick to learn operating skills, but in general men, when fully experienced, made better operators because they were steadier and could get up a good speed without losing their rhythm. Standards went down slightly as the Wrens took over, but I enjoyed working with the ships on my frequency, mostly minesweepers and small ships within range of port. Some of the work was acting as link for C in C Western Approaches at Liverpool; the Mersey was full of heavy industry which created bad atmospherics, particularly at night; and we were better placed at Holyhead and had a good transmitter, so I enjoyed picking up signals which Liverpool couldn't hear and passing them on. This made night watches more interesting than they would otherwise have been in our tiny base. In slack times it was tempting to doze off, though one's own call sign would bring one instantly alert again (I think it still would). Usually everything was coded, so we didn't know what we were sending. Only in emergency, such as the loss of a ship or an aircraft at sea, did we work in plain language, and then the Duty Commander would be breathing down our necks and dictating what we were to send. We used radio telephony for routine contact with the Skerries and Bardsey Island lighthouse crews, who were not above tacking a kindly 'nos da' onto their more formal communications.

My landlord kept the lighthouse at the end of Holyhead breakwater. He had come from the North Foreland, and spoke lovingly of Kent, but he and his wife took wartime conditions philosophically and gave me a comfortable home. Off watch I slept, walked on Holyhead mountain –

but never as far as South Stack, which was out of bounds – and made good friends in church and at the YWCA.

I had been in Holyhead nearly a year, and had just been recommended for my 'hook' (the anchor badge worn by a leading hand) when some higher powers decided I should go to the Royal Naval College, Greenwich, to be turned into an officer. This in some ways seemed a less important step than the hook, which was earned on the job and by hard work. There was sometimes a suspicion that recommendation for a commission came at least as much because of the way one spoke as because of OLQ (Officer-like Qualities), a funny naval phrase which was always cropping up.

Greenwich was undiluted privilege. For three weeks we were admitted to the Royal Navy's Holy of Holies. We dined, nay, *breakfasted*, in the Painted Hall where Nelson had lain in state; we worshipped in Wren's fine chapel and attended lectures from *real* naval officers. (Shall I ever forget the lecture on navigation to which I had omitted – for reasons seeming good at the time – to bring pencil or ruler, trying to lay off a course by scratching the chart with compasses!) I soaked up the atmosphere and traditions of the service. Squad drill was fine, except on the day one had to take it oneself and march a squad from quarters across a very public road to what is now the Maritime Museum.

It was decreed that I was to be a cipher officer, a logical progression from Wren telegraphist, so from Greenwich, still wearing the white band of officer cadet round my cap, I went to Portsmouth for a three-week course. While I hated the course, the only thing to do was to get stuck in, which I did, and passed out top in everything except typing, in which I was bottom. While at Portsmouth we ordered our officer's uniforms, selecting a tailor by fancy or family tradition – Gieves, Austin Reed or Moseley & Poundsford – and the tailors, working under pressure, would privately assess our prospects and arrange their priorities accordingly. My suits were not ready on the day; they had obviously not rated my chances very highly. However, within twenty-four hours the fine doeskin skirt and jacket with one blue stripe on the sleeve and the miraculous velour tricorne with its blue and silver badge were mine to wear. One never really stopped marvelling; it is such a beautiful uniform – though perhaps only the willowy blondes of Mountbatten's staff did it true justice.

My first posting as a cipher officer was to Naval Control Service Office, Belfast, which was at Bangor, County Down, on Belfast Lough. By now it was 1943, and the Atlantic convoys, largely of American ships, were coming into the Lough in large numbers. Our boarding officers, all Wrens, were kept busy briefing the convoy commodores: going out to the ship in a drifter, shinning up the side by rope ladder, leg over the rail and down to the captain's cabin – easy on a calm day but no fun at all in heavy weather. One of my colleagues, known as Tugboat Annie, took a heavy fall off the ladder in rough weather and landed – mercifully – back onto the deck (rather than between the two ships). She badly damaged her spine, but she could have been killed. My friend Juliet wore lorgnettes with her bellbottoms and tricorne (she had fudged the sight test and needed spectacles to find the right ship). I heard many a strangled cry from American seamen as she clambered over the rail in a heavy sea and raised her lorgnettes to her sweet English face. I used to go out for the ride when I was off watch from the cipher office, and made friends with some of the drifter crews, seconded from east-coast fishing ports for the duration. They were splendid people.

As D Day drew near everyone was kept very busy, and in the last few days the bombardment fleet, heavily armed, but old, French and British warships considered expendable, assembled in Belfast Lough. There was W/T silence, and the night before they sailed all orders had to be taken out 'by hand of officer', so I was pressed in to help as postman round the fleet. It was a very moving experience to board these ships, poised, as we all knew, for the assault. 'Pray for us,' someone said. By the morning they were gone, and we had to wait until the war was over to find out what happened to them.

A few weeks later I was posted to Portsmouth, glad to leave Northern Ireland though its sectarian hostility had not then exploded into violence. Portsmouth had been the command headquarters for D Day, and the enormous back-up base was still in action. We lived, ten officers to a cabin, in Fareham, a pleasant green village north of Portsmouth, and worked deep down in the hills behind the city. The air underground was none too good; in a 48-hour stand-off one could go by bus to Winchester, seemingly almost untouched by war, and take deep breaths, refreshing mentally and physically. I remember coming off watch at midnight on Christmas Eve 1944 and joining an assorted service congregation in a Nissen hut above Fort Southwick for the Christmas Mass.

In retrospect early 1945 seems to be near the end of hostilities, but at the time it didn't feel like that at all. Although the news from Europe, as far as we heard it, was good, the build-up for another D Day in the Far East against the Japanese was going on, with no indication that there would be an early victory. My sister Mary and I were both told about the same time that we were due for overseas posting, and by good luck were able to go together. Neither of us had volunteered; it had seemed hard on Mother to be left at home for a second war with husband (and, this time, all four children) away, but she had done a marvelous job providing a base to which we managed to return, sometimes with our friends, from time to time for food, baths and general nourishment. We cheerfully reported to Crosby Hall in Chelsea to draw our tropical kit. This was the time that the V1 and V2 rockets were coming over, and I remember my Portsmouth colleagues rooting round for a tin hat for me, insisting that I was not to travel to London without one. Nothing landed very near in the short time we were there, but the rockets were pretty horrible. After a few days we entrained for Liverpool and sailed almost immediately.

On Easter Day 1945 our ship came into Colombo harbour, actually while the Easter service was going on and the choir singing 'Brother James's Air'. We were to see the war out in Ceylon (as Sri Lanka was then called). Colombo was hot and very humid. The worst thing about being there was something we had not been told in all our preparatory lectures: menstrual flow is worse in a hot climate. Our working rig was white cotton blouse and white drill skirt, with as little as possible underneath, and one was in constant fear that the stain would come through. One's best friend was indeed the girl who came quietly up and said: 'I think you'd better change your skirt,' and if this happened when everyone else was waiting in the shuttle to go on watch, the effort of changing in a hurry might be enough to soak a clean shirt with sweat. Bugs in the wicker chairs, ants on one's sandwiches, spiders – well, *some* of them were tarantulas – were soon taken for granted, but the curse continued to be just that.

For the rest, life was glamorous, tropical beaches were plentiful, as were invitations to lunch on HM ships, and we changed watches at 2 a.m. so that the Wrens could enjoy a party without having to play Cinderella and leave too early. The Lanka Cambrian Club ran Eisteddfodau and hymn-singing evenings with Sub Lieutenant Alun Williams playing a prominent part. Sub Lieutenant David Jacobs was on Colombo Radio, and there was live music-making both private and public as well as gramophone recitals and concerts of various levels.

We celebrated VE day with a picnic before going back to work as usual, but a few months later the dropping of atom bombs on Hiroshima and Nagasaki brought hostilities to an end and we really felt like celebrating. The preparations for concerted landings on Japanese-occupied territory were no longer necessary, and VJ day was a great relief. Signals traffic diminished and became much less interesting, and the hectic social life soon thinned out as people began to go home for demobilization.

Also going home in easy stages were the British survivors of the Japanese prisoner-of-war camps, and some of the fittest were put ashore at Colombo en route. We were invited to meet them off the boat and help them get the hang of things, send cables home, buy socks, pick up the threads of ordinary life. They were very thin, but being sunburnt did not look ill, and there was no immediate sign of what they had suffered. Being Scots they had treasured items of uniform – kilt or glengarry – to wear when freedom came, and they came ashore to pipe music played by the Dogra Pipe Band, a Ceylonese unit in colourful uniforms incongruously playing like Scotsmen. At a quiet meal in the ward room, my guest was only anxious that he might have forgotten how to behave in mixed company and do the wrong thing, but of course he hadn't. The next day they went on their way home.

Travel was more relaxed now, and I spent my last leave in New Delhi visiting my brother who was in the Indian Army; on return I found my posting home for demob. had come through, and I was on my way before Christmas. On New Year's Eve, 1945, we were actually going through the Suez Canal, and because no bells may be sounded in the Canal this meant that we missed the chance to hear sixteen bells struck at midnight, instead of the usual eight, by the youngest seaman on board. We did, however, manage a conga which went all over the ship, climbing indiscriminately over bodies on deck.

As we sailed home everyone was planning what they were going to do when they got out, and there were long hours on deck in the moonlight exchanging dreams. For me there were also some hours below decks learning from a young Scot with a chanter to play bagpipe airs on my tin whistle. I did get to Oxford in the end – but that's another story.

To sleep, at 02.30

~

Lisbeth David

No, gentle friend, your time is not yet come;
There may be many signals and alarms
Fleeting for us – fatal perhaps for some –
Before I lay my head down in your arms.
O do not call so softly and so sweet,
Nor with enchantments ever seek to win
Me from this ecstasy of spite and heat –
My heart was yours before you could begin.
Wait only for the moment of relief
And I will come fleet-foot to seek your face,
Dwell on your kiss so lovely and so brief
And lose the morning in your deep embrace.
So Sleep, before unkindly dawn shall rise
Lay your cool bandage on my weary eyes.

Portsmouth 3.2.45

SS Queen Elizabeth

~

Muriel Graham

I volunteered for the Women's Royal Naval Service (WRNS) in November 1942. I was interviewed in Cardiff, sent to train as a coder at Lowton-St- Mary's in Lancashire and posted to Greenock on the Clyde, where I reported on New Year's Day, 1943.

For the first six months my work in the signals office, decoding messages, was routine, but at this time it became necessary to start bringing American and Canadian troops across to Britain in preparation for the Second Front. We heard rumours that some Wrens and cipher officers would be required for duty on the liners which were being used as troop transports. In July the First Officer sent for me and asked if 'I would like to take a trip.' Knowing what this meant, I was delighted to accept. That same evening, as I was walking along by the Cloch Lighthouse near Gourock, a wonderful sight met my eyes. There, sailing up the Clyde in her grey wartime camouflage, was the *Queen Elizabeth*, the largest and fastest ship in the world. I knew she was the one for me. Within a few days I had been kitted out with tropical uniform and was taken out by ferry to join the ship. Little did I guess then that this was to be the first of eighteen double crossings.

My first two trips were to Halifax, Nova Scotia, and all the rest were to New York, except one when we had to go up to dry dock in Boston, the New York facilities being occupied by the *Queen Mary*. The Wren complement consisted of two cipher officers, three coders and, on later voyages, a writer. We were lucky with our accommodation which was on the sun deck and we dined well in the officers' mess. Our hours of duty followed the standard ship-board practice of four hours on and eight hours off. Our work mainly involved decoding radio messages received by the ship: these were usually weather reports and intelligence on probable U-boat positions. Normally the ship maintained radio silence for security reasons. During the hours of darkness all external lights would be extinguished and no smoking allowed on deck. All port-lights were painted black and were secured at night.

Our main defence against attack was the ship's speed, exceeding thirty knots, and setting a zigzag course. When we left the Clyde and until we reached the open sea, where we could use our maximum speed, we were escorted by destroyers and aircraft. Similar procedures were adopted as we neared the eastern seaboard of America. Depending on weather conditions and the whereabouts of U-boat packs, we took a southerly route via the Azores, or the northern course sailing close to Greenland where icebergs were a constant danger. There was a six-inch gun aft and two three-inch guns forward as well as anti-aircraft guns manned by either British or American gunners. A U-boat did once, I believe, fire a salvo of torpedoes at the *Queen Elizabeth*, but they missed their mark.

We had lifeboat drill every trip. Sometimes there were high seas. On one of my crossings we sailed into the roughest sea even the captain had ever encountered. Vast waves crashed over our tall bows and smashed the glass enclosure of the bridge which must have been at least sixty feet above the water line.

On each eastbound trip to Gourock we carried some 16,000 American and Canadian servicemen, many of whom, coming from mid-western states, had never seen the ocean before. There were far too many of them to accommodate in the normal way aboard the *Queen*, but makeshift arrangements were made to sleep them all and meals were spread out over many hours on a shift system. Only two meals a day could be fitted into the shifts, instead of the normal three, so as a compensation for this everyone was allowed to eat as much as they wanted. The servicemen spent most of the four or five-day voyage resting. Had they known that there was only lifeboat capacity for one quarter of them I don't think they would have slept so well at night. On the westward journey we carried many thousands of RAF personnel to the USA and Canada for flight training.

The turnaround in New York harbour was very quick. We could usually embark our American allies and their supplies within three and a half to four days. Security at bay 90 was always very tight: we had to show our seaman's pass, complete with fingerprints whenever we went ashore. There was rarely much time but we made the most of our visits to America. We were always welcomed at the Whole World Club and often given tickets to Broadway shows. The Americans were lavish in their hospitality. One wealthy New York family put us up in their beautiful apartment, where we dined, served by footmen, and had breakfast in bed served by a maid. When the *Queen Elizabeth* had to be dry-docked we had a longer stay in America. Once we were posted to serve with the Navy Department in Washington but normally I used the three weeks or so that she was in dry dock to travel. I stayed with friends and connections in Rochester, Winchester and Toronto. I made new friends too, and still maintain close contact with an American Wave, the equivalent of our Wrens, whom I met when the ship was dry-docked in Boston.

I would return to Gourock laden with nylons, fruit and candies. The generosity of the Americans was greatly appreciated since our weekly pay did not stretch far in an expensive city like New York. We did get danger money – of sixpence a day – and a small shore-allowance in dollars, but it was never enough in that Aladdin's cave brimming with luxuries which were unattainable at home.

In the USA, they were genuinely surprised to hear that the *Queen Elizabeth* was a British ship, built in a Scottish shipyard. They believed that they were the only ones capable of building a ship that size. I shall always retain very happy memories of this wonderful ship that did such valiant work during a period of great danger. Although she was a prime target of the German navy for so many years, she outwitted her enemies time and time again. The tragedy is that she fell a victim to a welder's torch in peacetime.

Join the Wrens and Free
a Man for the Fleet

~

Pamela Barker

That is just what I did, or so I thought, on 24 May, 1944. I had to report to the General Service Training Depot in Tulliechewan Castle, near Balloch, by 14.00 hours. I travelled overnight from Rhyl to Glasgow, happy in the knowledge that my category was 'Boat's Crew'. The invasion of Europe on 6 June, D Day, closed many categories and Boat's Crew was one of them. On 7 June four of us were drafted to the Royal Naval air station at Yeovilton, to the armoury, where we spasmodically issued rifles. The lifestyle did not suit me: it gave me boils, which, in turn, gave me a change of category. I became a messenger, zooming around the camp on a pushbike with vital signals (i.e. typed messages). It was all highly hush-hush and secret. Eighteen months later I was demobilized and a sailor replaced me. So I achieved my ambition but not in quite the way I had expected.

At Tulliechewan we slept in bunks in Nissen huts, and were awoken by a 'Stripey' shouting, 'Wakey, wakey,' as he opened the stable door. We washed in ablution blocks with aluminium troughs, spent a lot of time scrubbing the 'decks' of messes, listened to lectures on naval history and procedure, had numerous hair inspections and squad drills and were finally issued with a pay book (no. 77311) and uniform. Until then I had never worn trousers but I was issued with bell-bottoms, money belt, square-rig shirts, blue shirts, white shirts, collars, collar studs, tie, hat, tally band with 'HMS' on it, passion-killers (knee-length woollen knickers), seaman's jersey, gym shoes, shoes (with laces to be threaded horizontally), skirt, jacket, great coat, mac, woollen stockings (which I replaced with silk ones as soon as possible), and a kit bag. We had a chit system for underclothes so chits made out for pyjamas were invariably used to buy civvies, if the shopkeepers co-operated.

The Bristol Holding Depot was very different from Tulliechewan. Locally it was known as the holiday camp: a large house on the Downs with six to eight people in a room. We were kept busy with domestic chores. On one occasion we went to Weston-Super-Mare to take part in a recruiting campaign for the Red Cross, marched up and down the pier in our woollen stockings and were part of the Drum Head Service on the promenade. It was a very hot day and several people fainted. I don't know if that helped or hindered the Red Cross campaign.

We were very anxious to be drafted to a real ship and pestered our petty officer for a draft to *anywhere*, to do *anything*, as Boat's Crew courses had closed. My friend Yvonne and I went to Yeovilton to be stores assistants. What a mistake that was! Our first night was in a Nissen hut on camp. All the plugs in the troughs were missing and we had to stuff them with Government Property (i.e. lavatory paper). The following day we were sent to Sparkford rectory, one of the 'dispersed quarters', which was very civilized. We were in a hut in the grounds of the rectory with our own ablution block – and plugs. The other girls were air mechanics. In our hut each bed had a counterpane with an anchor on it, which had to be the right way up so as not to 'sink the ship'. We slept well in our bunks especially after illegally made cocoa, warmed up on our black stove with powdered milk received in parcels from home.

At the first opportunity we went to Yeovil to buy silk stockings and to have our photographs taken. The photographer was very patient. We had one taken wearing the hat and jacket, one in shirt sleeves and one in square rig, which we had taken with us and changed into. Third Officer Knight had been at HMS *Spartiale* at Tulliechewan for my fortnight's initial training. Then, to my delight, she came to Sparkford. She organized cricket and our CO was the legendary C.B. Fry's daughter who helped to coach and bowled underarm. One of Knight's duties was to put our lights out and to check that we were all in bed: I'm certain she knew that there were pillows instead of bodies one night when Yvonne and I had gone to an army dance, but she did not report us. I was not so lucky with a stroppy PO who bounced into the cabin saying, 'Four of you were out scrumping and one of you had red hair.' I was on the next defaulter's parade – no pay for a fortnight and confined to barracks scrubbing the decks.

It was less boring than my store-keeping duties in the armoury, where Yvonne and I tried to occupy ourselves writing letters and reading. The daily visit of the mobile canteen and the table tennis at the YMCA helped to relieve the monotony of doing nothing. On our 'Make and Mends' (free time), we would hitchhike to anywhere within a ten-mile radius and then start the journey back again: the Wincanton milk-lorry drivers were very helpful. We spent a lot of time helping on Sparkford farm and felt that we were contributing to the war effort in a much more practical way than in the WRNS. The blacksmith's wife befriended us. We played tennis with her on the village courts in our square rig and brown gym shoes.

At the end of August I went to Southampton for a weekend course to learn scriptwriting and bookbinding. On my return, I learnt that Yvonne had gone to Plymouth to take up a boat's crew vacancy for one! I was devastated. Alma replaced Yvonne in the armoury but we had little in common and life became depressing. Net result – boils. I had injections in my left buttock and was told that my face would be clear by the time I was thirty! The MO recommended a change of category.

I became a messenger in the SDO, an underground air raid style building, with signals coming and going by telephone continuously: my job was to deliver these once they had been typed. Life was fast and I enjoyed being part of a busy office. I had my first leave in October. I could have got another fourteen days 'jankers' for that because I actually arrived at Rhyl station before I was supposed to have left Yeovilton. I suspected it was Third Officer Knight's 'Pipe Down' round, but I escaped.

Shortly after Christmas I was transferred to Speckington, a large manor house on the perimeter of the airfield. It was the Fighter Direction Centre, where Wrens and sub-lieutenants learned to be air direction radar operators. My seven months at Speckington were very happy. I cycled many miles with signals, enjoyed a round of parties, celebrated victories in Europe and Japan and played hockey, tennis and cricket.

When hostilities ceased I was demobbed at Yeovilton. I introduced my replacement to the control tower, hangers and stores and handed over my bike to *him*. I was satisfied. I was replaced by a sailor.

Radar Operator in the WAAF

~

Rhona Elias

Wireless operators we were not – in spite of wearing 'sparks' on our sleeves: this was meant to mislead the locals and enemy spies as to what we were really doing at those high-masted RAF stations on the coasts. In the beginning we were called RDF operators, short for Radio Detection Finder Operators, but the term 'radar' was introduced in the early forties and so we became Radar Operators. Around the coast of Great Britain a chain of stations sprang up under the control of the RAF while inland the vigilance moved to the Army Observer Corps. The stations were called Chain Home (CH) which picked up the high-flying aircraft, and CHL which had a low gantry similar to the one that can be seen scanning at Heathrow or any airport.

I was posted in the main to CHL stations in Pembrokeshire, Devon and Cornwall. We were always on isolated sites but usually billeted in a country house in the area. Our small group was self-contained, including administrative and technical staff. It was essential that we worked as a unit, and this made for a very close companionship of all ranks. As the men in our group were posted overseas we had to take over more of the technical jobs, including the maintenance of equipment and the operation of searchlights. We worked at cathode ray tubes (television screens) on which the aircraft appeared as small blips on a grid map, marked out for our area. The plots were read and passed by internal line to a filter room, usually based underground at a station well inland where they were marked on a huge relief map. From a raised balcony above the map, fighter command officers were constantly reviewing the situation: they were the ones that alerted fighter stations to scramble the planes to intercept the enemy.

We felt we were doing an interesting and worthwhile job when on our screens we could see by means of the lighted 'blips' that the enemy planes were being intercepted as they came into our area. Identification (e.g. Charlie Able 247) was given to all plots we passed to the filter room. As the planes moved out of our range they were picked up by the next station in the chain and so a picture was built up in the plotting rooms of all aircraft activities in their area.

When the war in Europe ended our work finished and

we were redeployed in other sections of the WAAF.

Radar Operator in the ATS

~

Betty Howard

Looking back on my 'army career', I regret that I did not opt for office work or driving. The first would have offered prospects of quick promotion and the second, which meant driving staff-officers around, certainly had its attractions. Instead I chose to train as a radar operator.

Candidates for radar training had to have matriculated at school and to show some understanding of electrical circuits. The training was no bed of roses but I passed out at the end of the course and was awarded a single stripe. Then I headed up a team of radar operators. When on duty we sat in a cabin, very close to a gun site, with our eyes glued to the screen for the first sight of any enemy aircraft. Our own planes sent out a distinctive signal known as Friend or Foe Identification so that we could easily recognize them. The enemy tried to fool us by using what we called 'window', that is dropping strips of aluminium from the plane, which would blur our screens with hundreds of signals. When that happened we were unable to keep track of them.

We had one task which had to be done outside the cabin and that was to look after the generator, nicknamed

Jenny, which provided the power for our receivers. She had to be kept sparkling clean, well oiled and always full up with diesel. When in action, we had to start her up in ten seconds by means of a cranking handle: it was neither an easy nor a safe operation.

My first posting was to a heavy anti-aircraft battery at Penarth near Cardiff. I was Number 1 of one of the three radar teams, each working an eight-hour shift. The duty team had to be at the ready when the alarm bells rang. It was a mad rush to start the Jenny and get ourselves into position. Only then could I report, 'Ready for Action'. When all was quiet the duty team slept in a nearby Nissen hut wearing battledress blouse and trousers, woollen socks and boots. In winter we also had leather jerkins and sheepskin mittens. We did not however get the perk of a tot of rum enjoyed by women sleeping under canvas.

After Penarth, I was posted to Swansea to a gun site at Blackpill. Known as Z battery, the site boasted a complement of sixty-four new 'rocket guns' instead of the usual HAA 3.7's. When these went off it was like a huge and very noisy fireworks display. The people of Swansea opened up their homes to us and they even staffed a canteen in a church in Sketty. After VE day the gun sites in Britain were disbanded and we operators were scattered to various units to continue the fight against Japan.

Kines

~

Daphne Price

At the outbreak of war I was a twenty-year-old Civil Servant in Birmingham. As such, I was in a reserved occupation and unable to volunteer for the Forces. I was quickly moved to the newly created Ministry of Home Security and then to the Assistance Board, where I spent the days interviewing distraught air raid casualties seeking compensation for injury and damage to property through the bombing. Nights were spent in our air raid shelter buried in the back garden listening to the German planes approaching followed by the explosion of bombs. In 1942, permission was given to volunteer and I was one of the first to join up.

After three weeks initial training in a Leicestershire barracks, being kitted out with our uniform and undergoing fitness and intelligence tests, it was suggested I should join the Royal Artillery as a Kine theodolite operator, whatever that was. Kine, I thought, would be something to do with a camera, theodolite was an angular measuring instrument but where did the operator come in? I was told this was something very new connected with the efficiency of our anti-aircraft batteries and also somewhat hush-hush. Matriculation in maths was a prerequisite. Our training took place at the Royal School of Artillery camp at Manorbier, where we were shown the Kine theodolite, how to load the 35mm film, how to operate all the dials and finally how to interpret what was on the developed film. The object of the instrument was to film a red target flag towed by a plane at which the gun operators fired their 3.7-inch guns for target practice. For this it was necessary to have two Kine theodolites positioned three miles apart, both focussed on the target. With the known distance between the Kine theodolites and the height recorded on the film, we were able to calculate from this triangle the accuracy of the firing. Each theodolite had a team of three 'Kines': one to spot the target and direct the instrument and the other two to operate the elevation and lateral dials. Apart from learning how to operate the machines it was also necessary to recall our knowledge of trigonometry and electricity and to learn how to use a circular slide rule. Because of the necessary qualifications in maths we all had at least a grammar school education and there were many who had attended boarding schools and came from a very wealthy background. However, we soon became a very close-knit group and because there were so few of us, we knew most of the members of the various KT detachments. I think there were about 500 of us altogether.

After passing the test I was posted to the Weybourne Artillery Camp in Norfolk where every two weeks anti-aircraft artillery batteries came in for gunnery practice. Now our real work began, as the men and women who actually manned the guns against the German raiders came in to update their skills and for a respite from the bombing. As well as operating our Kine theodolites outside the firing area, we had to work on predictors feeding information to the gunners alongside us. We were also initiated into the use of the GL cabins, the newly developing science of radar which had such an important part to play in the future of the hostilities.

After six months of enduring the east winds blowing on the Norfolk headlands, it was something of a relief to be posted back to Pembrokeshire. I was now attached to the Trials Wing of the School of Artillery and we were billeted in two Nissen huts in the grounds of Lydstep House, an Edwardian mansion situated on the beach of Lydstep Haven. Our work now involved the research and development of equipment to deal with the growing destruction by the German air raids. Information was coming through our spy network of new weapons which would cause widespread destruction and slaughter. Although we didn't know at the time, these were the doodle bugs and V2 rockets – unmanned aircraft which exploded on a given target. Our work took place alongside the guns on the headlands and all the computing work of the trials was done in the beautiful, panelled library of Lydstep House. Because the work was so secret, we Kines were involved only in working out the calculations given to us by the boffins, without knowing what it was all about.

When work allowed, we were able to discover the countryside by bicycle or on foot. Saturdays were usually free and we would take the bus or hitchhike into Tenby or, if the weather was suitable, stroll along the cliffs. Although we were well fed in comparison with the civilian population, a favourite treat was a meal in the café at the end of the lane leading to the camp. In the tiny room of what had once been the village shop, Mrs Walters and her two daughters would regale us with fried bacon, omelettes and any other ingredients she could find, including sometimes the delicious mushrooms we picked for her on the cliffs. The people in Tenby were most helpful and friendly, despite the shattering noise of our guns which they had to endure in what had been so peaceful pre-war. Our visit would finish in the Methodist Church schoolroom, where we were plied with tea and delicious cakes by the lady members of the church.

One memorable Saturday I arrived in Tenby to find the streets teeming with American soldiers. The following day, on my weekly visit to the morning service, I found every seat in the church taken by an American. The worship was movingly enriched by a solo from the New World Symphony. Many friendships evolved before they departed, as suddenly as they had arrived, to land on the Normandy beaches just a few days after D Day. Of those still alive today, like us aging Kines, they will have very fond memories of Wales and the Welsh people.

Women at War in Wales

~

Eileen Gillmore

The season was mid-winter, and cold: that biting cold one was getting used to by now. In wartime Britain everyone was feeling the pinch, and I was no exception. Not that I was particularly hard done by, but the chill, and those hard wooden beds covered by a wafer-thin mattress they actually called a 'biscuit', made me wonder what I was doing there. Both my brothers had gone to war, and listening to stories at home from my parents, both of whom had served in the First World War, had made me feel the call of adventure.

I had been in the ATS since January 1943, and now I found myself on a radar training course at a military camp 'somewhere in Wales', which was, in fact, on Anglesey. The training was unlike anything I had experienced before, but then radar was a comparatively new defence system then. We were quite a mixture of personalities and backgrounds, but we got on together well enough. Each and every one of us was kept far too busy to develop strong likes and dislikes. For much of the time we seemed to be changing into, or out of our physical training kit, or our denims for fatigues. These came rather hard to many of us. Most were unused to domestic chores, so that the sight of a heap of potatoes waiting to be peeled, or a huge stack of pots to be cleaned, with sand I seem to remember, was not our idea of fun or serving our country. The chore we hated most, it must be admitted, was being detailed to carry jumbo-sized dustbins of sanitary towels out of the ablutions block and across to the boiler house. How we longed to disappear into thin air on meeting any of the men on site, and, judging from their laughter, our red faces caused them plenty of amusement.

Those of us who had been selected for special training were housed in a hut forming a spider arrangement of other huts. On this particular winter's morning I was detailed to check that the ablutions block was empty of personnel, and to make sure that everyone was outside and on breakfast parade. We all knew the routine by now, and few of us were going to be caught missing one of the precious meals of the day. We seemed to be permanently hungry, and this made us turn out on meal parades promptly.

I breezed my way through the ablutions, calling out to anyone who might be inside. I rattled the doors of showers and lavatories, and hurried on, seeing the place deserted, as I thought, until I heard a groan. Back-stepping a few paces I saw that one of the cubicles had its door jammed, and I called out again, not wanting to intrude on someone's privacy. The only reply was another groan. Not being blessed with any medical knowledge, I decided that since I had no rank, the problem was not mine. I reported it to the duty sergeant knowing she would deal with it, and was gratified when we all were trooped into the mess hall for breakfast.

I mentioned the incident at table, but no one wanted to speculate during a meal. When we returned to our huts, we found a couple of orderlies packing up someone's kit. What they had to say shocked us beyond belief. The girl in question had had a baby they told us. Now, if we had been told that the war was over we could not have been more surprised. Babies were not a part of our scene at that time. Most of us were young, unmarried and in most senses of the word inexperienced. The idea of anyone having babies fitted more into idyllic pictures of happily married couples, than the situation we were in.

Sylvia, (though this was not her name) was one of a dozen or so girls in my hut. In such close proximity we knew each other reasonably well and liked one another for the most part. She was one we all got on with, but who kept to herself. She neither smoked, as we all did, nor drank, as most of us did, and she rarely came out with the rest of us when we managed to get a pass to leave camp. On her locker stood a photograph of a young airman, and she told us that he had been posted to Canada for training. We assumed that he was her boyfriend, and it would have accounted for her lack of interest in anyone else.

Sylvia was quite a big girl, portly rather than fat, and in retrospect we could see why. She was somewhat older than most of us. In my group, we were under twenty, and some of us were under eighteen, whereas Sylvia was well into her mid-twenties, making her appear positively staid compared with our high spirits. She had complained of backache, it was true, and someone had persuaded her to report on sick parade. The Medical Officer treated her for it, and prescribed physiotherapy which, Sylvia told us, consisted of a back rub. I can see her now trying to sit upright, hands on hips and stretching herself in that oddly uncomfortable way women have when they are pregnant.

We who shared Sylvia's hut were bustled out of the way while consultations took place, and the last we heard of her was that she had been sent home to the west country. The event became the subject of hilarious gossip throughout the rest of the camp, and it was made worse for us later that same day to be called out on parade for medical inspection. Perhaps pregnancy was contagious! When the furore had died down we were able to concentrate on what we had been posted to do – to train as radar operators. It had been no joke having ribald remarks aimed at us whenever we went on site, but I suppose a good laugh was worth its weight in gold at that time.

We wondered what Sylvia's family must have felt having her return, presumably in disgrace and lumbered with a baby. We hoped for everyone's sake that the child's father would turn up trumps and accept his responsibilities, but that we were not to discover. That she had given birth unassisted on the stone floor of an army ablutions block we already knew, and marvelled at. It was to her credit that her son apparently suffered little on such a chilly projection into the world.

W/185325 Private
Ruth Harris ATS

~

Ruth Newmarch

July 1942: the adventure began at Leicester – Glen Parva
Barracks. We were met from the station by fierce, efficient
ATS NCOs who bundled us into a three-tonner. One
girl wept all the way – it was her twenty-first birthday.
The next three weeks were a blur of learning to wear,
clean and use all the uniform, have jabs, more medicals,
aptitude tests and marching drill. As the Army wanted
girls to go into ack-ack (whether we had opted for that or
not) most of us went down to Blandford to join a Royal
Artillery regiment and I became a member of 567 HMAA
Bty RA. After initial training, we went up to Tycroes in
Anglesey for a month's firing practice. I remember the
aeroplane towing the sleeve as a target for us to shoot
at – the girls didn't fire the guns, we were height takers,
predictor numbers or spotters, and telephonists in the
control-room underground. The men loaded and fired the
guns – the shells for 4.5s and 5.5s are pretty heavy. The
aeroplane used to fly over us first to say it was ready, then
go out over the sea to fly parallel to the coast and let out
the sleeve some hundred yards behind. One day it came

in and swooped so low it hit one of the gun barrels with its wing and plummeted straight into the sea. The pilot was drowned, and the incident cast a blight over us all.

Our first base was at Eccles, Manchester, where we were often in the gunpark for six hours at night hoping to get a Jerry. Camp life was drill, more drill – both instrument and marching – PT, hockey, lectures on current affairs, music, cleaning instruments, barrack rooms, kit, endless cookhouse fatigues (porridge and gravy dixies when the water has run cold – ugh), peeling sacks of potatoes and carrots. I went on several courses – PT at Droitwich, and drill and duties at Beaumaris, where if not careful one could let the squad march into the sea! I could still drill a squad. It was freezing up there so we raided the boiler house at night to get hot coals and rushed back to the Nissen hut to light the stove.

For my twenty-first birthday I spent a half day at the cinema and, after a meal, went back to work! Soon after this we moved down to the Isle of Grain, doodle-bug alley as it was known, which in those days was the back of beyond with just one bus a day to Stroud and Rochester. We also spent some time in a mobile battery outside Maidstone in a field where you could just watch the V1s coming in one after the other, day and night. The fighter planes used to try and tip them over, but it was always scary when the engine cut out overhead and one waited for the bang.

In March 1945, the battery was disbanded and we had to remuster. Some of us went to a training school in Hampstead to become clerks. We were billeted in what I believe was Sir Henry Wood's house – stripped, of course.

There was snow outside, but no heating in the house which contained a beautiful black marble bath -with no hot water.

I then volunteered for the Far East and was sent to Ceylon. We sailed in the *Empress of Scotland* and once into the Med. changed into tropical kit and forgot all thoughts of seasickness. When we sailed through the Red Sea the soldiers on the troop ships coming back would yell across to us: 'Get your knees brown!' We landed at Colombo and took the train up to Kandy. I can still smell the spicy hot air. The journey took some two and a half hours. It was uncomfortable on the train in the dark but the air was clear and full of fireflies.

We were now part of the Allied Land Forces South-East Asia, and being shorthand typists were allocated according to ability to different branches from General Slim downwards. We lived in bashas, double storey in B.13 camp which was in a cocoa plantation. We worked all day – certainly not tropical hours. I worked in the company office, still a lance corporal. There were four of us, the junior commander, a company sergeant major, a sergeant and myself. The girls went off in trucks at eight in the morning to the various units, came back for lunch and flopped on their beds – and then off again from two till five. We worked every day and had one half-day and Sunday afternoon.

For a fortnight I went over to SEAC, Lord Louis' HQ, to the office where the signals were coming in thick and fast in preparation for the big push from Malaya. But the A Bomb was dropped and the war ended, thank goodness.

The HQ was then ordered to move to Singapore. After beautiful Ceylon, Singapore was so flat, but the roads were good and one was struck by the cleanliness. It was heart-rending to see the names of British troops written on the walls of our quarters and a line under the date when they were taken up to the infamous railway line.

In June 1947, I came home in the SS *Dilwara*, a small troop ship that had three times too many on board. After five and a half weeks we reached Southampton – a docker's strike rather delayed disembarkation. We arrived on a Friday evening – everyone away, hardly any food or greeting, and had to stay there till Monday. What a homecoming!

Turning Glass into Diamonds

~

Barbara Buchanan

I enlisted in the Women's Territorial Army in 1938. I was called up just before war was declared in September 1939. We arrived, after a long train journey, at an army barracks and were promptly given desk jobs – the only work women were *allowed* to do in those early days.

My last job before I escaped from a desk was sad and harrowing. I was with the Royal Army Records and Pay Office and we serviced the five Lancashire regiments. About ten days after Dunkirk the hospital trains started bringing the lads back to Lancashire and, at the same time, dropping off sacks and sacks of personal belongings of dead and missing soldiers. A small team of us was formed and given rubber gloves and face masks. One by one sacks were emptied out onto a trestle table. More often than not the contents were blood-stained. There were pay books, diaries, family snapshots, letters, rings, watches, identity discs and much more. We had to try and link up these items to an identity and ultimately to an army number. I would never like to see another Dunkirk.

When the conscription of women was introduced, I knew what I had to do. I fought tooth and nail for a posting to a conscription centre and I can honestly say that my years there were amongst the most rewarding of my life. Every six weeks there was an intake and we four senior instructors would be at Lancaster station waiting for the troop trains to disgorge 400 girls and women. We always felt so sorry for them. There were some with suitcases, some with carriers and parcels, some crying, some silent and fearful and some bravely hostile. Then came three days of bed allocation, kitting out, inoculations and documentation. Those three days also meant three nights. We and all the junior NCOs became mothers, comforting crying, homesick girls and soothing those who felt ill after inoculations.

Then the real work started – barrack square drilling, lectures on military discipline and a whole range of other training activities. Five weeks later the great day came – the passing out parade with a march past by immaculate, confident female soldiers. No one could ever know how proud we were of these girls and what we had achieved. We had turned pieces of glass into diamonds.

Down on the Farm –
the Women's Land Army

~

Eileen Jones

My call-up papers arrived on 28 December 1941: I had to report to a farm at Thirsk in Yorkshire. A train travel voucher was enclosed and I had to be measured for my uniform. I applied for the smallest size, as I am only five-feet tall. My parcel of clothing contained: wellington boots size 4, black working boots, brown shoes, canvas gaiters (buttoned at the sides), fawn knee-length socks – 2 pairs, beige corduroy jodhpurs, fawn overalls and smocks (2), green wool jumpers (2), cream linen shirts (2), airtex shirts (2), thick, three-quarter length coat, beige felt cowboy-style hat.

When I put my uniform on I looked trim and jaunty and I could not wait for my adventure to begin in the Women's Land Army . But at the station my mother and I were both crying as she passed my case to me and I waved goodbye. I was on a train alone for the first time in my life.

At Thirsk I was met by the farmer in his horse and trap. The farm was isolated and all I could see was cold, bleak, snow-covered hills. Joan, the other WLA girl billeted

159

on the farm, was nineteen. We sat down for tea at a big wooden table, the farmer at the top end, his wife at the bottom, two little boys on one side and Joan and I on the farmer's right. He always said Grace before meals. There were paraffin lamps and no electricity and it was very dark and cold. Bedtime was early, and shortly before nine p.m. we were given mugs of cocoa and a paraffin lamp to take to our room, where we were to share a bed.

Routine began in earnest the next day as the alarm went at 6 a.m. We got up in the dark and staggered down the cottage stairs and out to the cowshed before breakfast. I had never been near a cow before and was given a bucket of water to wash the cow's udders and rear ends, then a clean bucket and a three-legged stool and shown how to milk. I sat under the cow and grasped the cow's nipple. Nothing happened. I was beginning to get frightened as the cow became impatient and swished her tail, hitting me on the head and face. I looked around the dark cowshed. I was amongst strangers, cold and hungry, and then a rat ran across the floor. I rested my head on the cow and sobbed, unable to stop.

After a breakfast of fatty bacon and dry bread our next task was to feed the bullocks. They were jumping around in a big enclosed pen, about fifty big black beasts. I had to climb in the pen with them. I was much more frightened of the bullocks than of the cows. There was a big machine into which we had to throw swedes. Each one weighed three or four pounds. The machine then chopped them into smaller pieces and we took it in turns to work the heavy handle. We then carried the buckets of swede to troughs to feed the beasts.

Then it was time to muck out the cowshed. The manure stank, the pitching fork I used was nearly as big as me. I consoled myself with the thought that at least it was warmer inside with the cow's stench than out in the field. Later I was given a bucket of water to rewash the cows' udders. I could have passed out.

At lunchtime at the farmhouse we were given more fatty meat with two vegetables. After a break of half an hour the farmer was ready with the big cart and a shire-horse called Daisy. We were to go through the snow to pull up kale, fodder for the animals. I was given a sickle with which to top and tail swedes which I had just pulled out of the hard ground. We worked for a couple of hours, then it was back to the milking shed where I had another try at milking the cows. This time I was thrilled to hear the milk trickling into the bucket.

In between my other duties on the farm I learned how to chop wood, saw logs, pull sugar beet. I was very lonely as the only people to talk to were Joan and the farmer's family. The snow was still deep and the postman could not always get through. On Sundays the family went to Chapel. There was no Roman Catholic Church for me to go to. The farmer did not allow any activity on a Sunday. No wireless, sewing or reading. My wage for a six-day week, beginning at 6.30 in the morning and continuing until it was too dark to do more, was 32 shillings. Out of this the farmer took my keep. For the first month we received no wage at all, as we were on trial. One Sunday, utterly bored and homesick, I decided to go for a walk, but I could not get any further than the gate. The place was desolate and for miles around the countryside was completely covered in snow. When I realized I could not escape, I returned to the farm and was unable to control my misery and sobbed all night.

*

[*Eileen Jones was transferred first to a Women's Land Army hostel at Ripon and then to another at Wetherby. Here she worked with pigs.*]

The morning call bell would go at 6 a.m. I hated getting up at this hour in the dark and cold. Estna, the forewoman, said my job was to be on a pig farm. We had to cycle six miles. I was told it was a dirty stinking job and to put on my wellington boots and overalls. There were about five hundred pigs to look after. We arrived at the farm at 8 a.m., already tired. We could smell the farm before we could see it. Its fields adjoined the RAF camp and we could see the planes on the runway. The sergeants' mess hut was in the field next to the pig fold and barn.

Albert, the farm labourer, brought round a big shire-horse and dray-cart full of empty dustbins. We had to go to the RAF camp and collect all the swill from the canteens. I had to drive the horse and cart and Albert was to leave the empty bins and load the cart with the full swill bins. The lads were glad to see a new face and we were offered drinks of tea at each canteen. There was no need to lead the horse, it knew its own way back to the farm.

Albert unloaded the swill into big boilers which had wooden oars to stir the messy pig food. For the rest of the morning my WLA friend Doreen and I were left to keep an eye on the pressure of the boiler and to stoke it up with coke. We had to keep stirring the swill which looked and smelled revolting. It consisted of any leftover food, with bits of bacon rind, eggs, mouldy bread, floating around on top.

Whilst it boiled Doreen and I got a wheelbarrow, pitch fork, brush and shovel and went to muck out the pig sties. The sties contained a sow and piglets of all sizes. About twenty small sties surrounded the big square fold. I got to like the pigs, because they were a smaller animal. We would put clean straw in the top corner of the sty and the pigs would try to keep the straw clean for their young. We mucked out the manure and then used the hosepipe to swill the rest out. As the pigs got fatter they would be moved into the middle fold, to be picked out for slaughter.

At three o'clock in the afternoon the grunts and squeals from the pigs was quite deafening because they knew it was feeding time. We loaded the boiled swill into a bin on wheels, and poured it into the troughs. By the time we had finished we were covered in swill. The pigs would fight to be first by the food troughs, and would be climbing on top of each other.

At the hostel there was an ablution block which had six baths and sinks. The girls were glad to let Doreen and me have the first baths as we were smelling very badly by now. Our clothes had to be washed by hand, and ours took a lot of scrubbing.

[The Department of Agriculture, concerned at the amount of food lost to the country through pests, especially moles, rats and rabbits, called for volunteers to the Pest Department.

Eileen Jones volunteered and became a rat-catcher.]

As the war was nearing its end my transfer came through to the Pest Department. I was now billeted at home, and wore my dress uniform to travel to Garforth by bus. I worked on farms killing rats and moles. We had a Ford van. Written on the side was PEST DEPT. One day we came out of a café to find some soldiers had altered it to REST DEPT.

The work was not as hard as I was used to. We were given a small bottle of strychnine and told it was deadly poison and to use it sparingly. At the farm we would ask which field the farmer wanted us to go to. We dug for worms from the farmyard, collecting a jarful, cutting them in half and covering them in poison. We made our way to a field, looking for new mounds of soil where moles were making their new runs and ruining the field. With a walking stick, we would probe the field for the run and make a hole and put the worm in it. The hole covered over, we then went round all the molehills stamping on them to flatten them. Each day we would repeat the operation until no new molehills appeared.

We also had contracts with the farms to kill rabbits and rats. We poisoned the rats but the rabbits we gassed in their burrows.

One day the foreman, a Mr Barge, came to show us how to catch rats. We were in the loft of the barn, and he had a small Jack Russell dog with him that he brought to catch the rats. As the dog was chasing a rat, Mr Barge tripped over the dog and fell from the loft onto a pig in the sty below. It was bedlam, with girls, rats and pigs all screaming.

To kill rats took about a week. First we would have to find the rats' runs by new droppings. We would then lay rusks onto the rat runs or in the rat holes. We missed a day then so that the rats became hungry. We next mixed poison with the rusk and left it in the same place. The following day we would collect the leftover poison and the dead rats and bury them. People in the area had to be warned that we were using poison. One day we found a cat with the rats and had to bury that as well. The owner had not heard our warning to keep the cat inside.

Waiting for a Casualty Train: Whitchurch

~

Mary James

So drunken, moon, with your own beauty,
Cannot you even be veiled on this solemn night,
Full of half-heard commands, unrecognized
faces, and engines fitfully running.
You tactless jolly moon, I am infected by you
And, myself a figure dim to these others,
I turn away from your light and smile

Widely, half-wittedly, excited
By the bustle and expectancy
And you swinging overhead.

Irene Thomas, aged nine, with her
parents and younger sister.
The photograph was taken a week
before her father's death. (*War Child*)

Elizabeth Wroe in Girl
Guide uniform.
(*Up Penmaen*)

Gabrielle Capus, aged ten (on the right in the Panama hat), August 1942.
(*Don't you Know There's a War On?*)

Eva Pettifor with her younger
sister. (*Our Little Family's War*)

Lisbeth David in her new
officer's uniform, November
1943. (*One Wren's War*)

Mair Davies (right) at work
in the stores office.
(*The Royal Ordnance
Factory, Bridgend*)

Muriel Graham in a photograph
taken just after joining the
Wrens, December 1942.
(*SS Queen Elizabeth*)

Daphne Price (on extreme right) learning how to use a slide
rule on a Kine theodolite training course with the School
of the Royal Artillery at Manorbier, 1942. (*Kines*)

Daphne Price (left) on a tracker recording operation. (*Kines*)

Barbara Buchanan (left) as
senior instructor in the Women's
Territorial Army, 1943. (*Turning
Glass into Diamonds*)

Pamela Barker in her square-
rig shirt and bell-bottoms,
June 1944. (*Join the Wrens
and Free a Man for the Fleet*)

Ruth Newmarch (the one without
the hat) taking an elephant ride at
Kandy, Ceylon (Sri Lanka) in 1945.
(*W/185325 Private Ruth Harris ATS*)

Eileen Jones (left) on duty
(*Down on the Farm*)

Rat-catchers extraordinaire: Eileen Jones and colleague during
a 'victory parade' in Yorkshire. (*Down on the Farm*)

Eileen Jones (right) and colleague with the Pest
Dept. van. (*Down on the Farm*)

Maureen Kouroupis (aged sixteen) with Peter, September 1942.
(*From Gymslip to Wedded Bliss*)

Pamela F. Sanderson and her
two daughters, Rhyl 1944.
(*No Children should be Born*)

Portrait of Kusha Petts.
(*A Letter to my Wartime
Love, Figure in a Vestry*
and *In a Far Country*)

Polish refugees: Danusia Trotman-
Dickenson and her mother.
(*The Kaleidoscope of Youth*)

Mavis Machin Thomas, school
friend of three Jewish refugees.
(*My Quest*)

Patricia Parris with her mother, on
a break from evacuation, 1942.
(*Shadow Man*)

Hilda M. Howells (right) taking
a break from the hospital train.
(*Tunisian Journey*)

Emily Bond, whose work
took her to a concentration
camp in 1945. (*Belsen*)

Mary Morris in QA uniform, 1944.
(*A wartime Nurse*)

Captain Rona Price Davies in
Bombay, 1945: ready for duty.
(*From GP to Captain RAMC*)

CHAPTER 5

CONSCIENTIOUS OBJECTORS

Pacifists, who stood by their principles, faced job losses, fines and imprisonment. It took courage to adopt this stance in wartime Britain and Welsh women, as well as Welsh men, were prepared to accept the consequences of their beliefs.

A Woman Pacifist in Wartime

~

Rosalind Rusbridge

In the 1930s' internationally minded people watched with dismay as the governments of Britain and France turned a blind eye to Franco's rebellion against the democratically elected government of Spain and refused to consider economic sanctions when Italy invaded Abyssinia. As for Hitler's treatment of Jews, that was 'an internal matter' for Germany alone. Business was business. It was this cynical attitude that, long before Neville Chamberlain's pathetic gesture in 1938, gave the green light to Hitler.

War thus became inevitable. Many young people on the Left accepted conscription in no jingoistic mood but one of resignation. Others registered as conscientious objectors, feeling that they could not personally kill anybody. In Swansea, these young men were supported by women of two age groups. Some had experienced the First World War, and among these was my mother. My father had come home from the carnage of the Western Front with a Distinguished Conduct Medal, a constitution undermined by poison gas and the burning conviction that war was utterly evil. 'It isn't what it does to the body. It's what it does to the soul,' he said. Other 'oldies' belonged to the Women's Co-operative Guild. The younger group were mostly above conscription age and in 'reserved occupations'. Perhaps we would have got by, had we not maintained what seems with hindsight a naïvely high profile, holding advertised meetings, keeping up our Saturday Peace Stall in Swansea market and selling *Peace News* on the streets. We and our male friends were supported throughout the war by Plaid Cymru, nationally by Gwynfor Evans and Annie Humphries and locally by Aneurin ap Talfan with sardonic comments from behind the counter of his chemist's shop.

In the first months of the war, we met with remarkable tolerance. Then came the fall of France and the public mood changed. I remember a proposed meeting at Pontardulais being prevented by an angry crowd who shouted, as two of us turned our bikes round, 'Back to Swansea, you bloody conchies.' However, colleagues and neighbours were still friendly, albeit critical, and we might well have continued serving our country in our capacities had not an organization called the 'Swansea League of Loyalists' come into being. Its patron was the Duke of Beaufort and its president Lewis Jones MP. At its opening meeting the latter accused us of being traitors working for Hitler and harbouring a 'nest of communists'. The avowed aim of the organization was to accomplish the downfall of 'defeatism' and 'subversive tendencies'. The moving force of the League was one W.O.H. de Mattos who called a series of open-air meetings at which he whipped up crowds to anti-pacifist frenzy. On one occasion, he was reported to have said that all conchies should be castrated. I remember that because my mother did not previously know the meaning of the word. Pressure began to be exerted on the Swansea Borough Council, firstly with objections to the market Peace Stall, of which I was the official tenant. I received a phone call from the Borough Estate Agent, asking me to close the stall voluntarily as 'a nasty incident' was threatened. This I refused to do and next Saturday we found the stall closed and padlocked. A protest from the Council for Civil Liberties was ignored.

Then Italy joined in the war and the first bombs fell on Swansea. The League of Loyalists, joined by the British Legion and others, stepped up their campaign. A meeting of the Guildhall staff, chaired by the town clerk, called for the resignation of all council employees with pacifist opinions. A council vote was taken on this request and at first, by a narrow majority, it was left 'to lie on the table'. Then the press joined in the fray with letters and articles full of the vocabulary of hatred, and councillors themselves became the objects of bitter attack. When the matter came up for discussion again, a huge crowd gathered outside the Guildhall, singing hymns and songs such as 'Keep the home fires burning'. In spite of brave pleas for tolerance by some councillors, including the deputy mayor, it was resolved that a loyalty declaration should be given to all council employees to sign. This ran as follows:

I hereby solemnly and sincerely declare that I am not a conscientious objector or a member of the Peace Pledge Union, nor do I hold views which are in conflict with the purpose to which the Nation's effort is directed in the present war. And I further declare that I wholeheartedly support the vigorous prosecution of the war.

There is reason to believe that this was not sent to certain municipal establishments with strong trade unions but it certainly went to all schools. One headmistress preserved a copy in her logbook, noting that all the staff had signed it, but she had also sent a petition bearing fifty-eight signatures protesting at its imposition. Another headmistress, to the general astonishment, was herself suspended. While not a pacifist, she had encouraged in her school an active branch of the League of Nations Union with debates and discussions on international issues. She did not sign the declaration but submitted a plea for tolerance and freedom of conscience. Along with fifteen others, I received a note from the town clerk informing me that I was suspended, without pay, for the duration of the war. My headmistress, whose pupil I had once been, tried to argue with me. I was sent home immediately at considerable inconvenience to the school. We teachers found other jobs, though not easily. One headmaster told me that the more impressed he was by my personality the more he was determined not to employ me.

In September, the reaction began in Swansea. My own union, the old 'equal pay' National Union of Women Teachers (NUWT) had already protested on my behalf, though they all disapproved of my stand. Now came protests from the NUT, Plaid Cymru, the National Council For Civil Liberties and more influentially from the Home Secretary and the Ministry of Home Security. At a Council meeting in November the issue was raised again. The British Legion planned a demonstration outside the Guildhall but the Chief Constable had banned street marches. The resolution to suspend non-signers without pay for the duration of the war was rescinded, but only by a few votes.

Meanwhile, I was teaching at a boy's grammar school in Chester. I remember a colleague coming into the staffroom one morning and saying, 'Swansea have rescinded that thing.' But I did not go back. I felt loyalty was due to the authority which had taken me on when my hometown threw me out. Although married in 1942 to someone working elsewhere, I stayed on till the war with Germany had ended.

Sticking by my Beliefs

~

Iris Cooze

I became interested in Jehovah's Witnesses in 1940, when I was fifteen years old. At that time I was living at home, in Abercynon, Glamorgan, with my mother and brother and sisters. My father was away with the Royal Engineers taking part in the war. We had never been a religious family, although we believed in practising right principles. Through conversations with her brother, who had become a Jehovah's Witness, my mother became convinced of the rightness of their Bible-based beliefs. By the time I was sixteen or so, I had made up my mind to take up full time work as a 'pioneer' with Jehovah's Witnesses. This I carried out in Evesham, and I was then sent with a partner, a girl four years older than me, back to Wales, to Abercarn in Monmouthshire. When I was eighteen I received a letter directing me into work to help the war effort. I attended an Office in Newport where I was asked to become a receptionist in a hotel which was converted to accommodate young men, mostly from England, who were being trained to work in the mines. I declined this, explaining that I was fully involved in my Christian ministry work, and also that I did not want to be involved in any war-effort work, because as a Christian, how would I take part in a war where Catholics were killing Catholics, or Baptists killing Baptists, completely against Jesus's command that Christians should love one another? As full-time ministers of religion were granted exemption from war work, Jehovah's Witnesses claimed the same right, but generally speaking, this was not granted.

I had to make a written statement, and I had some interviews with, I suppose, probation officers. One woman in particular made it her business to point out that I was young and that I should be helping my country. I explained that I had a deep conviction and wanted to stand by that. Eventually, I received a summons to appear in court in Abercarn. I returned there seven times because the judge was so reluctant to sentence me. Personally, I was quite prepared to go to prison, as many Jehovah's Witnesses had done before me – Jesus and his followers were persecuted and suffered for their stand, and Jesus said his followers would suffer too. I just thought, well, whatever comes of this, it's a stand I've got to make. At my seventh court appearance, the judge said he was compelled to enforce the law made by parliament, and so he sentenced me to one month in Cardiff prison.

I was taken to Cardiff prison in the usual way, in a Black Maria. It wasn't a very nice experience, being in prison. I don't remember it too well now, but that month seemed like a year. There were grim looking wardresses who took your clothes away from you. They gave you an awful grey flannel prison dress, and underneath that, harsh calico underwear. They put me into a room by myself for a long time, for hours on end. I think that was part of the punishment. I asked for my Bible, and I was reading that for hours and hours before they gave me anything to eat, or took me to my cell. So that was my introduction to prison life.

For a few days I had the company of twin girls, very beautiful, who were Jehovah's Witnesses and had made a stand like myself. One wardress was interested in our beliefs, having spoken to others who had gone into prison before me. Eventually she became a Jehovah's Witness herself, and that happened more than once in the prisons.

The universal prison job was making mailbags. I don't like sewing but we did it all day long, morning to evening. Then they needed six women to paint the prison cells, and I was chosen. I must say I liked painting prison cells much more than making the mailbags. I had some little privileges. For example, I was passed over when the women were examined for venereal disease. I was a young and innocent sort of girl, and most of the women were prostitutes. Some of them were quite good sorts, and we talked. I had one or two letters when I was there, and on Sundays, a Jehovah's Witness from Cardiff came in, and we had Bible study together. When I got out, I had a marvellous letter of support from an American sailor who had been docked in Britain, and had read my case in the newspaper.

When I got out, I felt like a bird let out of a cage – even today, I hate being constricted. My mother met me, and she had great plans. She said, 'Come on, we'll go and get you something really nice to eat, we'll go and have a marvellous dinner.' But all I was interested in was the fresh air, and I think what we did most of the day was walk up and down Queen Street. I went back to my assignment in Abercarn. We rode about on bicycles, and I remember someone throwing a bucket of water over us. There were others who shouted after us in the street – 'Conchies!' But I'm glad I did what I did. I've always been glad I made a stand.

CHAPTER 6

ROMANCE

Romance blossomed in wartime. The threat of imminent separation and the dangers of war, caused young lovers to throw caution to the winds. The marriage rate soared and many young Welsh women were left to love from afar, wondering and worrying whether they would ever see their new husbands again.

Letter to my Wartime Love

~

Kusha Petts

Today the sun shines,
the almond blooms: so three things
are right with the world.

No Children should be Born

~

Pamela F. Sanderson

When war started I was in hospital in Oxford, rushed in overnight with a threatened acute appendix. I listened to the words of Chamberlain ending with 'We are at war with Germany', and felt it was a depressing end to the unrest of the last few years.

The ward was a very long one with a harsh sister in charge. There was no privacy. I think there were curtains round the beds, but they were never drawn. Everyone washed and used the commodes in full view of other patients. During the specialists' visits, the patient was never addressed, and if afterwards I asked what was going to happen, I was told curtly to wait and see, it would be Mr Abernethy's decision. While I was waiting, I started a period earlier than expected; when I asked for a pad I was told I must manage as I should have come prepared. However, as I made such a fuss, eventually I was given the biggest pad I had ever seen. This I was made to use for the whole four days.

Within hours of the declaration of war, many patients were discharged. Then all the wards were filled with evacuated patients from a London hospital – some very old and ill, some crying. Bombing was expected immediately, but after one fake alarm there was a long lull. My mother visited me in hospital and begged me to consider going home to her to think out what I should do next: my digs were now filled with evacuees from the East End. I worked in Oxford as a milliner and realized that, from now on, my skills would not be in great demand.

In 1940, another person joined my mother's household. John was a pilot in the RAF and had recently, in tragic circumstances, been left a widower, with a little girl of two years. My mother had not chosen to take him in, he had just been billeted on her. He was operating from Hampstead Norris and was instructing in between bombing raids. He had recently finished one sortie and was to do another, before returning to instructing.

It didn't take long for the RAF pilot and myself to discover that we wanted to spend our lives together – however brief they would be. He wasn't at all the sort of man I thought I would want seriously: he was a regular in the RAF and I disliked uniforms; we differed in our values, politics and way of life – but, nevertheless, we were both attracted to one another.

The news was by no means received with joy by my mother: 'You haven't known each other long enough. He is from a different part of the country. He is a widower. You will always be moving about,' and, last but not least, 'There's a war on.'

She even announced: 'No one should be allowed to marry during a war and no children should be born.'

Aunt Bess got cross and told her not to be so silly and Aunty Annie tried not to laugh.

It was cold and wet on my wedding day and I had

decided to wear my favourite bottle green two-piece. Scarves wrapped round the head like turbans were all the rage, so I borrowed a red scarf for my head. My mother had flatly refused to come as it was to be in a Registry Office, but at the last minute she arrived looking resplendent in blue and wearing her sables. I was sure she would be mistaken for the bride, and my cousin looked as if she didn't know whether to laugh or cry. A friend had lent a rather dilapidated car which was a long time starting.

Aunt Bess and Aunty Annie came to wave us off and Aunt Bess noticed I hadn't any flowers. 'Wait a minute,' she said and ran into the side entrance of the hotel, returning with a bunch of red carnations and maidenhair fern which she pinned on to my coat. We finally chugged off in the cold, sleety rain, along the muddy country roads. After the ceremony, Aunt Bess was waiting to grab the flowers back, sped into the hotel and replaced them in their vase. No one knew they had ever been borrowed.

During the next year I became pregnant. At that time we were living in a remote cottage with no electricity or running water. Once when John arrived on leave he brought Ann, his little girl. She did the most appalling things. She tipped over a cupboard full of china and every piece was smashed. She broke all her toys and tore up her books. But I tried to make allowances as she had lost her mother when she was very young and I was the sixth person she had been moved on to, all in different places.

I became very worried when I thought about the baby's birth, in case I was left all alone in the cottage. The district nurse was dismissive and told me I would have lots of warning. She ordered me to eat brown bread, which was unavailable. She ignored my complaints of severe back pain.

Suddenly, when I was alone with Ann, I went into heavy labour. We managed to get upstairs with a box of toys which I gave her to play with in the passage, and I undressed and went to bed. It was a dull, cold, misty day. There was no heating upstairs and I got colder and colder and more and more frightened. The experience was indescribable. Suddenly the doors opened and John stood there. He had had a feeling something was wrong and as there was a lull at the camp, he had borrowed a car and come home. He took Ann to my cousin's and phoned for the nurse. After three hours of labour a girl was born.

I was soon up and about as there was no one to look after me. The few days I was in bed, John came home each night. A lady in a cottage nearby used to send me in a cooked tea. People I would not have expected to sent gifts of eggs, a banana, an orange, things which were priceless. All the washing had to be done by hand with water heated on the kitchener, or cooking stove, and there were only candles to go to bed with. It was a lonely time. My mother didn't come to see me, as she didn't agree with me having a baby in wartime. I shall never forget that hateful war. I think mothers and housewives were forgotten women.

The Black Cat Tea Cosy

~

Nancy Walker

I did not believe in superstition until one day during the war something happened so unexpectedly it bewildered me to think of it. I had been clearing out and tidying a large clothes cupboard which stood in a recess on top of the landing in the house. While doing so, I came across the black cat tea cosy which had been given to me for a Christmas present. It was so like a cat sitting on the table with black silky fur and green eyes, it was used only once then put away and forgotten.

As I saw it lying there I thought about the black cat bringing good luck. I picked it up eagerly and felt the urge to use it again. Saying quietly to myself: 'Lucky black cat', I took it downstairs. I felt something had to happen.

I was living in hope every day of hearing some news of my husband, Arthur, who was sailing somewhere on the high seas, a prisoner of war on a German vessel. The anxiety was gradually having an effect on myself and my family. Every day was a day of hope and prayer. When the family sat down for tea that afternoon, the tea cosy was placed on top of a large teapot. One of my brothers asked who put the cat on the table and several other jokes were cracked.

That evening I retired to bed early with my baby girl as the air raids now were getting heavy. There were many times I had to get up in the early hours of the morning and go down into the air raid shelter for safety. I must have slept heavily and was suddenly awakened by the sound of raised voices downstairs. Then my father was tapping my bedroom door telling me to get dressed and come downstairs. We had news.

I felt quite dazed and tried to think clearly. The living room seemed to be full of people I hardly knew. They had all been listening to the radio and had called to see if we had heard the good news. The German newscaster known as Lord Haw-Haw had announced that the German sea raider *Altmark* had arrived at a Norwegian fjord and 500 British prisoners would be taken to Hamburg and interned in a few days. This was the ship on which my husband was a prisoner. I had already received notification from the War Office to say he was alive and well but still aboard an enemy raider which had not been named.

The Prime Minister demanded a safe return for the prisoners to this country from Norway. In twenty-four hours the Navy was on its way to rescue them with *HMS Cossack* and two other warships standing by. Few lives were lost in this gripping climax. The prisoners were released and landed at Leith, Scotland. My husband arrived at Cardiff General Station quite the worse for his gruelling five months on board the prison ship, but careful nursing brought him back to good health.

The black cat tea cosy had pride of place for a long, long time on the table. Where else?

The Landing

~

Phyllis M. Jones

Bill, my American soldier, had filled my life and occupied my thoughts for the length of time I had known him. Nothing else mattered. Every minute we had spent together seemed important; even our elusive friendship which had developed until there was a mute, basic understanding, seemed to count. Only now, the last evening with the prospect of never seeing each other again, surely this must be the time for honesty... if he would give just a small sign that he felt for me as much as I felt for him.

I knew my voice was normal when I spoke, and the way he answered. We might have looked more intently into each other's eyes. But eyes are deceptive. The only truth was in my own and he could not read this any more than I could see beyond the dark, cornflower-blue directness of his expression. I knew every detail of his face, the clean firmness of his mouth, the fresh brown of his skin; the way he smiled, his sensitive lips. I knew the casual way he would throw an arm around my shoulder, a gesture at once familiar, possessive and yet it held me away from him.

But tonight, there were no tomorrows, no more expectancy. It was only in the morning I guessed.

The drama of the morning made personal problems

insignificant. The words: 'To the people of Western Europe. A landing was made on the coast of France by the Allied Expeditionary Force...' were heard by the last patient in the line of beds which were being pulled out in readiness for cleaning. Still linked by his earphones to the wall, he shouted through the buzz of activity.

'We're there. We've landed in France.'

There was immediate reaction as those who were too weak called for nurses to push their beds back so that they too, could listen. Others got out of bed and pushed themselves. Nurses shared earphones with patients and over the faces of all there crept smiles of triumph.

Suddenly I knew where Bill must be. The increased sound of engines from jeeps and army lorries; the tang of excitement which mingled with the autumn air; the sad, lingering farewells which had no explanation now completed the pattern. My mind returned to last night. The way he traced a pattern with his finger on the top of the wooden gate. How I wanted him to go and then I met those dark blue eyes and for the first time saw desire... and now it was myself who wanted to get away. No kiss could satisfy the longings or ease the disappointments of the last nine months. I felt his hand on my arm, a pressure which should have turned me towards him but instead, I backed away.

'Write soon, Bill.' 'I will... we'll meet again, Margie, sometime... promise.'

I nodded.

'Thanks for everything.' He turned. The quick steps carried him out of my life.

A Joyous Interlude, May 1944

~

Hilda M. Howells

A notice appeared in the Sisters' Mess: 'The following Sisters should not make any arrangements for the 20th–22nd May…' We had no idea as to what was going to happen; we spruced up our uniforms just in case.

It was my privilege to be one of the Sisters chosen to join in the celebrations when the Swedish Mercy Ship, *Gripsholm*, arrived in Algiers on Saturday 20 May 1944. The *Gripsholm* was very colourful in contrast to the grey ships of the Royal Navy that were anchored in Algiers harbour. Broad bands of yellow and blue, the colours of neutral Sweden, were painted on the funnels, and along the whole length were sprawled in great black letters the words: DIPLOMAT GRIPSHOLM SVERIGE. She carried on board 900 repatriated British and Allied prisoners of war, and there was great rejoicing as she sailed into the harbour. The band of a British Armoured Regiment began to play and, soon everyone on the ship was singing. 'Take me back to dear old Blighty' and 'There'll always be an England'. Gangways were thrown out, and the women of the British and American Red Cross went on board giving out cigarettes, and sweets. The severely wounded and the very sick were carried ashore for treatment at Allied hospitals in Algiers. They would go home when fit to travel.

It must have been somewhat unreal, almost a dream for these men who had been prisoners for so long. After a day of celebrations, there was dinner on board to which the women of the British and American Services were invited. It was a great occasion. Some of these men had been prisoners for four years, since the early days of the war, and conversation was difficult at first. They were shy for we were the first women they had spoken to for so long. After a while the barriers came down and the pent up feelings released when they realized that they could talk freely. They spoke of Abyssinia, Benghazi, Tobruk, and the places they knew before their captivity. Then they wanted news of home. What was London like? What were the rations like at home? Was the country as beautiful as ever?

The following morning, a Sunday morning, we were down at the quayside, watching the *Gripsholm* slowly going out on the tide. But some of the prisoners, South Africans, Australians and New Zealanders stayed on to wait for transfer home at a later date. In the afternoon, those of them who were able attended a party in the Jardin D'Essai, a very beautiful botanical garden. It was wonderful: great long tables with all the delectable dishes to make it a party of the year, posies of flowers mingling with the delicacies. My escort was a South African, one of the many Dominion soldiers on board. Before the war he was a big-game hunter. As he lead me in for tea, he suddenly announced:

'I would like to give you some flowers'. He plucked

some flowers from a vase on the table and said, 'It is so long since I gave some flowers to a lady.' He was delighted and I was very touched. I have those flowers today pressed with others between the leaves of a book.

Suddenly, it was announced through the loudspeakers that coaches would take us to the zoo. 'Gee,' says he, 'This is great,' and I watched the happiness return to those sad eyes. In the zoo, I felt as if I was on safari, for he taught me so much. He had a great respect and love for all wild animals. He must have suffered so much to be confined in prison camps for four years.

The sacrifice had been made by so many. Their greatest assets, were their hope, their faith, their undaunted spirit and their pride in their homeland. These had sustained them during those long years in captivity.

From Gymslip to Wedded Bliss

~

Maureen Kouroupis

In silence we gathered around the radio to hear the announcement that Britain was at war with Germany. It was Sunday 3 September 1939. Never in my wildest dreams did I imagine, that I, a gawky schoolgirl of almost thirteen would be married to a foreigner and the mother of a baby girl by the time the conflict ended.

At the time I was just starting my second year at

Canton High School for Girls. As my father at forty was unlikely to be called up and I had no brothers and just one sister, Beryl who was younger than me, I did not think that we would be affected very much by the war.

On that same September Sunday, a young Greek sailor was aboard the SS *Mount Athos* in a German port. Under orders from the owners they hurriedly left port and by December were anchored in the River Plate awaiting a berth. Anchored close by, alongside the German battleship *Graf Spee* was a British vessel on which my cousin, Geoff Tucker was third engineer. Unknown to each other at that time, Geoff and the Greek sailor, Peter, watched the *Graf Spee* pull out into the river; and under orders from her captain, the ship was scuttled rather than face the British warships lying in wait for her outside the port.

The *Mount Athos* then sailed for England. On three occasions, Peter's ship was torpedoed after leaving British ports. The last incident led to serious injuries to his right eye and leg and he spent ten months in Manchester Royal Eye Hospital. On being discharged, Peter was sent to Cardiff. He came to live at the house of my best friend at school, Barbara Warren, whose mother, a widow, took in lodgers. Peter's cousin was already living at the house in between voyages and Peter was found a job at the Greek seamen's hostel by the Greek authorities as he was now unfit for sea service.

As I was a regular visitor at the Warren's house I knew all the residents and was friendly with them. That is how Peter and I met. Each day as I alighted from a tramcar at Canton Cinema he would be getting on it to go to work.

I wore school uniform but I knew he liked me.

At our house, the big worry seemed to be putting up blackout curtains at the windows or having to carry gas masks and identity cards. We had an Anderson shelter erected in our back garden and, at school, brick shelters on the playing field and 'iron rations' for each class which we kept in biscuit tins. At the beginning of the war we didn't mind frequent practice trips to the shelters. We were missing lessons after all. Some girls who lived near Canton High School in Cardiff were allowed to run home when the sirens went and sometimes I would go with a friend; nobody seemed to think we could have been killed on the way. At night, at home, my father stood outside our shelter with a tin hat on, passing us jugs of cocoa. I was more worried about any lurking spiders than the bombers. We all peeped out of the shelter to gaze at the searchlights. 'There's one,' we would cry if we spotted a plane in the fierce beams.

Then war events began to touch my life. Kenny Stone, a neighbour's son I had grown up with, was killed at Dunkirk. Another boy, Ivor Fox, went to India with the Air Force and was never seen again. His mother was devastated because there was no confirmation of his fate. In June 1940 the *Daily Mail* carried a small article, 'Ship your child to safety'. The government, in response to offers from the Dominions, was urging parents to evacuate their children, by sea, to the safety of Canada. Two sisters, one in my class, were to be evacuated. They sailed on Friday 13 September 1940 on board the *MV City of Benares* an Ellerman-Wilson passenger ship which was heading the convoy. Four days later her escorts having departed, the ship was torpedoed by a German U-boat which had been hovering in wait. Eighty-three children and 256 other passengers and crew lost their lives. Some of them died in the lifeboats; twelve Welsh children including my schoolmates Margaret and Nesta were lost.

By this time my father was in the Home Guard based at Ely Racecourse and my mother, who had never worked outside the home, was working at Currans' munitions factory at Cardiff docks. In early 1941, Cardiff had some heavy air raids. On the night of 2 January, the first major raid took place. My mother and two friends on the 2-till-10 shift, walked home through Grangetown and Riverside – the two worse-hit areas; they were terrified. My school in Market Road was badly damaged in this raid, and our lessons were relocated in a chapel before other accommodation was found. At the end of April, my form mistress and her sisters were killed when a landmine dropped on their house. Great sadness swept the school. After my class had been particularly horrible to the physics teacher, the headmistress warned us that Miss Coldbrook was already under great strain as all her family were in occupied Jersey. We had the grace to feel ashamed.

In the summer of 1942 I took the Central Welsh Board examinations and although I did well in them I did not want to stay in school. I wanted to go to work, to go out at night and, more especially, I wanted to see more of Peter. Barbara and I found jobs as trainee telephonists in the GPO Headquarters: I started there in September 1942, when I was sixteen. It was very spartan and strict but there were lots of young girls and we had fun. Everyone had a boyfriend. Free French, Norwegian, American and some British. Most of the British boys were fighting elsewhere but Cardiff had a huge floating population of eager young men out to enjoy themselves while they could. Although the blackout was strict and transport was terrible, once you went inside somewhere it was jumping. The cinemas and pubs were packed every night. Peter and I went out two or three times a week: to variety shows at the New Theatre, concerts at the Capitol and sometimes for meals at the Carlton where a band played every night and where mice actually ran across the floor. Nevertheless, we still ate there, and afternoon tea-dances were always packed out. I did not realize then that Peter often waited on card parties late at night to get extra money. The Greeks, being big gamblers, tipped well on a winning streak. He often brought me silk stockings and lipsticks that his friends brought home from sea for him. I had a present nearly every week. We were in love. In August 1943 I left the GPO and went to Cardiff Marine Department of the Inland Revenue. As a clerk my job was to go into the Shipping Registry and link up returns made by shipping companies with the files held on British seamen, in order to collect their income tax. I have never forgotten how many of these men I was trying to trace had died at sea. It was through this job that, unofficially, I discovered that the tanker *King Lud*, on which my cousin was an engineer, had been lost without trace after leaving New York out of convoy. This work really brought home to me the dreadful losses of the merchant fleet. Of course I was bound by the Official Secrets Act so I did not talk about it.

In the autumn of 1943, Peter and I asked my parents if we could become engaged. They refused: I was too young at seventeen and neither my father nor his family liked foreigners. That November, we bought an engagement ring and placed an announcement in the *South Wales Echo*. My father went mad. We had a small engagement party at my house and all Peter's friends sent me telegrams of congratulation. My father went out for the night.

The following year I wore him down and although he begged me not to marry, he finally consented. We were over the moon. By Greek law a legal wedding could only take place in the Greek Orthodox Church, otherwise I would not be recognized as Peter's legal wife in his country. On 15 April 1944, we married at Cardiff Registry Office and two days later, after the Greek Orthodox Easter, we married in the Greek Church of St Nicholas, Cardiff. I had another shock in store for my father: through my marriage I lost my British nationality and had to register as an alien.

Within a year we had a baby girl, born three days after my eighteenth birthday. When Victory in Europe was celebrated in May 1945, the change in my life from plain gawky schoolgirl to happily married young mother was complete. Our marriage lasted forty-six years until Peter died in August 1990, so I think we made the right decision even though everyone thought we were mad at the time.

Letters to the Front

~

Alison Bielski

I wrote to him in France
of ordinary workdays
in this evacuated
college where villagers
stifled us in silence

he replied with humorous
accounts of collapsing
field cinemas intensive
friendships no other news
allowed past the censor
anticipation deepened
his usual penstrokes

we lived in different
worlds my rigid lifestyle
progressing to qualified
success his trained alertness
controlled for swift attack

surviving war he left
with American prospects
far from insistent Wales
all correspondence ceased
safety destroying that thread
of comfort our fragile
relationship snapped by peace

All Leave Cancelled

~

Stella Morgan

Suddenly from his inside coat pocket Walter pulled out a folded sheet of paper and handed it to me. Silently I opened the document and for a moment couldn't believe what I read. 'It is a Special Marriage Licence!' I said at last.

Walter looked at me anxiously. 'It's all right, isn't it? It is what you want?'

'Yes, yes of course, darling. It's just that it's unexpected. I'm dazed by all the tumult and turmoil of recent weeks. I've been frightened for you, for me, and for the whole world.' I put my arms round his neck, 'Oh my dear, of course it is what I want.'

'It will not be the kind of wedding we've always dreamed of and so often talked about,' he said apologetically, 'but maybe, when this terrible war is over, we can have a proper ceremony in a church, and with all the splendour and trimmings you deserve. We'll have our families and friends there to share our happiness. But for the time being this will have to do. The main thing, darling, is that we love one another.'

We held on to each other almost fiercely, as if daring anyone to part us. I felt weak from the feelings that were surging through me. Then, he held me at arms length, kissed me lightly on the nose, and said, 'We must hurry, we have to be at Paddington Town Hall by 9.30, so we haven't much time.'

Panic gripped me, 'What on earth shall I wear? All my best clothes are in Newbury, and the rest are packed.'

Walter chuckled.

'It's all very well for you,' I said. 'You have your fireman's uniform, and very smart you look in it too.'

The blue suit that I'd travelled up in from Newbury would have to do.

Thank goodness I had it cleaned only a few weeks ago, and I'd had my hair washed and set during the week. A last critical look in the mirror left me in no doubt, that in the circumstances, I had reason to feel pleased with the way I looked. I rejoined Walter and asked, 'Will I do?'

'You look wonderful,' he assured me.

The town hall was only a short walk away. The ceremony was a chillingly impersonal affair and seemed to have nothing to do with either Walter or myself. My heart was thumping so loudly, I felt sure everyone in the room could hear it. I tried in my mind to imagine there were coloured glass windows as in a church, the polished table an altar, the first couple before the Registrar as my sister Evelyn and Walter's brother Trevor, as bridesmaid and best man.

Then it was our turn: Walter's voice reached me breaking through the brittle shield of my imagination. He spoke in a steady confident voice. But when it came to my turn I stumbled and stammered over the words. It was hard to believe that we were uttering words that were to bind us together for the rest of our lives in the most sacred and intimate bond of all. Two of the staff were called to witness our signatures then we left to return to the flat, where we just had enough time for a coffee and a slice of toast, before Walter had to rush away to report for duty once again. What should have been the happiest day of our lives proved to be one of the most wretched.

'I will let you know as soon as I have some leave,' said Walter, 'So you can come up to the flat, no use me coming to Newbury, until you find a flat there.'

We clung to each other fiercely and desperately. Then with a final kiss he was gone. I pushed back the tears and my throat ached with the effort. This was my wedding day and I was alone with no idea when I would see Walter again. The rest of the day was spent in packing and arranging with a removal company to store the furniture if I failed to find a flat.

On my return to Newbury, I wasted no time in looking around for a flat, and was fortunate to find a very suitable one right in the centre of the town over the fifty-shilling men's outfitters shop. This would be our first real home together but because of the war would be rarely shared. There was the no-married-women rule of my employers, the Anglo-Saxon Oil Company to be considered too. This would mean my marriage would have to be kept a secret, for the time being at least. And for this reason I could not wear my wedding ring.

Newbury experienced little of the immediate violence of war. At first, when the sirens wailed their moanful sound across the town, everyone hurried to the nearest air raid shelter, but, as time went on and alarms signalled raids that were directed on other towns, the sirens were ignored and everyone continued with their work. This indifferent attitude to the warning of possible attack by enemy aircraft almost cost me my life. On leaving the office with other members of the staff, we heard the sirens sounding their doleful warning. As usual, we ignored them. I reached my flat and began to prepare a meal when, through my kitchen window, I saw a plane which seemed to be heading straight for me. The warning completely forgotten I assumed the machine was one of our own which explained why, as I dived under the table, I shouted out, 'You fool! What do you think you're doing?' Even as I spoke, there was a terrifying screaming sound ending in a loud thundering thud that shook the whole building.

My whole body froze with shock. I tried to move, but it was as if I was paralysed. After the plane flew out of hearing, there was a deathly silence. Shaking violently, my heart leaping and lurching, I dragged myself to my feet and made my way downstairs. The lady in the flat below mine was standing stiffly in her doorway, her face ashen. Beside her was her nine-year-old daughter. All of a sudden the child plunged into hysterics, letting out a high-pitched yell. Her mother, as if in a trance, stared at her daughter for a while, then she too lost control and screamed. Fearing my head would burst, and quite unaware of what I was doing, I struck the child's cheek. She threw her head back, gulped and was silent. At the same time, her mother became calm and took the now quietly weeping child into her arms.

The bomb which had screeched through the air had done no serious damage. It had fallen into an open field blasting a large hole in the ground. Nevertheless, I never again treated air raid warnings so carelessly.

In the weeks that followed, the wail of the sirens were heard frequently as the Germans stepped up their attacks. These were mostly by night and a number of bombs were dropped in the Newbury area. The one that caused the worst devastation was during the day, when it fell on a school, killing children and teachers. This tragic event cast a gloom over the whole town and spread to neighbouring towns and villages. It was heart-breaking that innocent children were being wiped out in this way all over the country.

I was alone on the top floor of the building, and for safety reasons, made up my bed on the corridor floor with only pillows and cushions to protect me from the hardness of the boards. It was a grim and savage period with the thought of being maimed for life more terrifying than of being killed outright.

It was three weeks after our wedding that I saw Walter again. I was by then firmly settled in the flat. He came down whenever possible, usually on twenty-four hours leave. There was no advance notice of this, and when it did happen, the time was so short that neither of us could be completely relaxed with each other. Time after time we looked forward to a four-day leave but, as it came nearer, the raids on London would be intensified and all leave cancelled. The bombing and fires were so fierce that the firemen could scarcely afford time to rest. They would take odd moments to lie on their bunks in full uniform ready for the next attack.

Once when I expected him on a four-day leave, he didn't turn up. I thought little of it when he failed to arrive at the appointed time, as travel was very uncertain and trains were likely to be delayed. But as time went on I became anxious. Day turned into night and yet another day. I was numb with fear, particularly when I read on the news placards that the hospital near Paddington Station had been bombed. My fear turned to terror. Walter's fire station was behind this hospital. I had no telephone in the flat, so went to the nearest kiosk, and phoned the station. There was no reply. This could mean the station had been hit as well as the hospital. I spoke aloud, 'Please God, please make someone answer!'

Frantically, I rang hospital after hospital, each time told, no patient of that name admitted. I went back to the flat. My stomach was on fire, my throat was dry, the pain in my head made me wonder if I was going out of my mind, or did the ache around my heart mean I was due for a heart attack? There was no one I could turn to for advice or reassurance. I wandered aimlessly from room to room, then unable to endure the confinement of four walls, I went out to the street. Panicking again when I realized that Walter might arrive in my absence, I raced back to the flat. In an effort to ease the burning of my forehead, throat and cheeks, I went to the bathroom to bathe with cold water. I caught sight of my face in the mirror and was frightened at what I saw. Startled by the ringing of my front doorbell, I dashed downstairs. It must be Walter, it must be! It wasn't, it was Miss Alexander from the office. 'Are you all right? We wondered why you didn't turn up today.'

I poured out my story. It was a comfort to talk to someone and to someone fifteen years my senior. 'London is having a pretty rough time just now, and Walter would hardly be sitting around in the fire station, so if the station was bombed, he wouldn't be there.' She paused, 'And didn't you say the phone was ringing?' I nodded. Then I realized what she meant. 'Of course, how stupid of me. If the phone was ringing, the station hadn't been bombed.'

I got through to the station this time, and was told that the men were working all hours, that I was not to worry, that my husband would be home with me shortly on leave. Three days later I heard familiar footsteps on the stairs. I rushed to open the door. Walter walked in slowly, and unsteady on his feet. If he had been a drinking man, I would have said he was drunk. I made to take him in my arms but he pushed me away. He mumbled some words of explanation, at least I thought that was what he was trying to say. I suddenly realized that he was over-exhausted, and helped him to a chair. His face was black from smoke and his eyes were circled red. He looked ghastly.

The next day Walter slowly began to tell me of some of the experiences he had been through. It was hard to believe that he had survived when men had dropped dead alongside him. It had meant constant nights and days of heavy bombing, allowing no respite. Fires were springing up everywhere. Firemen were simply transferred from one fire to another without reporting back to their stations. The sustained battering and the increasing devastation had caused confusion and had developed into a state of complete disorganization.

It was a relief when London was given a respite even though it meant that the attacks were diverted to other places. Cardiff, Swansea and places in the south of England suffered badly. During the latter part of the war, Walter was transferred to the ocean-going firefighters. These came under naval control and patrolled the sea between the south coast and the French coast. They were called upon to put out fires on vessels bombed by the enemy. I did not see Walter for this period. We exchanged letters, though these letters often went astray, perhaps arriving weeks or months later, but some never reached their destination.

CHAPTER 7

EVACUEES AND REFUGEES

Millions of children were sent to the country at the outset of the war, many to return shortly to the big cities because their parents felt their initial fears were unjustified and many because they could not live where they were sent. Not all evacuees were fostered in suitable homes; they were often shuffled about for the convenience of their carers. Refugees arrived with their merest possessions sewn in to their clothing. Some children never saw their parents again.

Evacuee School

~

Mimi O. Hatton

In the summer of 1944, as V1 flying bombs rained on Kent, I taught in and out of school air raid shelters – long brick buildings with blast-proof entrances. Not far from Biggin Hill Fighter Station, we had a ring-side view of the Battle of Britain. Everyday, after school, we escorted the children home, dodging the shrapnel (from our anti-aircraft guns) which the small boys wanted to pick up, not knowing that it was burning hot. Finally, our area was declared a danger zone. Children were evacuated and I volunteered as an 'evacuee teacher' and was told to report to Porthmadog, a place I had never heard of.

As I travelled on the train through Bangor and Caernarfon I was amazed to hear what was to me a foreign language. When I reached Brynkir I found myself alone on the train – I had not understood that I had been told to get out and continue my journey by bus. When, at last, I neared my destination I saw, down below, a magic place in a faint haze with a mountain rising above it and the sea shining silver. 'That is Porthmadog!' I was told. It looked so beautiful.

I found lodgings with a Mrs Gibson, an elderly lady who only agreed to take me on a temporary basis. On the Sunday night, Mrs Gibson came home from chapel and told me that an announcement had been made that school would start at 9 a.m. on Monday at the Sawmills. It sounded an odd place for a school!

Over the following weeks teachers arrived from Kent. School started officially on 4 September with 188 on the roll. As acting headmistress I was given the task of finding extra classrooms and completing the organization. Miss Merkl and I had the top junior classes in the Tabernacle vestries; Miss Gandhi had Standard 1 in a small room at the Sawmills; Miss Diamond had an infant class and Mrs Ivans a Roman Catholic group sharing the large room at the Sawmills; Miss Evans had the senior class of thirty in the Science room, Central School.

The children had a third of a pint of free milk each day which arrived in churns, delivered by Mr Tom Pugh on his horse-drawn milk float. Sometimes the Tabernacle vestries were used for a local health clinic and then we had to take the two classes on expeditions, nature walks, sketching or physical training in the park. We collected cones and beach nuts in Tremadoc woods; walked to Morfa Bychan for seashells and seaweed for handicraft; we did bark rubbings with cobbler's wax, begged from Mr Ensor's shoe shop.

Because I was interested in self-government and the educational ideas of A.S. Neil (*The Dominees' Log*), I encouraged the evacuee schoolchildren to elect a Children's Committee, one member from each age group, eight and over. The Children's Committee produced a magazine once a month. Some of the poems submitted for these issues were sent to C. Day Lewis, who ran a children's poetry competition, and had an honourable mention. The children also helped to organize events and to deal with problems such as bad behaviour, delinquency and homesickness. One deprived boy, John, was frequently pilfering and had been warned by PC Jones, the young Porthmadog policeman. The Children's Committee decided after much discussion that John should not be punished, but they would arrange that those with enough pocket money would give a penny a week to provide pocket money for John, so that he would not have to steal.

To help the people with whom the children were billeted, we set up a play centre at the Sawmills, open most evenings, using toys and games, collected locally and some from parcels from the American Red Cross. The play centre was a special help to the 'billet mothers' as there were sometimes discipline and language problems. In many billets only Welsh was spoken. Many of the evacuees learnt some Welsh, but the Welsh children did not learn to speak English until they were about seven years old. On 22 December we had a Carol Service and readings in the Tabernacle and invited the billet mothers and friends. It was a happy day. Slowly the children drifted back to Kent and, after Christmas 1944, we only had about a hundred left and only three teachers.

Bertha Merkl, (who since September had shared lodgings with me at the home of the motherly Mrs Roper Morgan), explored with me all the local mountains. We had no car, only bicycles and there were few buses, so mountain trips often depended on lifts – in that time of petrol rationing mostly on lifts from commercial vehicles. One day, walking along a mountain track near Cwm Pennant by myself, in pouring rain, I met an old shepherd. 'You like the mountains in the rain?' he said. 'Ah! How much more would you like them, when you put the sheep on the grass and you see the lambs come. Sharp as a rock is life, but it has beauty like the hills.'

On VE night, 8 May 1945, Bertha Merkl and I thought we would be very brave and go into the Sportsman Hotel and have a drink to celebrate; women did not go into pubs in Porthmadog. When we arrived there was no one there. Outside the town hall was a large crowd of people singing hymns in Welsh, with Dick from the shoe shop standing on a soapbox in the middle, conducting. When Bertha and I arrived on the fringe of the group, I remember him calling out: 'And now for our English friends, we will sing "Abide with me" in English!'

The school finally closed in July 1945. During that year, Leslie Morgan, the son of the house where I was staying, returned home after serving with the Army in the Middle East. We fell in love but, the following year, while on 'demob' leave, he died before we could be married. I can still see the canon from St John's, Porthmadog, in his flowing robes, against a backcloth of mountains, standing at the cemetery gate at Bethel, like an Old Testament prophet with his long white hair, raising his arms and saying, 'I am the Resurrection and the Life!' Although I returned to Kent, I always came back 'home' to Wales, to 'Mum Morgan' in Meadow Drive. Now alone, that is where I am today.

Evacuee Roulette

~

Beryl Mills

At about 7.30 p.m., we were marched into the Memorial Hall. We each had a glass of milk and some Marie biscuits, while all around us was a mass of waiting people.

My name was called, 'Beryl Mills, please!'

Two strange women came forward to get me. My instant reaction was to draw away from them as I did not want to go anywhere unless my friend, Rosie Hills, came too. I wanted to go with Rosie, I needed someone. I cried and struggled, but it was of no use. With one firm hand in each of mine, we marched off. I held a stiff reluctant body, I was not going anywhere with these strange women who spoke in a language I didn't know.

One said, 'Come on, come on, we'll bring you back to see your friends tomorrow.'

Lurking beside tall trees was a large semi-detached house and I was led up the short path, and indoors, where I found out who my two companions were. One was Miss Elizabeth, the other Miss Nesta and there was another, Miss Florence. They were the unmarried sisters of the Revd Jeffery Jones. There was also a maid, Mabel. In the kitchen I was given a glass of milk and, without much ado, shown the way up the narrow flight of stairs to the attic bedroom where I was expected to sleep. It had a cold, eerie feel. The door was shut tight behind me, and I stood alone, shaking like a leaf on the limb of a bare branch. The spasms in my tummy fluttered like caged butterflies trying to get out. The silence scared the life out of me. Looking out of the window I thought I saw a lone flickering light in the sky way out over the sea. I asked 'Mother are you, too, daunted and alone? I am thinking of you.'

My heart leaped at the suddenness of the bedroom door being opened.

'Why aren't you in bed?' Only when she saw me with the blankets over me did she leave, shutting the door behind her. I shivered, out of control, the nervous vibrations throbbing through my body. Even the bed seemed to shake with me. I must have dozed off, only to wake up the whole household with screams. After that they came in every night. They were concerned about my well-being; I could hear their whisperings and their breathing so near to my face.

I had breakfast, dinner and tea with Mabel. I would have died had she not been there; I began to look at her as my sister-mother companion. There was no life, no laughter, no joy, in the vicarage. Days and weeks went by, and I slowly became accustomed to my surroundings and the humdrum existence.

The first morning was a sombre start with everyone up for breakfast at eight o'clock. I was having some porridge beside Mabel when the three stern-looking women came into the kitchen. Miss Elizabeth, Miss Nesta and Miss Florence had come to inspect me and acknowledge me; they had weak smiles but said hardly a word. They talked together and walked out, one after the other, each giving me a careful look. I was so scared of them I could hardly swallow my porridge. It was not at all easy for me, or for them to accept me, in their nunnery-like existence. I was frightened of everybody and everything, and there was no one around to talk to about my fears. The only way was to hold and keep the fears to myself. Away from mother, I did not have any faith or trust in anyone.

Life at the vicarage was strict (there was no playing around), and I had to learn to adjust to far slower and calmer ways, to be quiet, to be seen and not heard. They were reserved and quiet people who led private lives. If I was for some reason challenged about something or other, 'What have you been up too?', even if I did not know what they were talking about, I felt the red-hot colour flare in my cheeks. Outside school hours, I was not allowed to bring any of my friends into the vicarage grounds, all had to stay outside. If there was any playing to do, I had to do it elsewhere.

I was able to visit my friends some distance away, but first, I had to tell the sisters where I was going and with whom. Delightful Newport, Dyfed, within walking distance, was a kaleidoscope of colourful views and historical events at one's fingertips. We hardly knew that a war was going on, we were protected on all sides by wonderful countryside, sandy beaches, river, and the wide blue sea. We could go for walks, play the fool in the narrow tree-lined lanes or run along Parrog sands. All bright and beautiful by day, but the night had me struggling back to consciousness, trembling with fright and sweating profusely with fear. All of us children thrown together by the uncertainties of the war were trying hard to adjust to new surroundings, holding onto the loose straws of personal existence, and identity.

At Christmas I was most fortunate to be presented with the loveliest porcelain doll, from a kind-hearted lady called 'Miss Christmas'. Sometime later, I sat the doll on some washing on a chair and, to my horror, she slipped off, and broke to pieces, and so did my heart.

One day my excitement knew no bounds. Mother asked if she could come down to see me. But when she was refused, my world blew apart. I never saw her ever again.

Early during the summer school holiday, without any hint or warning, events once again engulfed me. Mr Chin, the Evacuee Officer, had parked his car outside the vicarage. I had no idea what was going on. There were tears of apprehension and fear in my dazed eyes, for inside the car were all my belongings, packed and ready for me to go. I was told to get into the car. There were no goodbyes from anyone, and no one saw me off. I was not allowed back into the vicarage for an explanation. I was taken to the Nanyfer Hostel for Evacuees below St Mary's Church, off Goat Street. It was sheer delight to have the company of other children.

At the hostel I had freedom and understanding I had not thought possible, but it was only a temporary place to stay until suitable homes and people were found. My stay there was far too short, just three weeks, when some of us were told that we would be leaving. Some people wanted a girl companion for their young daughter, and it seemed that I fitted the part. There was no question of not going.

When Mr Chin called at the Nanyfer Hostel to collect me, everything seemed to fall apart. My world was again full of fears and uncertainties. I was taken to live at Penybryn, a public house out in the countryside. When I first set my eyes upon it, it had a claustrophobic air, surrounded by hedgerows and narrow lanes. I arrived about noon. Customers were drinking at the bar, and to my alarm, I was introduced in Welsh, 'Dyma Beryl yr ifacwî sydd wedi dod i aros gyda ni. Rhowch croeso iddi!' (Here is Beryl, the evacuee who is going to stay with us. Give her a welcome!)

I felt so embarrassed that I shied away. What a topsy-turvy contrast to the vicarage.

'Come in,' a friendly woman's voice invited. It was a welcome into their home, hearts and lives. There were two women, Bessie and Mrs Davies, her white-haired mother. Our eyes met, then Bessie took my arm in a gentle, silent grip, and I was led to the kitchen to sit beside the fire. A bold ticking clock broke the silence.

I felt so tight that words were impossible; inner fears tormented me. They were friendly and I began to ease among them, but they didn't have much time to spare me; it was a busy place. I was shown my bedroom, at the front of the house, above the passage and the bar.

Before I was fully aware of it myself, I was accepted as one of the family. Everyone was known by their first names. There was never a dull moment and there was freedom to go where I pleased and stay up as long as I wanted. There was no isolation nor stillness because everyone was preoccupied with something or other.

Waking up in the pub with the sun rising above the opposite villa, the roadside grass damp and shiny with dew, and everything green, caused my heart to lose a few beats. All roads led to Penybryn. Bessie knew that I understood a lot of Welsh; everything was Welsh. She told the customers not to speak to me in English: 'Siarad Gymraeg gyda hi.' (Speak Welsh to her.) Sooner than I had expected, I was speaking fluently and could understand all the wonderful events that happened all around which were discussed at the pub daily.

They made me one of them, they made me feel wanted, and gradually the loneliness in my heart began to fade. I was taking on a different identity, I was becoming Welsh in thought and speech; I was becoming a local.

Margam Abbey

~

Alathea Thomas

Every day, with her toy
                  brush,
the little girl
made the Abbey graveyard
her own chattering
                 village.

Morris

~

Sally Davies (as told to Barbara Roberts)

Harold was a driver on the railway and he was bringing the children down. I had to go to the Model School to collect a little girl, but when I got there Mr Jenkins, the schoolmaster, said to me, 'All the children are nearly gone, now.'

'When am I going to have a little girl, Mr Jenkins? Where is she?'

'Oh, you can't have a little girl,' he replied. 'They're all gone. But there are two boys here that won't be separated. You'll have to take the two.'

'I don't want boys,' I said. 'And I don't want *two*.'

But he persuaded me to take them home with me. When I asked them their names, one of them told me he was Mickey Mouse and the other was Windy Williams.

'That's not your name,' I said.

'Well that's what they call me,' Morris said.

I gave them supper and they went to bed. Now, in the meantime, Harold was coming home from work. 'What's the row I can hear upstairs?'

'There's two boys there.'

'Two boys!' he said. 'I thought you were going for a little girl!'

He went upstairs. The curtains were down. They'd been having pillow fights. Playing about they were, you see. So he went into the room and said, 'Now you two, get into bed and stop this nonsense. And if you don't you'll be in the hostel tomorrow. You won't stay here another day. I'll take you myself to the hostel.'

We never heard a sound afterwards.

You couldn't help but like Morris. But Rodney was a bit queer, a bit funny. Do you know what his ambition was? I asked him one day, 'What do you want to do, Rodney?' (He was older than Morris.)

And he said, 'I want to be a sailor. I want to get drunk, and I want to beat my wife.'

'Well,' I said, 'I don't think much of what you want to be when you're older.'

Morris wanted to work to earn money to have war

savings certificates, and indeed he found a job. They wanted a boy in the fur company shop of King Street. It was a nice shop, too, and I knew the manageress there. She wanted a boy to go out on Saturdays to deliver goods. So he went in and he asked for the job.

'Oh, I don't know,' she said, 'I'll think about it. I'll let you know.'

And he said back to her, 'Can't you tell me yes or no now? You might as well say yes or no.'

And indeed she told me afterwards, 'For his cheek, I gave him the job.'

He never looked back. He used to go out delivering, out to gentry's villages, delivering their furs. Fur coats, they were, and fur hats. I remember one particular night. The war was on of course, and the siren went. I said to my mother, 'Morris has gone to deliver a fur coat and I'm frightened for him.' The siren was going, you see, and we had a blackout. We were all frightened. I went to meet him. I went down Orchard Street and when I got down there Morris was coming, whistling, happy as a sand boy.

Rodney of course was jealous of Morris. He wanted his own job. Well, I said, 'Right. I'll try and get you a job.' And I did. I got him a job at the printers as an errand boy there. He was no good there really because he didn't want to do the messages they were asking him to do.

'How is he getting on?' I asked his boss.

'Oh,' he said, 'he's not much use,' But he added, 'We'll keep him a little while longer.'

He got ink on his collar, on his cuffs, on his shirt. I couldn't get it off. It wouldn't come off. It was spoiling all his clothes really. He was like this all the time, you see, playing about with his collar and his cuffs. There was more ink there than there was on the paper.

One morning we were having breakfast; we had an old-fashioned grate then and I had a long toasting fork and was toasting the bread. I could see them scuffling, the two of them, Morris and Rodney. And I said, 'What's the matter with the two of you?'

'Auntie,' Morris said, 'he's looking at you all the time. He doesn't take his eyes off you.'

'I can't stand any more of this,' I said. 'You'll have to go from me. I don't know where you'll go or what they'll do with you,' I said. 'But I'm not keeping you here to quarrel with Morris.'

They were fighting and I got frightened. So Mr Daws, the schoolmaster, came to see me and arranged for him to stay with someone else. I knew the person he was staying with and I told her, 'You're going to have an outing with this boy, you know.'

Morris had such good ways with him. There was a woman selling oil. She and her husband had a little cart and were selling paraffin oil round the houses. And he used to go out with her and wheel the cart for her. And he wasn't paid for that. But he always wanted to be doing something.

And he was quick. He would say to me, 'Auntie, what is so-and-so in Welsh?'

I would ask, 'Why are you asking me all these questions, Morris?' and he would reply, 'Well, I went to the mart and I heard two farmers talking.' He was finding out what they were talking about, about the cattle. He was interested, you see, he was listening.

He used to sit and look at the fire a lot, you know. He was meditating a lot, thinking. And I often used to watch him and I'd say to him, 'What are you thinking of, Morris?'

'My mother hasn't written to me.'

'Oh, you'll have a letter tomorrow. Or perhaps you'll have a letter the next day.'

The next day would come and he'd have a letter. And he'd say, 'I'm sure you're a fairy, you know, Auntie. You know when my mother's going to write.' I knew he was worrying about it. And yet he didn't want to go home.

Then Morris caught a dirty germ. He had what they called Bull Neck Diphtheria. The neck swells. He had it bad. I asked the doctor to come down to see him but he replied 'I'm a sick man myself.'

The next morning the doctor did come and told me, 'He'll have to go to Llanon.' That was the isolation hospital. The next day the MO came, the Medical Officer of Health, and there were seven or eight other doctors and they all said that he had to go away. Well they took him as far as the front door, my front door. The ambulance was there to take him, and my sister came in and she said to me, 'They're giving Morris brandy, Sal.'

'What are they giving him brandy for? Why don't they take the ambulance away? Why don't they go with him?' But he didn't go further than the door. He died outside my front door.

They brought him back in dead.

'You let that little boy die,' I said. 'He needn't have

died. He could have stayed in London and the bombs would have killed him. And yet he had to come to Carmarthen and have diphtheria.'

I had to phone his mother and father. His father was a bomb tester in Bridgend. His mother was in Lewisham in London in the War Office. I phoned his mother first and told her that he was going to Llanon, that he was ill. And then afterwards I was phoning again telling her that he had passed away and would she come down to see me. She stayed up in my mother's house because all my house was sealed up through the diphtheria.

When he was buried, all the children came to the funeral. I asked Rodney, the other boy, to come, because they were together and I thought it wasn't very nice to leave him out. He came to the house to me. The others were at the graveside, of course, the schoolchildren, but Rodney came from the house. He went behind Morris, then. He was in the first car. And I was there with him, of course, and Harold. It was just pathetic to think that he'd come from London to escape the bombs.

After the funeral when everything was over, I said to Mrs Caney, 'I'd like you to come up and see the doctor. I want him to tell you what really happened because I want you to know that I couldn't help what happened.'

'I don't think for a minute that you could,' she said to me.

The surgery was full, but the doctor called us into the room straightaway and the others had to wait.

'Now this is Morris's mother, the little boy's mother,' I said. 'And I'd like you to talk to her and tell her what really happened.' He saved me from blame because it all happened so quick, within a week. He told her, 'This lady has given him everything and done everything she could.'

She didn't think that I'd done anything but I wanted to clear myself and I wanted the doctor to tell her. I was grieving too much, to tell you the truth.

'I quite understand,' she said. 'I know. I lost Morris when he went to Mrs Davies,' she said. 'That's the time I lost him. The letters he was writing said he wasn't coming home any more.'

There was an inquest, but they wouldn't let me go. They said I was too ill to attend but that was wrong. I know what they were afraid of. I had called the doctor a murderer, you see, and I supposed they wanted to clear him. Of course he couldn't help that Morris died. But I was annoyed that they didn't come soon enough to him. I went up on that night and the doctor told me he was too ill himself to come out. It was snowing, the snow was coming down, but I did go up.

I was a long time coming to myself. I spent a lot of time in the cemetery. I used to go up nearly every week. And I'd sit and think about him, you know. But that didn't bring him back, of course. It was a terrible time.

[Morris died in January, 1940. In the three months before his death 106 patients were admitted to the county isolation hospital for diphtheria. Four died. On 9 January 1940 the County Medical Officer submitted a plan to immunize all children under five against the disease.]

Shadow Man

~

Patricia Parris

Boom! roared the guns. And boom boom boom rumbled the answer from across the Channel. At school it was whispered that we should be evacuated once again. On Friday, rumour became reality. A long train stood at Ashford station. Our 'unknown destination' was Wales.

Hundreds of us milled around the trestle table where Mr Price, the Billeting Officer, sat in Air Force Officer's blue. He worked down the list, pairing hostesses with children: 'Next!' – just like the doctor's surgery.

The sun burned as we stood in the school playground, each clutching a tin of condensed milk, a tin of corned beef, and a large bar of chocolate, to hand over to our prospective 'mothers'. The chocolate started to melt, so I ate mine.

Lunchtime passed. Still we waited. Only a few of us remained. At four o'clock I stood alone. Mr Price looked round helplessly, then said curtly, 'You'd better come with me.'

'Neat' was the word to describe his house, called 'Kensington'. Mrs Price was a suburban, genteel housewife. She had no children. Next morning after breakfast, I went to the stairs to go up and fetch my books. Mrs Price barred the way.

'Where are you going?'

In astonishment, I explained.

'You may go this morning, but in future you must bring everything down at breakfast time. You'll be wearing out the stair carpet.'

Mr and Mrs Price always addressed each other by title and name. Mrs Price told me that there was such a strong rapport between them that if she had a headache, Mr Price would know it immediately. To prove this, when it was time for him to return from the school where he both taught and ran the Air Training Corps (hence his uniform which he wore whether it was training day or not), instead of having the table laid, Mrs Price slowly took out the tablecloth, and languidly laid the plates. Mr Price watched this charade for a few minutes then asked,

'Have you got a headache, Mrs Price?'

'There you are,' she said triumphantly, darting a look at me. Her point established, she laid the tea in her ordinary manner, bringing in a pure white sandcastle of a blancmange. The bland, perfect whiteness tightened my stomach muscles. I replaced the spoon.

'Eat up,' said Mrs Price sharply, 'I expect you're not used to good meals decently served.'

On the Saturday, the Prices dragged me to the pictures. The film was Dr Jekyll and Mr Hyde. I begged to stay behind.

'Certainly not. I'll not trust you in my house on your own.'

What did they think I would do? Smash their china?

Run away? I sat in the cinema alternately covering my eyes and ears.

The mistrust extended to out of doors too. No matter whether I was going swimming at Caswell, staying late for school choir or drama club, or going out with friends, there was an inquisition before I left and another when I returned. I could not help thinking of home, where with a large family, my mother was only too glad for some of the children to go out for an hour or two. Mrs Price was a walking example of failure of imagination. Childless, she could not imagine a healthy adolescent plucked from a warm family, exhorted by the school not to burden parents with complaints, and wanting to talk to friends and take part in all the activities provided by the school to keep us from thinking of home. Mrs Price never conversed. Her speech was limited to short apoplectic orders: 'Keep off the lawn. Mr Price doesn't want your clumsy feet on it. Take your homework to your room, don't disturb Mr Price when he's marking books. Keep a civil tongue in your head. Don't argue with Mr Price.'

Mr Price said nothing for himself. He obediently marked books, ignored my arguments and kept his lawn smooth.

On Fridays Mrs Price did the weekly baking. Towards the end of the session, she made currant Welsh cakes. Each week she hid these in a different place. It became a challenging game to find them and steal one. She always knew. I justified myself on the grounds that she did not exchange my meat ration – which I did not eat – for cheese. Malnutrition led to my fainting in school.

This resulted in a teacher bringing round a seven-pound tin of cod liver oil. Mrs Price was furious at what she saw as a disgrace. She revenged herself when she found that I hated the stuff, by standing over me three times a day and watching me drink it.

Neither of them struck me, but Mrs Price withheld my letters. When the postman called 'Happy birthday,' I knew. I rushed into the house like a whirlwind.

'Give me my letters,' I shouted.

Mrs Price turned white but she handed them over. In my unheated room, I sat on the bed with blankets hugged round me and looked at the improbable roses on the glossy cards from my sisters, silently thanked my father for his postal order, and turned to the book from my mother and her letter. She told me that my brother had been killed. 'Taking a pot shot after a battle,' in the desert, he was blown to bits; a stupid, senseless killing from a random shell. Nothing was left but a beer bottle stuck in the sand to mark his papers when the padre came round.

After a while Mrs Price called me to tea. She was ashamed, and passed me the plate of cakes. I did not want any, but I took two. Mr Price tunelessly, maddeningly, whistled through his teeth as he rustled the 'ocal paper with its lists of casualties.

'Only a fool gets himself killed,' he observed.

Then I exploded. I told him he was a jumped-up, cowardly buffoon, a nothing man, in his peacock clothes, who thought himself too good for the poor bloody infantry, where he might get blown up and run around like a headless chicken. And that's what he was, a mindless, brainless, heartless, strutting turkeycock, not good enough for the pot.

He left the room without a word.

One day they went to fetch Mr Price's idiot sister. Far from appealing to my compassion, they said nothing about their journey. When I came back from school I found myself locked out.

The idiot sickened me with her slobbering lips, crooked eyes, awkward movements, and white hands covered with red splodges. Opposite me at the table, she giggled, pointed, made speech noises. The Prices were used to interpreting her noises and gestures. Their family took it in turns to keep her. Each morning Mrs Price carefully made up the idiot's face, dressed her like a doll and set her in the window. She was grotesque.

The doses of cod liver oil continued until Mrs Price caught me with a very small spoonful. She seized a large spoon, twirled it to cut off the long treacly thread, and the idiot laughed and pointed.

'Ah, she wants some,' said Mrs Price, and put the spoon in her hand.

The white, red-spotted hands held the spoon as she licked and dribbled, then put it back in the tin. That was it! I was not going to eat any more of that seven-pound tin of goo. I tipped the tin. The thick, viscous mess rolled across the cloth, over her bib, into her lap, down her legs, onto the carpet. The idiot blubbered. Mrs Price stood transfixed. Then she lunged. She grabbed my shoulders and shook me until my teeth clattered. With ears exploding and lungs bursting, I thought I should die if I could not draw one more breath. Then she flung me away from her.

In my room I sobbed, not just for the awful fracas, but for my brother's death, and the whole horror of being parted from my family. I cried for my lost childhood. I wept for the misery of war.

After six years of war, the school was to return to London. I packed the night before. No one would be seeing me off. I was to label my bike and take it down to the station, then come back for my cases.

I went down to the shed with my bike labels and was stooping to remove the pump, when out of the shadows Mr Price pounced. He grabbed me, one hand over my mouth, the other fiddling with his clothing. His rubbery lips were like his idiot sister's. His eyes were hard as blue glass marbles. As I struggled, he slapped me viciously across the face. Shocked, horrified, numbed, that slap galvanized my desperation. I still held the pump and hit him across the head. I knew now. Mr Price hated women. He hated his sister. He hated his wife. And he hated – my God how he hated – me!

Back home I did not write the prescribed letter of thanks. Maybe I should have, for Mr Price gave me a touchstone. Of the various men who made a pass at me over the years, not many have been in love. But every one of them had the gallantry to simulate the feeling, if only for half an hour.

My Quest

~

Mavis Machin Thomas

As 1989 neared its end my quest was almost completed. Two-thirds completed to be exact – fifty years since the first dark wartime Christmas. Of course my quest did not commence so long ago when I was only a little girl. I set out on it about ten years ago, fuelled perhaps by television programmes of reunions and the unfolding of the horrors of the Nazi concentration camps, or perhaps as a result of increasing age, when one tends to look back instead of forward.

The story started in 1938 or 1939, before the outbreak of war when three Jewish girls joined my class – Sonja and Gertrude From Vienna and Ella from Berlin. I was intrigued. I believe it was my first encounter with someone who could speak two languages – how wonderful English sounded with an attractive accent. And leather boots! I had never seen girls wearing boots before, and how I longed for a pair. The girls spoke little of leaving their homes and parents, and I, in my youth and naivety, did not realize how brave they were and what they may have been suffering. They did, however, tell me of travelling from their homeland with money, watches and other meagre treasures sewn in the hems of their dresses.

Sonja and Ella and their sisters lived in a hostel, together with several other girls. Gertrude was fostered by a Jewish family. In no time at all, they outclassed us in maths, even in English. Whilst we were content to enjoy *What Katy Did* and *Pollyanna* they were reading the classics. Their brilliance promoted jealousy and prejudice, particularly in the girls who had always been top of the class.

Then there was knitting. We could all knit quite well and struggled with comforts for the troops, but they could knit continentally and absolutely flew along the rows. Another trick I envied was the diablo – two handles attached by string with a separate wooden egg cup-type device which was meant to run up and down the string and to be jerked into the air and caught again on the string. My brother and I had never succeeded in even one run up the string, yet these little wonders could toss it as high as the school and catch it. They could even sing 'The donkey serenade' in German.

Time moved on, we sat exams for scholarships to grammar schools. Here again we were surpassed and, with the confines of the wartime blackout, curtailing of social activities and my parents being naturally protective, we lost touch. But I could not forget my friends. When the war ended and the devastation of the concentration camps was revealed, I thought of them, and grieved on their behalf. I read books of the holocaust over the years, saw films, documentaries and interviews with inmates of the camps. I was deeply moved, and more moved than most because of my short friendship with these girls. I felt personally involved, until in about 1960 it became an obsession; I had to trace my long-lost friends. I had to know if they had been re-united with their parents, yet was almost frightened to learn the truth.

I contacted local rabbis by letter and telephone. I wrote to television programme directors and producers who either lost or mislaid my letters or merely sent acknowledgements – 'You will be contacted in due course'; the due course never materialized. It all looked so completely hopeless, I almost shelved my resolve.

Then in the summer of 1989, a large reunion of Kinder Transport was organized in Harrow. A film was shown on television. My friends must be there. I searched faces, almost expecting to recognize the young faces I so well remembered. I wrote yet another letter and was sent a copy of the souvenir programme of the reunion, and my name was included in the circulated list of those seeking relatives and friends.

At last I felt there was a chink of hope. I had read that Gertrude had gone to Israel in the 1950s to join a kibbutz. I finally tracked down an address in Lower Galilee. 'I know you will not remember me,' I wrote, 'but I have never forgotten you. Please, please write to me.' Joy of joys two weeks later, a letter from Israel, a letter from Gertie, now a widow, a reservations manager in a kibbutz hotel with photographs of herself and her eleven grandchildren; and even more than I expected to hope, still friendly with Sonja who lives in Essex.

Sonja's father had died in a concentration camp, and she was not reunited with her mother until 1947. Her mother had travelled to Israel via illegal transport on a ship called *Patrie* which was not allowed to land and was blown up in Haifa harbour by the refugees rather than be sent back. Fortunately her mother was rescued.

Gertie was re-united with her mother, who had survived the war by continuing to nurse in Vienna. Her father and all her uncles were deported from Vienna in 1939, and all perished in a concentration camp.

My quest two-thirds completed, I have yet to trace Ella. Where is she?

The Kaleidoscope of Youth

~

Danusia Trotman-Dickenson

Memory shatters images of the past and, over the years, reassembles them in ever-changing patterns. Childhood memories are vivid, selective and egocentric. Mine certainly are. The diaries that I started keeping in 1939 bear this out. I was ten years old when the war broke out.

My introduction to Wales, where I have subsequently lived for over thirty years, came about indirectly as a result of the export of Welsh coal. We were afloat in the Bay of Biscay in a small fishing boat. Although the storm had not abated the boat had to take out to sea by noon, when the French surrender came into force. To have stayed would have meant being captured by the Germans. There were other boats ahead of us. As the French army disintegrated, Polish units fought their way through

France towards the Spanish border. Those that made it to Saint Jean de Luz regrouped and were ordered by Polish officers in command to embark on anything that could sail and make their way to England.

Families were to be left behind. My father said goodbye to us. Mother and I stood on the water's edge and watched the boats go off. There were few people left on the shore. The remaining boats were ready to weigh anchor when somebody shouted to us that they still had some space. We waded out and were wedged in. One of the soldiers took me on his knees and this gave a bit more room to the others. So there we were, tossed about, getting very wet, the waves creating a big-dipper effect except that this was not the fun of a fair. I glanced at my mother: she was very white but then most of the others in the boat looked seasick too. I hoped that nobody would actually start being sick. The others were bound to follow and we would have a horrible mess. I was rapidly losing my enthusiasm for a sea voyage, when a British coal ship rescued us. Having unloaded its cargo of Welsh coal somewhere in Africa, it was heading home. Heavy seas made it difficult for our boat to come alongside the cargo vessel. No sooner did we get close than we were swept away. Sailors threw ropes overboard. Somebody tied one round my waist and I was hauled up.

The next few days and nights we sat on the deck and watched the sea. It was very crowded on board and in any case there was nothing else to do. We zigzagged across the Atlantic to escape a German U-boat that had been reported to be hunting in the area. It must have spotted us. The word went round that it was following, but if it was, then its attention must have been diverted by a more worthwhile prey. The U-boat disappeared and we reached Plymouth. It was June 1940.

Our destination was Fulham barracks in London. I liked the barracks. The gates were closed and we were under guard. When I had nothing better to do I used to go to watch the guards. I did not think they could see me – or for that matter anything else – from under their extraordinary headgear, that seemed to cover half the face. It would have been easy to escape I thought; not that I was considering this. In the barracks, there were beds and food, one could eat as much bread as one liked and each person was issued a daily portion of margarine and jam, and that was just for breakfast. There were two more meals each day. This was a great improvement on the last few months. The Red Cross gave me a blue-and-white cotton dress, so I no longer had to stay in bed when the one that I had arrived in was being washed. Once deloused and with our real identities established, we were told that we were free to leave the barracks. I was not that keen to do so. After all, one does not lightly give up the certainty of three meals a day. I clearly remembered the bowl of lentil soup which was all we had day after day when we lived in Paris. Even if there was a lot of food in London, I did not see how we would pay for it. My father, too, had reached England but had disappeared again and all we knew was that he was somewhere with the British Army. My mother, as yet, had not found a job and we had run out of possessions to barter.

As it was, things turned out much better than I had expected. Living in London was fun. We walked for miles, looked at Parliament and Buckingham Palace. Bombing had not yet started properly. The huge barrage balloons floating over the city created a sense of security. Our life was becoming more normal again and my mother began talking about my going to school. We also began attending church regularly and there I ran into trouble. To take Communion, as a Catholic, I had first to go to confession. The problem was that I only spoke Polish and had a smattering of Rumanian that I had picked up in a prison camp. The priest understood neither language. My predicament was shared by other people and a system of confessing by numbers was devised. The principle was simple enough. All that one had to do was to hold up the appropriate number of fingers for the commandment that one had broken. That was all very well, if one was sure of the order of the ten commandments. I was somewhat vague on the numbering and as one was not supposed to talk about one's confession, I did not feel I should ask. I remembered enough to be sure that I did not have to worry about the commandments at the beginning and at the end. I had not made a graven image and had no intention to make any such thing. Also, I did not covet my neighbour's ox and could not really see why one should want one, let alone the neighbour's wife. I decided that it was the commandments somewhere in the middle that I was most likely to have broken. As it happened the number that I plumped for turned out to be for adultery. This I went on confessing for several weeks to the priest's evident dismay. It surprised me. At last in desperation he wrote on a piece of paper 'not adultery' and told me to take it to my mother. That much I understood. I asked her what the message meant. She looked a bit blank and said we would have to find an English-Polish dictionary. When my mother eventually managed to buy one, I looked up 'adultery'. The dictionary defined 'adult' as a grown-up person and 'adultery' as acting falsely. This, I thought, could stretch to cover not telling the truth and nothing but the truth. So I went back to confessing adultery. Faced with such persistence on the part of an eleven-year-old, the priest must have accepted this as one of the things that were sent to try him. He no longer protested.

My thoughts were now increasingly reverting to food. Air raids became more frequent. This made shopping and cooking more difficult as we spent considerable amounts of time sitting in shelters. Food figures prominently in my wartime diaries. The entry for 6 September 1939 I intended to be a rather grand opening. Roughly translated it reads, 'To the sound of exploding bombs and crashing buildings we left Warsaw as the German tanks rolled in.' After that, as we made our way through Poland, Rumania, Yugoslavia, Italy and France, the entries get shorter and shorter and increasingly more repetitive: 'Today we had food', 'Today we had no food', 'Food again'.

Our progress through Poland was slowed down by diving for cover as German planes swooped, machine-gunning anything that moved. Pilots flew so low that some planes barely cleared the treetops. This was the undoing of one of them: a single shot brought him down and he burned. There was little time to bury the dead. It had been a hot summer and the soil had dried up.

Anyway there were no spades. When we got to Lvov the oil refinery had been hit and was burning fiercely. There was a lot of smoke and the fire was spreading. Lvov was still a Polish city then and had as yet not been annexed to Russia. My mother's family had lived in the area for generations. I would have liked to look round but as the fire got out of control we moved on and eventually reached the spa town of Zaleszczyki near the Rumanian border. Here a military hospital was being set up to receive the wounded from the Western Front. Soon there were no empty beds left. Men lay on stretchers everywhere. Some moaned unconscious, some prayed out loud, others screamed. Many just lay quietly waiting to die. The stench of vomit, diarrhoea and gangrenous wounds was all-pervading. There were a number of children around and we were told not to run, make a noise or get in the way. Several of us made ourselves a tree house on a magnificent old chestnut. It was from this vantage point that we spotted the arrival of British Embassy cars and watched in fascination as an immaculate figure of a man emerged. He wore pin-striped trousers and a fresh flower in the buttonhole of his jacket. A small dog that looked equally impeccably groomed followed on a lead. We were convinced that we were looking at the Ambassador. He may have been a butler, but whoever the man was he was splendidly unperturbed. The news the Embassy staff brought was bad. Some Polish detachments were still putting up resistance. There were reports of cavalry charges against heavy German armour, but these were symbolic gestures. Men on horses were not a match for tanks. It was the end, the diplomats said, and drove off to Rumania. I heard the grown-ups saying that there was still a hope that the Russians might come to help us as they had a treaty of friendship or non-aggression with Poland. I was not sure what this involved or what was the difference but it sounded reassuring.

Then the Russians invaded. Some doctors and nurses stayed with the wounded who could not be shifted. Anybody who could move or be moved crossed the bridge into Rumania. My mother and I followed. It seemed as if there were hundreds of people pouring over the border, columns making their way slowly eastward. There was little food and water. Polish currency lost its value and was no longer accepted. We bartered what we could but at times lived off maize. There were acres and acres of it. Cobs were now ripening and could be eaten uncooked; some of the farmers let us pick the corn.

The problem for Rumanian officials was what to do with all of us. Their government too had a treaty. It was with the Germans. It seemed that under the terms of the treaty we were to be locked up in some sort of prison camps. The trouble was that there did not seem to be any available. Our first place of incarceration was an asylum for the insane. Women and children were accommodated with the inmates who wore what looked like nightgowns and appeared to be very, very mad. The ones that were particularly violent were put into straightjackets. We all shared the wards and it was a noisy place. Nurses carried huge keys and locked all doors.

After a time we were moved to a makeshift prison camp. The commanding officer at the camp was a kind man and appeared to interpret his orders liberally. His wife asked my mother and I to their house for tea. Their daughter and I got on well together. Coca began to teach me Rumanian and I taught her Polish. To simplify communication we invented a language that contained elements of both, plus some Russian she knew and words of French that I had learnt. We then added 'ula' to the words. Spoken quickly it was incomprehensible to anyone else but us. This was a great advantage. I spent many afternoons with Coca. In the corner of the sitting room there was a blazing stove and a samovar simmered on the table. It was nice to be warm for a time.

Hard winter set in. The room where seven of us lived had no curtains or floor covering to give insulation and there was little heat from the small iron stove. We collected bits of wood to burn in it but as everybody else was looking for sticks too, there were few to be found. We cooked on the stove when we had fuel. As children were allowed to go outside the camp I would sometimes go to the slaughterhouse outside a village to get scraps of meat. It was a horrible place and I thought of becoming a vegetarian, but as the only vegetables we had were potatoes I decided against the idea, until such time as we got out of the camp.

My father escaped first. Shortly afterwards there was a message that he had made arrangements for my mother and I to follow. We were to meet up in Bucharest. He was waiting for us there with false passports. We crossed into Yugoslavia at night by train. At the border a customs official came into the compartment to check papers and luggage. Our belongings were in a sack. He put his hand in, rummaged and pulled out my father's uniform jacket.

I looked at the official to see if he would call the guards to take us off the train. He winked, waved the other official on down the corridor and tied the rope round the sack tightly.

We changed trains frequently. Once we were in Italy, my father explained, it would be dangerous for us because the Italians were allies of the Germans. He asked me not to speak in Polish in public places so that we did not attract attention to ourselves. I thought our clothes were odd enough to do that, but nobody bothered about us and we got to Paris.

It was not what I thought it would be like. It was grey, cold and wet. I had expected Paris to be full of cafés, bubbling with conversation and overflowing with artists and writers, served by White Russian waiters who would break off to play their balalaikas and be joined by Hungarian gypsies singing sad songs. We could not afford to go to the cafés but as we walked I observed them closely. They did not seem to be very lively places. My parents found a tiny room at the top floor of a pension and there we waited.

The French government, it seemed, could not make up its mind whether to enlist volunteers from the Polish army into the French Legion or to incorporate Polish units into the French army. Some minister or general must have made up his mind, as my father went away again promising to send for us if he could. Sometime later we joined him in Combourg. Its claim to fame was the château where Chateaubriand's father had confined him. I became interested in the story and, now that I had acquired a bicycle, would cycle to explore the surrounding area.

One day a French general arrived to lecture on strategy. He told his listeners that the Maginot Line would stop Germany's advance into France. With this assurance he left. Father did not believe that but thought that my mother and I would be able to stay in Combourg for some months. My parents decided that I should go to a local convent school. I protested to no avail that the school year was almost over. The nuns could hardly believe that anybody from a civilized and Christian country could be as ignorant of the French language as I was. They proceeded to remedy this defect in my education by teaching me irregular verbs. Before I could get to nouns, we left.

It happened very quickly. We lived in a house on the outskirts of the town. There was a machine gun nest manned by French soldiers just across the road from the house. As the nights were hot, we slept with the windows open and, going to bed, I found it reassuring to hear the distant murmur of voices and see cigarette lights in the darkness. Then one morning, as I was getting ready for school, the nest was empty and the French soldiers were gone. The Polish unit moved up. A train was commandeered. Wagon doors were pulled open and machine guns mounted. Women and children who wanted to leave were ushered to passenger compartments. French families preferred to stay. We set off. Before the train approached the Loire, a message was sent that there would be a few minutes stop before the bridge so that civilians, if they wished, could get off. The bridge was mined and might blow up. We sat still. Soon the train began to cross the river very slowly. I looked down, the waters of the Loire were muddy brown and I wondered how long it would take the train to sink. I was not much of a swimmer and stopped speculating. When we finally stopped it was near the Spanish border and there the last stage of our journey began.

It took us nearly a year from the time we left Warsaw until we reached London.

The Bombing of Stettin

~

Johanna Wilkins

Vera closed her eyes and before her emerged the street just as it was before. She saw herself as a little girl skating along the asphalted street with her new roller skates, her brown curls tightly pulled back by a big ribbon, her eyes shining with excitement, and Mutti waving at her telling her to be careful. She was once again that happy carefree child before her whole world would fall to pieces all around her.

As she continued walking the streets of her childhood, the memories came flashing back, like a flood tearing down all obstacles in its way. Standing on the big empty space which once had been Number 7 Berg Strasse, one by one the pictures emerged in front of her eyes: the wide road at the end of which the Elisabeth Schule, her old grammar school, stood; the museum, the Haken-Terrasse, the wide softly curved slopes, covered in green lawns and framed by trees leading all the way to the banks of the river Oder. Towering high above stood the ancient, proud-looking Prussian Government Building. Its towers seemed to reach into the sky and could be seen for miles and miles across the water greeting ships approaching the harbour of Stettin.

What joy it had been to walk through the fish market on her way to school, where stall after stall stood alongside the river, starting by the railway bridge and ending near the Haken-Terrasse. There was always a smell of herrings in the air, mingling with the fresh salt breeze from across the sea. She remembered the noise too, quite deafening at times, between the shouting of the fat women behind their stalls praising their fish, and the screeching of the ever hungry seagulls riding on top of the waves, eagerly awaiting their share. Then there were the sirens of the many ships steering their way into the harbour. Vera loved every minute of it, the smell, the noise and all the hustle and bustle, this was the place where she could hear the pulse of the big city beating its loudest, and to be part of it, if only in a small way, had always filled her heart with pride.

Papa's shop was doing well in those days of 1938, as people had more money to spend than ever before. Hardly anybody was out of work since Adolf Hitler had come to power in the spring of 1933. He had created new jobs by building roads all across the country, the Auto-Bahns, which linked all towns and main cities in Germany. Large housing estates were built at the outskirts of every town, mainly for families with three or more children who paid very little mortgage for the privilege of living in their own houses with a small plot of land for growing vegetables and where their children could play. After years of depression, the ordinary working-class people had yielded to the man who had brought them new hope of a better life and the promise of more to come.

Mutti, Papa and Vera carried on living in their carefree little world just as before, and without giving too many thoughts to the new leader and his régime. Vera did not remember much of the happenings and events after the Party took over, except that instead of the morning prayers in school, the girls had to sing the German National Hymn, holding up their right arm until it ached. Papa used to get quite annoyed when customers came into the shop who previously had murmured a Good Morning, or Good Day, suddenly shouted, 'Heil Hitler' at the top of their voices. Mutti smoothed things over, as she always did, by saying, 'Do not upset yourself, my love, can't you see that all these people have been brainwashed? The best thing is to be quiet, it will all blow over soon.'

To make matters worse Vera would come home from school with stories about this genius, this man called Adolf Hitler. 'God, not her as well,' Papa would say under his breath whilst listening to what his daughter had learned in school about this great leader of Germany.

The opinion that the war was not going to last very long was shared by most of the German people. They were sure that Hitler would win in no time and that everything would be back to normal again soon, except that Germany would have gained the territory which, according to Hitler, it so desperately needed. In the meantime, Papa went on to prepare the cellar, as he was told to do. He put chairs down there, and a settee, even an old carpet to cover the flagstones. It looked quite cosy and seemed safe enough with the huge stone walls surrounding it.

The flat on the first floor was occupied by an elderly couple who had no children, and Papa did not like Herr Neumann very much. 'I do not trust this man,' he told Mutti, 'I look at the way he is showing off his Nazi badge, as if to tell everybody that he belongs to the National Socialist Party.' Papa carried on, 'I am telling you, that man is not just a member, but a spy who noses around people like you and me who have not joined the Party.' Mutti did not share her husband's opinion, she liked Herr Neumann who was always friendly and polite; he had even helped her to carry the washing basket up to the attic, where the big drying-room was, a few times. 'Perhaps he had to join because of the job he is doing as a Judicial Officer,' Mutti suggested. 'Nobody has ever bothered you or me to this day to become members of the Party, or have they?' To this question Papa could only just shake his head.

Contrary to what people had predicted about air raids and bombing when Papa had prepared the cellar, it had come into frequent use since that day. At first, the bombs did not do a great deal of damage. Most of them were dropped by planes returning from an attack on Berlin. It soon became part of their everyday life to spend a couple of hours down the cellar a few times a week; Vera did not remember too much about it, except the one evening which stood out vividly in her memory. She had arrived rather late from school one afternoon and found a visitor in Mutti's kitchen. It was Max Springer, Uncle Max, Vera called him. He was the owner of the textile shop who gave Papa a job when he first came to Stettin. They had become friends over the years, a friendship which carried on even after Papa had left the firm to open his own little business. A pile of clothing was spread on the big table in Mutti's kitchen, and Max was sitting in the rocking chair in the corner, away from the light of the big lamp hanging from the ceiling. Their conversation stopped as Vera walked in and, as Max sprung to his feet to greet her, she noticed the big badge he was wearing, the Star of David printed on it.

It was not long after that the sirens sounded and Mutti had stayed behind in the kitchen with Max, much to the surprise of Vera who had followed Papa down to the cellar. Since Papa had been made Air Raid Warden of Berg Strasse and neighbouring streets he had to be there at all times to make sure that everyone was seeking shelter in the cellars of their houses. Downstairs he pulled Vera to one side and whispered in a low voice, 'Listen, your mother has gone out tonight, visiting friends, in case anyone should ask where she is. Do you understand?' And as Vera just nodded her head somehow bewildered, he carried on, 'I do not want the people here to know that we are friendly with Jews, you never know who you can trust these days.' He glanced at Herr Neumann who had just arrived with his wife.

They never saw Max and his family again but they knew that they had escaped Germany when they received a postcard with a simple message, 'Best regards from your old school friend, Max.' The incident with the Springer family shattered Vera's belief in Adolf Hitler as the chosen being. Why did he have to persecute the Jews and everyone else who opposed him?

There was little to celebrate any more, at Christmas or any other times, but when Vera came home on Christmas Eve in 1943 from the little church at the end of the Berg Strasse, where she had gone for as long as she could remember, it was still a bit like the old days. They had sat in the kitchen which was always nice and warm, as Mutti kept the big iron stove going day and night. Papa sat in his rocking chair, smoking a cigar instead of his normal pipe: he had just returned from his rounds to make sure that there was no light shining through any of the blackout curtains in Berg Strasse and neighbouring streets. Mutti was knitting for the Red Cross and the little wireless was playing Christmas carols. The silver candle-holder from the cabinet in the front room stood on the middle of the kitchen table, a bit out of place, perhaps, but the light of the flickering candles created some sort of Christmas spirit, whilst the smell of the big goose, slowly cooking in the stove, completed the picture of a happy Christmas, or perhaps an illusion of it.

Uncle Hermann, Papa's brother, had brought the goose for them a few days before Christmas like he had always done in the past. Vera loved her Uncle Hermann, he was so tall and broad and good-looking with his thick hair and twinkling blue eyes, and always full of fun and ready for a joke and a laugh. Only this time he seemed different, quiet and somehow withdrawn. He followed Papa's eyes which rested on the small Nazi badge on the lapel of his coat, 'Oh, did I not tell you? I have joined the Party, they asked me to, they need someone like me in the village to keep the spirit going, since all the young ones have gone to war. There are a few privileges involved, you know,' he added with some of the old sparkle returning to his eyes.

The first of January 1944 dawned a bitter cold morning, the town was unusually quiet, as if holding its breath in anticipation of things to come. Vera did not exactly remember the day or the month when the bombing raids on Stettin started. She only remembered how her hometown died, bit by bit, stone after stone, and how the ruins had grown bigger and bigger after each attack. She saw her beautiful city crumble before her eyes and, as she walked the streets she hardly recognized anymore, with the smell of burning still hanging in the air, she thought she was dreaming; all this was just a terrible nightmare from which she would wake up at any minute. But no, all of it was true. Where had all the shops gone – the big stores like Karstadt, Defaka, Kittel which once was called Schwartz and Co., an old established Jewish firm? There was a sign sticking out from under the rubble, Vera could only read the latter part of it, '...do not buy from Jews.' In helpless anger, she kicked it out of sight and then she turned and ran all the way home to collapse in Mutti's arms with tears streaking down her face, 'Why, oh why did they do this to us, what have we done?' She only calmed down after Papa had talked to her. 'The men in those planes did not enjoy what they were doing, I am sure of that. They just follow orders, they only want to hit military objects, and sometimes it goes wrong. No doubt their target was the harbour which is quite near the shopping centre. And you must not forget, it was us, the Germans, who started it all, and our bombers are doing the same to their cities.'

The people of Germany still believed that the new invention, the V Bomb, would swing the pendulum of war back into their favour. After all, Hitler was shouting about this *Wunder Waffe* in all his speeches, so why should they not believe him when his voice was drowned by cheers of the thousands more who did.

In January 1945 Mutti closed the shop for good, seeing no point in keeping it open; there had been no more fresh supplies from the warehouse and Papa had been killed. The town seemed empty; most of the soldiers had gone, probably engaged in combat with the fast-approaching enemy troops.

It had been one of the worst winters they had ever experienced as if nature too had turned against them and formed a pact with the enemy. Vera remembered Herr Neumann coming to see them and talking to Mutti in a very serious-sounding voice. He had urged Mutti and Vera to leave Stettin before it was too late. Mutti was adamant to stay, she could never ever live anywhere else. 'They would have to carry me out dead before I leave this town,' she used to tell everybody who tried to get her away. But it was Herr Neumann, who had finally won her over.

'My wife works for the Red Cross and was summoned to help out at the Haupt-Bahnhof, [the main station in Stettin]. You should hear the stories she is telling about the refugees from East Prussia, about rape and killing in the wake of the Russian troops.' It was then that Mutti had finally agreed to leave. 'It will only be for a short time, only till the war is over,' she had said to Vera. 'We shall be back in a few months.'

'I managed to get the tickets for you, it was not easy, believe me,' Herr Neumann said. 'There is a train going next week, reserved for mothers and children only. I hope you will not forget this, Frau Bauer, that I helped you and Vera to get out, I mean. I have never done anybody any harm, you know that don't you?' His voice was more steady now, but his hands, holding on to the table, were shaking. 'Only they might investigate the members of the Party after the war. You would only say good things about me, in case you were asked?'

Vera was cold and tired, feeling rather depressed as well and not at all in the mood to listen to Herr Neumann's plea. Looking up at him she noticed that he was not in the full rig-out of his brown-shirt uniform. Come to think of it, she had not seen him wearing it for some time, and as she looked more closely she could see that the little Nazi badge on his grey jacket, the one he always wore for work, was missing too. And at that moment something inside her snapped. Standing up from the seat by the stove she looked straight into Herr Neumann's eyes. 'Oh, you do realize then that your days are over, your days of playing the big man, trampling down the people who did not agree with you and your party. Now that the war is over and lost, oh yes lost and you know it is, Herr Neumann, now you are afraid for your own skin. I shall have to carry the shame of what you and your fellow Nazi members have done to other human beings. Every decent German will be branded with your stigma for as long as they live.'

She ran out of the kitchen after her outburst to collapse in tears in the big bedroom which she now shared with Mutti. 'Oh, what have I done? What have I said? I'm sorry, really I am, but I did mean everything I said.'

'It's all right, my love, it's all right, don't worry. Herr Neumann understands, he knows how upset you are about Papa being dead and the thought of leaving your hometown you love so much. He will not report you.' And, with a little dry laugh she added, 'They are all too busy right now destroying their documents and burning their membership cards.' Herr Neumann never mentioned the incident at all. In fact he came to see them a few days before they were leaving. He brought a couple of rucksacks which were left over from his camping days. 'Don't forget now, Frau Bauer, just pack what is absolutely essential to manage for the next few months. There is a limit to what people are allowed to take onto the train.'

Mutti packed one of the rucksacks with their goose-feather beddings, pressing them down hard so they did not take up too much room. They took most of their warm clothing and a few pots and pans, as was suggested on the list they had received from the Red Cross. All their documents were in the briefcase they used to take to the air raid shelter. Mutti added a few photos of her and Papa, and some of Vera as a baby and when she was a little girl.

To their utmost horror, they lost the case. Their most precious possession fell under the train, as people were pushing their way to get a seat. Vera was nearly out of her mind and refused to follow Mutti into the train. 'We can't go without the case,' her voice was barely audible above the noise of crying children. 'All our documents are in there, you know,' she told the woman in the uniform of the Red Cross.

'Don't worry, my love, we'll send it on to you. Just remember to register with the Red Cross as soon as you arrive at your new address.' With that, she pushed Vera into the seat next to Mutti's.

Herr Neumam had been right, there was room for everybody on the train with a ticket. She did not see the crowd who had been left behind, the ones without tickets. But she did not open her eyes until the train had left the station. She could not bear to see Stettin disappearing in a cloud of smoke, knowing that her life was never going to be the same again. The happy child and carefree teenager stayed behind in her hometown on that bitterly cold morning in March of the year 1945.

CHAPTER 7

HORRORS OF WAR

Thousands of civilians were killed in bombing raids over the cities and towns of Wales. Bombers often dumped their loads on small villages and on the countryside, as they turned home. The people below wondered why they had been hit; they were not military or industrial targets. Not even the farthest corner of Wales was completely safe from such dangers.

February in Wartime

~

Menna Bassett

It is February 1991 and it is cold, very cold; the Gulf War dominates the news; and I hate February. There it is every year, with twenty-eight interminable days to be endured between January and March, like an albatross around my neck.

It was cold fifty years ago in February 1941, and we were at war then too; but living as we did in a small village far away from the big cities, we were of no interest to the German bombers and our lives carried on very much as usual. I lived with my mother and father in a tiny bungalow on a hill, called 'Haulfryn' – it was aptly named. Made of asbestos and wood, it had been delivered in sections which had to be slotted and nailed together onto a foundation and then a roof added. This was the original DIY house of the thirties, meant to last only a few years; but the foundations, dug deep into the side of the hill were, as my mother would declare proudly 'solid as the Bank of England'. We had our own 'ready-made' air raid shelter.

Although tiny, before the war the bungalow was always bursting at the seams; with food (a combination of my father's green fingers and my mother's miraculous cooking), with furniture (bargains tracked down at local auction sales), and with people. Uncles, aunts, cousins, first, second, cousins twice removed – removed to south Wales to find work, many of them – all wanting a few days by the sea.

Things changed little when war was declared. The young men in the village had been called up but I was too young at eight for that to worry me unduly. The most exciting change was the arrival of the evacuees; children from Liverpool and, later, from London. In order to make them feel at home, we had to speak English all the time, and almost overnight English became the order of the day, except in chapel.

My childhood was a happy one. When my mother wasn't shouting at me, or quarrelling vociferously with her sister who lived a few yards down the road, she was full of fun. She was known, all her life, as 'Mrs Roberts, the bungalow'. Like most daughters, though, it was to my father I clung.

'Don't get her out of bed now. Leave her alone,' my mother used to say, when she went out in the evening; but no sooner had she gone a few yards down the lane, than I would call out for a drink, a hot water bottle, any excuse and I would soon be curled on his lap in the kitchen listening to a story. When my mother came in, we would both be fast asleep. But I was never spoilt; he was too wise for that.

I was never lonely either. I played with my two cousins who lived just down the lane and I had an extended family. My father had two younger brothers Glyn, twenty-seven and Gerallt twenty-four. Glyn had married a few months after war was declared but before that he practically lived with us. I loved him. He used to breed budgies as a hobby and I had been given one for my birthday – we were busy trying to teach it to say, 'Down with the Germans', but all it ever said was, 'Joey, pretty boy Joey.' In 1940, Glyn joined the Army, but he was stationed quite near and we saw him and his wife quite often.

Gerallt had been called up early and was training to be a bomber pilot. When he came on leave, tall, Brylcreem smooth and very handsome in his uniform, he was always full of high spirits. He had given me a brooch - RAF wings. I was very proud of it.

The third close member of my father's family was his favourite sister Lona. She was about thirty-six, sophisticated (she had worked in London!) smart and single. 'It's high time you found a man,' my mother would tell her relentlessly, 'You're not getting any younger, you know.' She was working in the munitions factory in Bridgend and had two silver bracelets of threepenny bits made there for my cousin and me (strictly illegally, I should think). They were beautiful.

I loved it when they were all at home together. It seemed their laughter would crack the thin asbestos walls, and when forced to go to bed I would strain to reach the keyhole of my bedroom door, afraid of missing anything. I was caught too, often, but after the obligatory tap on my backside, they would all come in and kiss me goodnight.

In 1940, we had a lady evacuee to stay, a Londoner; her name was Mrs Walsh. She was the manageress of a feather duster factory, which had taken over the outhouses of the big house in the village. They were flighty, useless things, when I come to think of it, to be making during the war. They were actually made from dyed sheep's wool, all the colours of the rainbow and bright as butterflies. The strips of wool were wound and tacked onto a slender black handle and then combed and combed until they were soft as silk and light as candy floss.

Mrs Walsh (I never knew her Christian name – only families called each other by first names in those days) quickly made herself at home, despite our primitive bathroom facilities. Running water from the tap outside in the lane, and the *tŷ bach*, literally in the bowels of the earth in the cellar, must have been quite a shock. She spent most of her free time with us in the kitchen and used to say she had never eaten so well in her life.

Early in February my father was admitted to hospital

for a routine operation and was recovering well.

On the 19th I woke earlier than usual, put my nose out over the blankets and hastily put it under again – it was, as usual, freezing. My feet fumbled for the stone jar at the bottom of the bed, but that, too had grown cold during the night. I don't think I had any premonition that this was to be a day different from any other, but, although I wriggled back down under the ton of blankets, I couldn't get warm. I reached for my blue woollen dressing gown under the pillow and went through the usual contortions, using the bedclothes as a tent, to get it on without exposing even my face to the biting air. I found my warm furry slippers and shuffled over to draw back the curtains. I couldn't see out, but the frost had made pretty patterns on the window pane. I picked up my koala bear, called Bogey, who was my constant companion – a present from my father's eldest sister who had emigrated to Australia – and went to look for my mother and a fire. And I heard voices... and I could smell bacon frying.

As I opened the door, the voices stopped – that was strange. Normally grown-ups carried on, unaware that little ears picked up far more than they should. The room was quite dark, but everyone was sitting near the fire, and I could see who was there. My mother was in her usual place attending to the frying pan. Auntie Lona was sitting upright as always, even in the easy chair; Uncle Glyn was holding his head in his hands and Uncle Gerallt still had his RAF cap on; the smell of Brylcreem mingled with the bacon... Mrs Walsh was there, too, moving plates round the table.

I was still very sleepy, but wary now. Why was no one

looking at me? I went over to the fire to warm my hands and turned to Uncle Glyn who was crying. (He cried on his wedding day, too. My mother said it was because he was making a mistake.) He lifted me onto his lap, wiped his eyes and held me close. The others, I noticed, were looking at each other almost furtively and then shaking their heads and saying, 'No.' If I hadn't been so sleepy I might have understood. Then Mrs Walsh picked me up and said, 'All right, I'll do it.'

I remember we went into her little room; that had a fire too, but not as warm as the other one. 'Now,' she started in a brisk voice, 'You have to be very brave. Your father was much worse yesterday, he had complications (what were complications?) and your mother decided to send for the family. You see,' she faltered, 'he's had to go away for a long, long time and you won't be able to see him.'

'A sanatorium,' I asked, 'Has he gone to a sanatorium?' I knew that word. Uncle Glyn's wife was there for three years before they were married. She had TB and she came back cured.

'No, love. It's not a sanatorium, it's somewhere where he won't have any pain any more. He's gone to heaven,' she finished hurriedly, not looking at me.

I tried to speak, but suddenly my tongue and lips seemed to have changed places and only a squeak came out.

'Now, you must be very brave,' she repeated, brisk again, 'and help your mother.'

I don't think I really took in what she was trying to tell me – I could only see my father's face as I had seen him two nights before, when I was frightened of the hospital

254

ward and the smell of disinfectant. Then the familiar smell of bacon drifted through from the other room. Somehow I didn't think it strange that my mother, who should have been distraught, was cooking for everyone else. She was always cooking. We went back into the crowded kitchen, so small for so many large people. I should have gone to my mother, but I didn't know what to do. It was to Uncle Glyn I went and he held me tight.

'Don't worry, bach,' he said. 'Things will be all right.' He held me; all the time he ate, he held me.

Later we were all caught up in the arrangements for the funeral, and to keep me occupied I was allowed to comb the feather dusters in the factory. I wasn't allowed to attend the funeral, but watched from my friend's house near the chapel and the cemetery. The chapel was packed to the door, (just like the bungalow) and when they sang 'O Fryniau Caersalem' by the graveside on the hill, the sound carried down all over the village. They talked about it for years, it was the biggest funeral they could remember. He was special, my father.

I didn't cry. It was wartime and you didn't.

Within a couple of weeks we had a postcard to say that Glyn would be home for two days on embarkation leave and would be coming to see us. I was very excited, even when I realized what it meant. He and his wife came to supper and I went with my mother to the station to see him off. He said goodbye to us all in turn. 'Don't worry, bach,' he said to me, 'I'll soon be back. Keep trying with that silly Joey.'

Shortly afterwards we heard he had been taken prisoner

by the Japanese and in a couple of weeks had been drowned. They were transferring British prisoners to Java; American bombers, not realizing this, had destroyed the ship. He might have survived if he had been able to swim.

Before we had time to draw breath, we heard that Gerallt had been shot down over Germany. He was missing, believed killed. Confirmation came very soon.

It was still only June. In less than a month another of my father's sisters, Eunice, a young widow, was killed in a bicycle accident in Kent. She was working for the ARP and a storm blew up. It was in the evening, in the blackout. My cousin, who was two years older than I, was now an orphan and came to Wales to live.

There was a war somewhere.

Figure in a Vestry

~

Kusha Petts

In slanted light, the nave
is full of ancient grace and grain.
But through this door,
as guard from stain
old newsprint lines the vestry floor
and on its litter sheets now lies
a salvaged Mary with unseeing eyes.
Comely, full-fleshed, a figure in two modes:

the upper torso classic in repose,
(fast in her arms her naked child)
the lower half disordered, wild,
– the latest rage –
the void below the knee
a shadow missing on the printed page.

From loins of disarray
two charred stumps point
impertinent in vestry air,
each thigh like Sunday's joint
burnt to the bone,
one smooth patella, glistening white
in the wonted candor of the morning light.

The blast is 1941,
when stones of makeshift morgues are not surprised
to witness any remnant rite,
oblation such as this
abrupt Madonna of a Swansea night.

Forgive One Another

~

Betty Lucking

The first air raid on Birmingham happened on 9 August 1940 and a major raid on 23 August wrecked much of the city centre. Night after weary night through the following winter, I and my family took to the Anderson shelter at dusk, emerging each morning to more and more devastation. We never knew what to expect. My father stood helplessly by as his own office burned. The local cinema received a direct hit, killing all the brave souls who had sought a little light relief from their dreary existence. Water mains burst making fire-fighting almost impossible. I was part of a human chain stretching from top to bottom of the street, passing buckets of water hand over hand, in a desperate attempt to quell the fires caused by incendiary bombs. By the end of it all, the city was on its knees, with two thousand people dead and nearly seven thousand injured.

Our house took the full blast from a bomb which demolished three houses on the opposite side of the road. One was the home of my best friend. I stood with my mother in the cold damp street as a neighbour approached.

'All the Claytors are dead. Suffocated in the cellar.'

It registered immediately. My friend was gone: I burst into tears and the well-meaning neighbour rammed a toffee – a rare treat, into my mouth. That was me dealt with. Their chat seemed more important than my instant grief. As a child I had no words to express my feelings, I could only cry and, as I stood shivering, the salt tears ran into my mouth mingling with the sweetness of the toffee. I thought I would choke. The awful acrid smell of dust and debris was everywhere and a pall of filthy smoke hung over the city. Small groups of people stood helplessly by, their pinched grey faces dull with fatigue.

That night I cried until my head ached and my throat was on fire. My parents must have offered some comfort but I don't remember it. I can recall an overwhelming feeling of loneliness knowing that my friend was gone, along with our childish games and innocent secrets. For the first time in my life I had to face emotional turmoil alone, for I knew that whatever anyone said or did, nothing would be the same again. No one could help me. The next morning I saw things as they actually were, not as I wanted them to be. I had turned a corner and was well on the way to growing up.

That day my parents were busy trying to salvage what was left of our home. The blast had ripped through the house blowing doors off their hinges and breaking all the windows. The result was wall-to-wall glass in thousands of tiny splinters. Clothes spilled out of overturned wardrobes, all the china was broken and there was no gas to cook by. Our breakfast that morning was a slice of bread and dripping and water from a tin mug. I went to school, picking up odd bits of shrapnel as usual. My head ached and I was not looking forward to another day shivering in an icy unheated classroom. The week before, I had fallen down half a dozen jagged stone steps in the blackout and the cold bit into the sores and abrasions on my legs. I was so tired and cold, I half hoped the school wouldn't be there. But it was still standing alongside the pathetic concrete structures called air raid shelters which littered the playground. The teacher glanced at the empty seat beside me.

'Kathy was killed,' I whispered.

That morning extra prayers were said, then the teacher

instructed the class to write a poem about the war. She told us to put our feelings into words, explain our loathing for the Germans and describe what we would do if we met one. All the vitriol I could muster was poured into my effort. It was read to my peers and displayed on the notice board. At ten years old I had castigated and written off an entire nation because I knew no better. Worst of all, it was seen by my teacher as an excellent piece of work. Such was the collective hate whipped up against the enemy during those six years of carnage.

Twenty-five years later, in a café in Germany, a man struck up a conversation with me. He was with a German bomber crew during the war. He rolled up his trouser leg, pointing to the scars that were his legacy. He wanted to talk about his experiences and it soon became apparent that he still carried his bitterness along with his war wounds. He had bombed Birmingham – a prime military target – and had heard that the damage was major. I sensed pride in his voice. Then he asked me where I had lived during the war. I told him all.

'Perhaps I killed your friend,' he said quietly.

'Yes, perhaps.'

Sadly he pushed a glass of schnapps across the table towards me. 'I'm sorry,' he said.

'I'm sorry about your leg.'

'It doesn't matter. It doesn't seem to matter at all now.'

For every action there is a reaction. It may take fifty years, but sooner or later there will be one.

Cardiff Burning

~

Violet Williams and Maud Prescott

In 1941, I was living with my parents in Cardiff, together with my older sister Maud, whose husband was in the RAF. Because Maud had no children at this time she was required to undertake essential war work, and in 1941 she started as a munitions worker at Paton's Factory in Taffs Well. Although I was then only fifteen, my sister applied for me to join her at the factory, and I became the youngest worker there.

On a cold heavily frosted night as our shift ended on 2 January, the massive German air raid on Cardiff began. The bombing became so bad that the management of the factory gave the workers the option of remaining in the shelter for the duration of the raid, or for the local people to return to their homes. My sister and I and another Cardiff girl called Maureen decided to go back home. We saw flares and searchlights crossing the sky, and heard the explosions and ack-ack fire in the distance, but we girls did not fully realize the danger. But as we reached Whitchurch Common we could see the vast panorama of the city on fire, and the stricken cathedral at Llandaf.

In the dark wake of one fearful explosion, I lost sight of my sister and her friend. We were outside one of the communal air raid shelters, and while my boyfriend searched outside, I entered the nearest shelter to see if the girls had taken refuge there. I walked the whole length of the shelter, up one side and down the other, in pitch darkness, calling out her name. As I stumbled over the feet and knees of all those people, no one moved, no one spoke, no one helped me regain my balance as I fell. There was an awful, eerie, heavy vacuum of no response.

With great relief I caught up with Maud and the others outside the shelter, and we continued through the noise, the smell of swirling smoke all around us, and the glow of fires about the city. Then there was a crash right beside us. Forced to take shelter in the doorway of the Cross Inn, we were showered with tiny pieces of shrapnel dust and were enveloped in a choking black cloud of smoke. The noise shattered our eardrums and we all clung together, almost unable to breathe, expecting death at any moment. We later learned that an unexploded bomb had dropped nearby.

Shocked and shaken, but still intact, we neared home. We found my father, a tank driver in the First World War and now a Home Guard, frantically fighting a cluster of incendiary bombs which had fallen in the garden of our home and on the house next door. The ground was so hard from the severe frost that the men had extreme difficulty in loosening earth to smother the flames. (The obligatory bucket of sand had long been used up.) Using pick-axes and spades, the men worked like demons until the flames were doused and the adjoining houses saved from danger. Worn and exhausted, we rested under the stairs, under tables – anywhere we felt might afford protection, however slight, from the turmoil outside.

Many Cardiff people were killed in that air raid, and I have often wondered if this explains why I received no response in the air raid shelter. With what relief we greeted the breaking of the dawn. Work was as usual, for the factory had sustained no damage during the night. We were at our machines, as expected, for the following shift.

Bomb Victim

~

Alison Bielski

every weekday morning
we crawled laden to school
but today that crater
appals as I approach
her cordoned-off garden

KEEP OUT

this crater in my heart
gaping unfillable
terrifies as I step
back from beckoning rim
stare over bleeding ground

Night of Terror

~

Mary Evans

It had been an ordinary school day. I was eight years old and bedtime was around 8.30 p.m. Later that night a warning siren sounded. My mother's young sister arrived home and told my mother to get me from bed, and we three went to shelter in the *cwtch* under the stairs. My grandfather had gone to his allotment behind the house to tend his greenhouse and my father was out on ARP duty.

We heard a bomb drop and soon my father came into the house to tell us he was going to Treorchy to investigate. No sooner had he gone out of the house than a bomb dropped directly on our back garden. We heard nothing, we simply felt a thud. Up we were thrown into the air. My father had only had time to walk two doors away before the bomb dropped. Now all he could see was the house, a pile of rubble. He knew we were buried underneath but he did not know whether we were alive or dead. As he had been a miner in his younger days, he had some knowledge of safety measures when a fall occurred underground to ensure that the top of the debris was made safe. So, he set about working on the rescue. Soon he was joined by a young man who had come up off an afternoon shift underground. Together they worked for hours until all was ready to try to get us out.

They began with me, as I was nearest to the small opening. I was freed except for my left leg which remained tightly trapped. It took the young man approximately two hours to free me. This meant that I had been buried for six hours altogether. My mother was brought out two hours later and taken to the local miners' hospital. Then, the last of our buried family, my mother's young sister was freed but died as they lifted her out. She was twenty-four years old and was to have been married in a few weeks.

My mother remained in hospital for three weeks with no serious injuries but in a great state of shock. I was X-rayed for any broken bones; there were none but I couldn't walk for months afterwards. We were taken in by an aunt and uncle who lived in Ton Pentre and we remained there for the duration of the war. The casualties on that one night in one street totalled twenty-seven. Among them were two sisters evacuated to the house next to us. When the bomb fell, the younger sister was killed outright. Their two brothers were rescued from a fire which had broken out when an incendiary bomb hit their house. They were taken to a house lower down the street where a lady had opened her home to be used as a first aid centre. A short time later another bomb fell and hit that house and all inside perished. That mother from London who had been evacuated with her children to be safe from the London bombs had lost three children in one night from bombs which fell on the sleepy mining village of Cwmparc.

There was a mass funeral the following week when the main roads of Cwmparc and Treorchy were black with people as they followed the cortège of lorries which carried the coffins of adults and children. No one could find an explanation as to why this small village had been attacked.

A Welsh Woman in London

~

Betty Howard

I was in my last term at Kensington College when war was declared. My first job after leaving was as a private secretary in the City (at a salary of £3 a week). I moved into a bedsitter in Lancaster Gate and immediately joined the ARP. We met once a week in a nearby basement room, were issued with a uniform, steel helmet and respirator, and when the air raid siren sounded we would dash up to the street and report to the warden in charge.

Our worst experiences came in May 1940 when the enemy started dropping incendiaries all over London and many well-known landmarks were on fire, including Selfridges and other stores in the West End. My particular patch was in W2, covering Leinster Terrace, Lancaster Gate, Bayswater Road and Craven Hill. My main duty as warden was to write out messages and send them by runner to the fire-fighters, ambulance men and other officers as required.

There were several of us girls in the ARP Service and no one seemed afraid. We had a job to do and we got on with it. Mind you, we experienced some gruesome sights. After the incendiaries had been put out, we would make a final search for casualties. Once I pushed a front door that was slightly ajar and out tottered the body of a man who had been killed by the blast which had wedged him behind the door. On another occasion a volunteer fire-fighter slipped and fell while hosing water onto an incendiary in the street. I heard a shattering explosion – another life was sacrificed. The people of London were on the front line and we were not allowed to forget it.

Bombs were dropping thick and fast, particularly in December 1940 and through to May 1941. One of the wardens lived in a flat below mine. By day, he was a masseur to the 'élite' and every morning after breakfast would be seen walking to work. His clients included a rich lady staying at the Dorchester Hotel in Park Lane and a film director living in Swiss Cottage. This man had one disadvantage – he was deaf and during the day wore a natty little deaf aid. However, he liked to remove this deaf aid at night so he arranged that if the siren sounded I would wake him.

One night the two of us set out along Bayswater Road. We could hear the bombs falling, mostly in the docks area. Suddenly we heard the tell-tale whistle of one approaching – much too near for comfort. We had been told that we were less likely to be hurt by blast if we lay face-down on the ground. This my partner and I did and not a moment too soon. The bomb scored a direct hit on the Odeon Cinema, Marble Arch, causing the building to cave in, and many people to be injured or killed. The pavement on which we lay cracked beneath us. We got up, brushed ourselves down and reported for duty.

The time came when the enemy started to send over landmines. These were terrifying weapons dropped by parachute. One advantage however was that fire-watchers on duty on the roofs of buildings could spot the white silk parachute in the air and send word over to the next district. The warning given would enable us to get civilians into their underground shelters before the bom fell. Landmines caused much more widespread damage than high explosive bombs. One Monday morning, returning from a weekend with my parents at Aberystwyth, I set off to visit some friends of my father's who kept a large dairy and shop off Tottenham Court Road. I got out of the Tube and was horrified on turning the corner to find the whole street flattened. There were no survivors.

By the time the flying bombs (V1) and rockets (V2) started coming over, I was out of London and in the forces. A friend in the ATS was posted to a south coast gun battery defending against the flying bombs – if they penetrated the defences and you heard the engine cut out, she told me, you knew the bomb was on its way down. They were a short-range weapon launched mostly from the coast of France. The V2 was a long-range rocket landing unexpectedly with a far-reaching impact. My friends in London told me afterwards that these were the most frightening as they came over so silently and without warning.

I shall never forget the bravery of the thousands of Londoners who poured into the underground stations every night with their bedding and food, to lie on platforms huddled like sardines and always cracking a joke to keep their spirits up, not knowing whether their home would still be standing when they emerged in the morning.

In a Far Country

~

Kusha Petts

His house has gone;
his wife lies stiff and strange;
his daughters are small reddened heaps.

The texture of his hair
is unlike yours or mine;
his eyes are narrow
and his cheekbones broad and high.
But the cry that breaks his face,
the grief that wells his breast,
sounds on the air the same
both East and West.

CHAPTER 8

MEDICAL WORK

Welsh women served in the farthest reaches of the global war as well as in the local hospitals. In Sri Lanka and India they nursed civilian and military casualties and in Llandough they nursed shell-shock victims. The horrors of war cannot be more graphically illustrated than in the hospitals where its victims are treated, comforted and laid to rest.

Finnegan's Fair

~

Roberta Powell

Llandough Hospital, Penarth, October 1942

Dear Uncle Dan,

This is the first chance I've had to write you since I came here, a few weeks ago. I wish you could see this modern hospital high up on the hill, the sea in the far distance.

At present, I'm on an orthopaedic ward which receives accidents of all kinds. The work is heavy and hectic, but we have time off for lectures, (usually mid-morning) when we all sit at desks in 'classroom' and scribble the notes dictated by our Sister Tutor.

Wartime conditions have made nursing much harder. Besides all the routine jobs, there's the hated one of doing the hospital blackout, when we have to go round putting up heavy wooden shutters on every window. This is sure to give you a permanent ache in your side. Then there's fire-watching at night. If there's an air raid warning and it's your turn to fire-watch with your group, you have to get out of your nice warm bed and go out in the cold (not forgetting your tin hat).

Sunday is 'visiting day' and while the patients are besieged by relatives, we have to shut ourselves away and scrape the wheels of the trollies to get them clean.

The food here is made up of grey porridge and stodgy puddings – but they have to fill you up with something to give you energy to rush round the wards.

The only thing I *really* dislike is getting up at 6.30 every morning. We're terribly short-staffed and our time off (apart from mealtimes) amounts to about two hours a day. When it does come round, you're too tired to do anything at all! – But we're lucky enough to have one evening off every week, and also a day and a half on which I can go home. We're on duty until just after 8 p.m., and we sometimes have to fire-watch after that.

Forgive the short letter – I have to rush off in a few minutes.

Yours, *Bobbie.*

Throughout the war I kept up a correspondence with my uncle in Fallon, Nevada. Most letters survived the censor's blue pen; many were published in Fallon's local paper, the *Eagle*. But at Llandough I had few spare moments for letter writing. 'I'll never get finished!' we would mutter, in a frenzy of brass-tap cleaning, bath-scouring, disinfecting and drowned hopes. Our Irish staff nurse on Orthopaedic christened the more hectic days 'Finnegan's fair'. Like a dancing dynamo, she would shriek, 'When you're finished with the sputum mugs and kidney basins, take those specimens up to the Path. Lab. And don't throw them out, for God's sake, or they'll shoot you down in flames!'

Our side wards were all occupied by wounded Army officers, to be plastered, poulticed, dosed and cured, before being sent to the west coast to convalesce. Brought back from Italy, all suffered in varying degrees from a condition known in the forties as 'bomb-happy'. One lieutenant, in particular, tattooed his own rhythm on the drum using the bedpan as a drum in his mad moments. Another found relaxation in composing topical jingles, in which even I featured:

'And after breakfast (tea and kippers),
Nurse Bowen comes with silver slippers.'

Meanwhile, the world outside still beckoned us invitingly, despite barrage balloons floating in the sky, barbed wire on the beaches, overcrowded buses with masked headlights and blacked-out trains. For, besides these things, it also offered packed cinemas showing Betty

Grable and the Andrews Sisters, and odd cafés where romances blossomed between soldiers with the flashes of occupied countries on their sleeves and girls wearing turban hats, wedge-heeled shoes and bright red lipstick. People were kind to one another, simply because they never knew whether they would ever meet again.

Complimentary tickets for the theatre were often available to us, as nurses. A blunder in the blackout on returning from one of these outings with my friend Kathleen, a pretty girl from the west of Ireland, as our train hurtled past unknown stations in the dark, resulted in our being carried five miles beyond our destination, and half an hour beyond our curfew-time of 10 p.m. Ploughing across country in the utter dark, we feared the wrath of Night Sister far more than breaking our legs.

Christmas Eve was taken up with gathering prickly holly in the woods above the concrete blocks manned by the Home Guard. On Christmas Day, we cleaned the cutlery.

Christmas Night, 1942

Dear Uncle Dan,

This is the first Christmas of my life away from home. Perhaps one of the Fallon boys has been able to get leave and spend it there, in my place.

The patients here have had a really merry time. We've decorated all the wards and the Lord Mayor has paid his visit. On Christmas Eve, we went around the beds singing carols, carrying lanterns, with our cloaks turned inside out, to show the red lining. Some of the patients were crying. Today, the Medical Superintendent came into each ward to carve the turkeys, which we were very lucky to have, considering it's wartime. We're having our own dinner tomorrow night, when the doctors will carve the turkeys and wait on us. The puddings will be brought into the hall in the dark so that the lights show up around them, when they're set on fire. After that, there'll be a dance.

Sorry I can't write you long letters, now. My two hours' off-duty goes like lightning. The strains of 'Music While You Work' on the wireless mean it's time to return to the wards and, when one's on duty, there's no time to think of anything except work.

They're trying to improve working conditions for nurses in this country, because they can't get enough girls, and they need so many, with the war on. Any increase in wages will only amount to a few shillings a month, but the thing to which we're most looking forward is the promise of a month's vacation every year. They may try to solve the problem by conscripting girls, but hospitals just don't want conscripts. Nursing means long spells of duty and a lot of standing and rushing about. It's different from other jobs, because you just can't 'clock off' at a certain time. We all know there'll be a lot more fighting before the war's over, so it's more important than ever to really want to do the work. Nearly every doctor is doing the work of two, because all the young doctors who can be spared are in the Army.

I must say 'goodnight', now. It's 'lights-out' time and Night Sister will soon be on her rounds to see if we're asleep!

Best wishes and love, *Bobbie*

By now, we were duly familiarized with the varying whims of Sister Tutor, Home Sister, Office Sister and Sister Housekeeper, not to mention Matron, of whom I was petrified. I had come on to the Children's Ward, a pleasant place with a jovial Sister. The children themselves, of all shapes and sizes, came from homes both average and poor. Some had been bombed out, some deserted, most were underfed. With Sister out of the way and the ward to myself, I would skim headily along with the breakfast trolley, reciting the murder scene from *Macbeth* before an audience of thirty astounded little faces. Later would come the less congenial task of combing their hair for nits, my uniform well-covered with a voluminous gown.

Feeding the children resulted in my first vivid encounter with Matron, in the form of a head-on collision. Out in the corridor, I was struggling along from the main kitchens with a giant container of soup for the children's supper, Matron striding just ahead of me.

'The Solarium doors, Nurse – I feel a draught...' She swung around. Too late! Matron was now feeling more than a draught, as the hot soup slopped over her uniform before my horrified gaze. Sister, stunned for once into silence, rushed into the ward kitchen to find her most junior nurse mopping up Matron's ample bottom.

No one could understand why I had been mad enough to leave the haven of college for the comparative hell of a training hospital. Sister herself christened me the 'University Bolshevik', but having taken a dislike to a nurse three months my senior, she would send me down to theatre in her place, an experience I relished. This was mainly because I had only to keep silent and stand, gowned and masked, near my tiny charge on the trolley. Theatre Sister, like a whirling dervish in the heat, made mincemeat of everyone, except, of course, the surgeon who was operating, as he dramatically flung swabs and anything else to the ground.

A brief stint on the Babies' Ward under a draconian sister nearly killed me. I could do nothing right. Soldiers coming on hurried leave to visit their screaming offspring would be forcibly expelled when Dr Merton, the consultant paediatrician, did his round.

'Naarses!' Sister would shriek in a frenzy. 'Dr Merton's morning! – See that all the babies have clean coats! See that all the babies have clean bibs! – Dr Merton's morning!'

Having screamed herself hoarse, she would rush to the clinic room to powder her nose, and emerge, as her paragon appeared through the swing doors. 'Ah – Dr Merton!'

Escape miraculously came in the form of my being sent on night duty on Men's Medical. Instead of the 6.30 a.m. call, it became 'Seven o'clock, Nurse!', with the same slamming of doors, only this time in the evenings. Life was turned completely upside-down. Our breakfast over, we went to our respective wards in twos, carrying little cases with slippers, cardigans and books, notably *Anatomy for Nurses*.

At ten o'clock the first night, my Senior left me to go to dinner. She called out a few last-minute instructions before disappearing down the corridor. The red light flashed on above the first door along the corridor. I hurried in.

'Lieutenant Gooding, get back to bed!'

A thinnish young man was fairly dancing around, the blackout pulled back, his eyes on the moonlit window.

'But look! A Jerry caught up in the searchlights!'

I looked up at the sweeping searchlights stabbing the sky, pinpointing a tiny object high above.

'Back to bed!'

Miserably, he crawled back. The walls were by now reverberating to the sound of the big Naval gun across the road and the ack-ack fire in the docks.

It was always a relief when one's Senior came back. The patients at night were 'our children', and we would work to keep them alive, all the long hours through. Antibiotics had hardly been thought of then and people often died of what would now be considered minor infections. If things were reasonably quiet, we could have toast and jam in the kitchen about four o'clock, before cutting the patients' bread and scraping it with marg. Next, the seriously ill people had to be attended to. Then came the mad rush of waking them all up about 5 a.m., with cups of tea, giving bowls of water to wash, handing out mouthwashes and collecting specimens.

The worst thing that could happen to you on nights was to be delegated to being a 'Runner'. This meant you could be sent anywhere, more particularly to wards that were a hurricane of happenings. You were given the worst jobs, and at 3 a.m., felt at your lowest ebb, legs aching and ready to drop. Later on, you began to recover your energy, catching a glimpse of the sun rising as the 'all clear' sounded. Worse than air raids, we hated East 3, a hopeless ward of men 'jumping in and out of cot-beds' as another girl put it. Bending over one of these forlorn old men, I received a black eye from a well-aimed fist. The next night, we laid out his worn-out body and, accompanied by an ancient porter (young men being unavailable), I trundled the heavy trolley down to the mortuary in the blackout. The drawers containing the bodies were barely visible in the weird light of a bulb which was painted blue. Looking round, I realized I was alone, the porter having vanished into the blackness. After what seemed an age, he reappeared without explanation, and I was thankful to return, meeting another nurse coming towards the lift with her own particular body as I was coming back with my blissfully empty trolley. She waved cheerily as we passed one another, 'Happy days!'

It wasn't that we were unfeeling, but if you didn't laugh, you wouldn't have lasted five minutes. As it happened, I never stayed the course, ending up with a spell as a hospital patient myself. Afterwards, the thought of returning to be junior to my friends, who were now senior nurses in a rigid caste system, was not to my inclination. By now, D Day was approaching and fierce fighting would follow, with terrible loss of life. We could not believe it, yet, but after five years, the lights would soon be coming on, countrywide.

A Tunisian Journey

~

Hilda M. Howells

The seriousness and the excitement of the war gripped everyone in the land. I was in London during the Battle of Britain, and in Kent during the evacuation of Dunkirk. The future was misty, and I stood hesitant. At last I joined the Queen Alexandra's Imperial Military Nursing Service Reserve. I joined my unit in Scotland, and soon we were mobilized for service overseas.

Hospital ships always sail alone, and never in convoy. One morning we were sighted by a German U-boat. The Commander came on board to inspect our little ship and if we had one gun or one ounce of ammunition on board the two hundred nursing sisters may well have been lost at sea. I can only speak well of the compassion of that German U-boat Commander.

Early in 1943 we arrived in Algiers and were taken to Phillipville to join our Unit, the 300th British General Hospital. Soon the convoys began to arrive, two hundred or more every day, and we were very busy. After treatment according to the severity of their injuries, some were transferred to base hospitals, and some were returned to their fighting units. Sometimes we saw these men admitted a second time with more severe injuries. Their courage gave us courage too.

After a while I was transferred to a prisoner of war camp attached to our unit. Had I volunteered to come 2,000 miles from home to nurse these men who were my enemies? They were Germans and Italians, some very severely wounded, some mobile. I tried to analyze the situation. Some of these men did not want war any more than we did. Whether in peacetime or wartime, nursing knows no frontiers. When I was on night duty, morning after morning there was one thing that always upset me. This was a tented hospital, we lived and worked under canvas; outside the wards we had ablution benches, and in the mornings the patients used to wash and then proceed to lace up their great army boots. For me this always symbolized the oppression of the Nazi heel.

Within a few months, many of us were posted to forward hospitals in Tunisia. The last phase of the campaign in North Africa was fierce, long and bitter. Casualties were heavy. April and May 1943 were the crucial months of the North African offensive, when the armies were grouped strategically for the final victory. The British 8th Army coming from the Middle East took Enfidaville on the 20 April 1943. The British 1st Army in Tunisia retook Longstop Hill on 26 April, and finally the 9th Corps of the British 8th Army took Tunis on 7 May 1943. The 2nd US Corps took Bizerta on 8 May 1943. The German Armies surrendered on the Cap-Bon Peninsula on 10 May.

Following the invasion of Sicily, casualties from Italy were evacuated by air and sea to hospitals in Tunisia, and after treatment they were transferred by hospital trains to base hospitals in Algiers. The hospital trains were very primitive, almost like converted trucks. We were able to accommodate 200–250 patients. Stretchers were arranged in three tiers on either side, with a narrow corridor down the centre; lack of space caused great problems when meals were served and dressings renewed.

The gruelling 850-kilometer journey from Tunis to Algiers was usually accomplished in two to three days. Some patients were in intense pain and discomfort. Some of the men were blind, and one man had both arms amputated and was blind in both eyes. How I admired his courage. One afternoon I asked him, 'Would you like a cigarette?'

'I haven't had one since Italy. I would like one please.'

He was on the bottom stretcher so I sat on the floor and held the cigarette for him to smoke. He needed this opportunity to talk more than anything else. He had four children. A fifth, born whilst he had been away, he would never see. I was hoping that he could not detect the emotion in my voice.

A Wartime Nurse

~

Mary Morris

Normandy, 19 June 1944. The landing craft was attempting to draw alongside us with very little success. Each time it drew near the ship, a huge wave tore them apart. It looked distinctly alarming from where I stood looking over the edge of the deck and down onto the craft way below. The sailors had attached a scrambling net to the side of the ship and in theory we were to descend in agile fashion down this net, whilst the sailors on this side helped us over the edge. The men on the landing craft were ready to catch us as we jumped aboard. But the heavy seas made the synchronization of these events highly unlikely. The wearing of a 'Mae West' although essential in such weather, increased our girth and made the effort of climbing down the scrambling net very difficult. It couldn't have been more difficult if we had all been eight months pregnant.

Our strange silhouetted shapes were lit up periodically by the flares as we stood in fear and trepidation as to who should go first. I volunteered not out of bravery but because of feeling seasick again. Anything to get off that ship! I was all right whilst the sailor lowered me over the edge of the deck, and whilst I could feel his strong arms, then I was on my own. Voices from above and below said, 'Hold on carefully and don't look down'. The 'Mae West' bulk constantly pushed me away from the too-mobile scrambling net. I thought I was almost there when a voice behind me said, 'Hold on until the exact moment I say and then jump backwards.' I was soaked in spray by now, cold, wet and frightened but when someone shouted, 'Now!' I fell straight back into waiting arms.

The relief was instantaneous and my spirits rose as I encouraged Driscoll and Wally who came down next. The sailors on the landing craft were a very jolly bunch, full of jokes and laughter. We were the first British women who had literally fallen into their arms in Normandy! Matron was the last to come down, which she did without too much loss of dignity. We watched all the activity around us, as the landing craft crept towards Graye-sur-Mer. When we got there the tide was in and we had to sit and wait until it ebbed before going ashore. Some of the sailors had landed the D-Day troops and told us about their experiences. We got ashore eventually and are now sleeping on stretchers on the floor of an old barn alongside the beach.

I am too tired to write anymore and listen to the screaming shells in the distance before going to sleep.

9 p.m. 19 June 1944. Writing this in an apple orchard 'somewhere' in Normandy. Sitting on the grass outside my tent. We left Graye-sur-Mer about twelve hours ago. This has been such a long day and so much has happened that I feel disorientated. It would be lovely to be alone for a little while just to think, but we have strict orders not to leave the camp. There is constant activity, and too many people and always so much noise. The fighting must be quite close.

My first look at the Normandy beach came when I woke up this morning about 8 a.m. The beach was a deserted battlefield in the daylight; smashed amphibious vehicles, the remains of concrete embattlements, a confusion of scrap metal, tin hats, broken rifles etc. It was easy to visualize the bitter battles that had been fought there less than two weeks before.

We clambered aboard a 3-tonner open lorry after breakfast and set out inland. It was a warm sunny morning and my first impressions of Normandy as we left the coast were of clouds of dust, a flat countryside, straight poplar trees standing like sentries on the skyline and the sound of ack-ack guns and screaming shells. The roads, trees and fields were covered in a mantle of white dust. It was in our hair and eyes and stuck to our damp battledress. I felt dirty and hot and dreamt of a cool shower as we moved along. As we neared Bayeux, the parting of clouds of dust revealed huge tanks on the side of the road, black from burning, dozens of them with the dead crews hanging half in and half out of the turrets and escape hatches. There was mile after mile of destroyed armoured cars, trucks of all kinds, and always the dust, heat and stench of decaying maggot-ridden bodies. There were dead cattle in the fields.

We met up with our Pioneer Corps escort at Bayeux. The Cathedral mercifully undamaged, the city surprisingly intact. The shutters were up on the shop windows and the place looked deserted apart from some troops in battledress wandering about, many of them Free French soldiers. Then we drove off on the long, straight road leading to Caen, and arrived in this orchard. There is not any sign of farming activity here although there is a dilapidated farm and a disused barn nearby.

20 June 1944. There is a RC Padre attached to our Unit. Heard Mass in a tent and received Holy Communion.

The water supply is nearly two kilometres away. The resourceful Pioneer Corps have found some water barrels in the disused barn, and we now have a special water tent. All drinking water must be boiled.

The Pioneer Corps are our armed guards, rifles at the ready standing on the edge of our compound. They are delightfully unmilitary, rather untidy soldiers. Many are basically conscientious objectors. They are multinationals from all walks of life, some very well educated and with useful specialist skills. There is an officer with an unpronounceable name whom I call 'Chezzy'. He has told me a little of the background of some of these men. Many were refugees from Germany before the war. Chezzy speaks fluent English and German, also Polish and Russian. I think he is a Polish Jew. He loves music and is a professional pianist in civilian life. Short and dark with a big nose and the most beautiful deep brown eyes, Chezzy has so much warmth and personality that it knocks me over.

Our large hospital tents are now erected, also the operating theatre (a bell tent) thanks to Chezzy and his men.

There was some rapid gunfire this evening in the vicinity of the farmhouse. A Pioneer Corps Corporal found the sniper, he cannot be more than fifteen years old. He was wounded in the leg and ironically became our first casualty! Fritz told Chezzy when he was interviewed that he had been ordered to stay behind to 'fight for the fatherland'. The wound in his leg is superficial – a flesh wound. Fritz is very high and mighty, the product of Hitler Youth I suppose, but he did not refuse the food we offered. He was ravenous.

The Pioneer Corps completed our new canvas latrines today. There is alarmingly little privacy. Driscoll and I are reducing our fluid intake, in order to minimize the embarrassment of being escorted to the latrines by an armed guard (Matron's orders because of the snipers). There are some terrible jokes about 'pot' shots.

23 June 1944. There was a great deal of bustle everywhere this morning. The word has got round that 101 British General Hospital is in business, and we are expecting our first casualties today. Two of our first patients are Germans, picked up by a Canadian officer in a jeep. One is a frightened young boy about the same age as Fritz our sniper friend. Fritz is still hobbling around with a stick, tending to exaggerate his leg injury. He is quite 'cocky' now that he knows we are not going to poison or shoot him. The other German is a man in his thirties with a kind sensitive face. His name is Hans and he has a wife and two children in Frankfurt. I do not know what he was doing wandering round roads in Normandy, probably a deserter. He is delighted to be with us and apart from malnutrition and some superficial cuts and bruises he seems to be OK. We cannot chuck him out to starve and there are not any POW camps here; so he will probably do odd jobs on the wards or around the camp to earn his keep. Hans is quite unlike the jack-booted Hun whom we had anticipated. He is polite and timid and makes me feel that he is one of the many 'pawns' in this game of war.

I was going off duty at 5 p.m. when the ambulances rolled up, three in rapid succession. It is now midnight and I have come off for a rest but may have to go back on the ward later if any further convoys of wounded come in. We have a mixed bag in the ward now, Germans, Welsh, some Canadians, a few Cockneys, several Poles, one or two Free French soldiers, a civilian member of the Maquis shot whilst escaping from somewhere, one Latvian and two Americans. Chezzy and his men are of enormous help in interpreting Polish, German, even Latvian for us. It took many hours to clean them all up, put on temporary dressings and give them food and drink. The ones who were shocked through loss of blood were put on a plasma intravenous drip. There will be a long operating list tomorrow.

24 June 1944. Hans brings me a cup of tea as I sit at my desk to read the night report. My mind wanders for a while as I think of this ward and my charges. This multi-national microcosm of a Europe at war is interesting and sad. A badly wounded Cockney says, 'Thanks, mate,' to Hans as he gives him tea and fixes his pillows. Why are they all tolerant of each other inside this canvas tent, and killing each other outside?

In my training days in a civilian hospital it was considered good policy not to tell the patient anything, but just 'fob them off' by saying, 'it's all right, dear'. Consultants were only slightly below God and Matron ruled the roost. It is very different here. I decided that all the conscious patients should be given a detailed list of their own treatment, diet and medication and asked to remind the day and night staff at the right time and to 'nag' if necessary. I hope this works, for with so much to do it would be impossible for me to keep track of everybody's therapy. I can now concentrate on the seriously ill cases who are unable to help themselves. I call it 'patient participation' but I dare not imagine what

Matron will say when she finds out.

25 June 1944. There were several 'repair of gunshot wounds' on the theatre list today. I boiled all the necessary instruments, including a bone saw, should an amputation be necessary, and prepared the table and anaesthetic trolley. Determined not to incur Col. Cordwell's wrath by any incompetence on my part. The heat of the tent was heavy and oppressive and the flies were very worrying. I stood there for nearly six hours silently handing Col. Cordwell the instruments at the right moment. He never spoke and I had to watch carefully to mop his brow periodically. We were all exhausted by 4 p.m. and went to sit on the grass outside to drink a cup of tea kindly provided by Taffy.

The two worst cases were still to come. One, Private James, is only twenty years old. It is frightening to contemplate the future effects on these men, but there is no hope of repair when there is extensive damage such as theirs. They both lost a leg, and my own personal sadness for them was intermingled with exhaustion, and the nauseating job of clearing up the blood-stained theatre afterwards, and carrying away the legs to an incinerator and watching until they were completely burned.

26 June 1944. Good news this morning, some replacement uniform and underclothes arrived from England including ghastly khaki knickers. These pants are hilarious – huge and elasticated at the waist and legs. But we could hardly have expected army supplies to have equipped us with glamorous cami-knickers. It will be blissful to feel clean. My battle dress is dirty and blood-stained. Hot water is such a luxury. We are becoming anxious about hygiene in general, particularly as some of the girls have developed a mild dysentery. We are so short of Sisters that we can not afford to have anybody off sick.

27 June 1944. We had another very serious case of gun-shot wounds and blindness brought in today. He is very shocked, but talks on and on interminably and cheerfully about his incredible experiences. He has a nice voice, and the warmth of his personality comes over as he talks and talks. He completely ignores the appalling state he is in. The British are renowned for the stiff upper lip – but this is ridiculous. He stinks to high heaven, and tells his story to Taffy and me as we endeavour to cut him out of his filthy, smelly, blood-stained uniform.

He is a Normandy veteran, one of the shock troops who arrived at Leon-sur-Mer in the early hours of the morning of D Day, complete with a folding bicycle on his back. His first memory of Normandy was of being dragged up on to the beach and landing face downwards next to a dead German soldier. He eventually made it to Cazalet Wood but his 'wheels' unit was sadly depleted by then. He and the remnants of his unit got 'dug' in there and apparently 'all hell was let loose' around them. They were surrounded by minefields and the shelling went on day and night. Their battle for survival went on for two weeks. They kept their heads down and stole eggs from farmhouses at night. They were completely cut off from the rest of their unit and were unable to make any contact. Len and his friends eventually got out of the predicament in Cazalet and joined up with Monty's men somewhere round the Odon and Orne area. It was here that Len's real troubles began. During a particularly tough battle he dived into what he believed was a slit trench but it turned out to be a German latrine. Whilst sitting there a massive shell landed nearby. The impact blinded him completely and although he is too shocked to realize it yet, most of his right leg has been blown off. His face is completely blackened from impacted shrapnel.

Len talks on as we bandage up the remains of his leg. It is a terrible mess. He tells us how he forced himself to crawl out of the latrine and under a tank. He banged on the underside and shouted above the noise until someone with an English voice found him. He then helped this other soldier to put a makeshift tourniquet on his thigh as he was losing so much blood. He then remembers being strapped on to the top of a jeep and being driven over the agonising bumps on the road. As if this were not enough, a screaming shell blew the jeep over, on its way here, with Len still strapped on top. The jeep was righted and incredibly Len is with us. The bleeding has stopped now, but Len is weak although still talking bravely. I fix him up with intravenous plasma and give him a shot of morphine. He will need sleep to prepare for major surgery in the morning.

I get off duty at 1 a.m. and am too tired to sleep. Wearing my tin hat in bed as there is a great deal of shrapnel flying around!

28 June 1944. The new wonder-drug penicillin is a great help in the fight to save the lives of young men like Len.

This is the first time that I have seen this antibiotic in action. It is not yet in use in the civilian hospitals. It seems to be particularly good in preventing gangrene infections in gunshot wounds.

Len is subdued as I give him his pre-medication. Anxiety about his blindness, and the pain of respiration is quite enough without the added fear of major surgery and amputation. The other patients sense his fear and try to cheer him up. He tries to respond but by now it is time for Taffy and the other orderlies to fetch a stretcher and take him across to the theatre. It was just at this point that 'Jerry' utterly disregarding the red cross on the roof of our tent hospital decided to strafe us. The Luftwaffe planes swooped low and then were away. The two orderlies, having seen a bomb drop harmlessly on the ground panicked. They dropped Len and his intravenous bottle of plasma and ran. Col. Cordwell heard Len shout, came out of the operating tent on his hands and knees wearing his gown and mask, saw what had happened and went back in for his revolver. There was shrapnel from the ack-ack guns flying around but the CO found the men and forced them at gun point to pick up the stretcher and bring Len in to have his anaesthetic (very necessary by now). These orderlies should be put on a charge but I doubt if they will. We are too short of personnel.

4 July 1944. The mud is still with us and today we had some disgruntled visitors out from England. War photographers from the magazine *Picture Post.* They took formal photographs outside our hospital tent and less formal ones as we worked. They were unable to hide their irritation and disgust at the sight of their muddied boots and were in terror of dropping their precious cameras. It was unkind to laugh at their discomfiture.

5 July 1944. We had a convoy of young Canadian casualties brought in this morning. I was called for duty at 3 a.m. and was appalled at seeing their condition when I entered the ward. There were stretchers all down the middle of the tent, there were charred bodies everywhere, some were quiet and dying, others screaming with pain, all with severe burns. We gave them morphia and more morphia and watched helplessly as they died. We moved the dead out of the ward and got on with trying to save the living. They were all so young and frightened. Extra beds were put up, and we cut off the remnants of their uniform and gently laid them naked on their beds. Coverings were not possible because they could not tolerate anything touching their bodies. We tried to replace the fluid loss with intravenous plasma and saline, and we were glad of the human heat, generated by the over-crowded ward. They were so cold. We gave them penicilin in the hope of preventing infections, but we are very conscious of the fact that this is the worst type of condition to deal with in our inadequate surroundings and with so little equipment.

A young officer, Jock McCabe, one of the few able to speak, told me what happened. There was bitter fighting somewhere near Carpiquet aerodrome. The Canadians wore a darker shade of khaki uniform to ours, similar to the Germans. Our troops attacked them with flame-throwers, thinking that they were an enemy target. Such is the stupidity and futility of war.

We did everything possible for these young men, but nineteen in all are dead. Spent the afternoon in the depressing task of trying to identify the dead, filling their labelled details and laying them out. Their average age was twenty years. They had so much living to do. Feel tired and depressed.

18 July 1944. We had a small convoy of patients in today. On the way to Falaise, our troops captured a German hospital and released some British prisoners. The stretcher-wounded English and Germans filled the one ambulance, the other German cases had to walk.

Col. Cordwell was very impressed by the skill of the German surgeons. Our boys said that they had been well treated, but complained that the Germans did not have any pretty nurses like us.

20 July 1944. Matron was upset at breakfast this morning. Fortunately not our fault; *Picture Post* magazine was the culprit. It had published photographs of us at work, some of which were reproduced in *The Times* and *Morning Telegraph* under the invidious caption of 'First ATS in Normandy.' Sally was incensed on behalf of her QAs and bustled off to write stiff letters to *The Times* and the War Office.

21 July 1944. I was doing a duty in the reception tent this morning when I saw a bedraggled group of soldiers arriving. The smell came first. They were German prisoners without an escort. Some were wounded and they were all very tired, dirty, hungry and frightened. I sent for Chezzy to act as interpreter. They are a small pocket of resistance troops, who had been captured on the road to Falaise, had been relieved of their weapons, turned around and pointed back to us. The war is moving on fast. This situation could not have arisen a week ago.

We sorted them out, gave any necessary treatment, fed them, deloused them and made the usual arrangement for them to go to POW camps in England. The wounded are on the ward. Chezzy is keeping the others under guard. They are too tired to be any kind of threat.

Came off the ward at 9 p.m. They were still playing housey-housey and I could hear their shouts as I walked across to my tent. The rain has stopped. The silence is uncanny. There is a strange feeling of change and movement in the air – a rather unsettled feeling.

Two World Wars a Nursing Sister

~

Elsie M. Hughes

As a nursing sister to the Dafen Division Home Nursing Class, I was privileged to accompany a soldier who had had both legs amputated. He was brought back from the invasion of France, and was healed enough to be taken to hospital in Leeds to have artificial limbs fitted. I wore my St John's Ambulance uniform of a Nursing Sister and we left by first class carriage for the first part of our train journey. At the station other St John's personnel were ready, waiting to assist me in carrying him in our arms to the Leeds train. He was so depressed at his condition and I had difficulty in raising his spirits on the journey. Trains were very much slower then and it was dark by the time we reached the hospital. The soldiers already there for treatment knew of his impending arrival, and on opening the ward door came forth a terrific shout of welcome. When I left him next morning for my return he had been transformed overnight into a most delightful, happy soldier and I left again for Wales, a very happy nurse!

I find it hard to believe that I nursed soldiers in the two world wars. At the end of the First, I worked as a VAD in Maindiff War Hospital in Abergavenny, Gwent. It was in this hospital that Rudolf Hess was imprisoned during the Second War.

Please excuse this writing, my eyesight is poor but at ninety years of age I am not grumbling.

From GP to Captain RAMC

~

Rona Price Davies

My own personal grudge against Hitler came when my autumn cruise up the Norwegian fjords had been cancelled and I found myself making blackout curtains instead. After that, as a young doctor in north Wales, I drove my car to calls after dark at about five miles per hour, the headlights covered so that only a hole the size of a shilling was left. Then petrol became rationed and so, at my mother's request, I returned to within striking distance of my old home and became an assistant in a busy practice in Cardiff. I began to save petrol by doing the nearest calls on a bicycle but was somewhat put off when a well-meaning woman, coming to the door to see me on my way, said: 'It's not so easy as one gets on, is it?' That did put years on me.

One night, two nearby streets were destroyed by landmines. There were casualties of course, and many were dug out but most were saved by being in their own or large public air raid shelters. There were some heart-rending cases in our own practice. I remember a mother with asthma who would not use the shelter. She was killed and her young son blinded. There was also a disabled and diabetic man who lost his house, wheelchair, and even his insulin. He found the strength to crawl half a mile to the nearest hospital to ask for an injection.

It was at that time I had my call-up papers. My boss appealed saying, 'She is doing a man's job here,' to which he received the reply, 'Then she can do a man's job in the Forces, can't she?' So I found myself in the uniform of the Royal Medical Corps – a first lieutenant. I was assigned to the South-West looking after the health of the personnel on the ack-ack (anti-aircraft gun) sites. I remember one incident when neither I nor my driver, who was no better than I was at map-reading, were lost on Exmoor trying to find a camp site. We were in a village. All place names had been removed, and seeing a group of interested villagers, I told my driver to ask them where we were. He did so and came back to me grinning and saying, 'They won't tell me, ma'am.' At this we both laughed so heartily that the villagers softened, thinking this could not possibly be the reaction of Germans in disguise, and then told us exactly where we were.

By now, anyone who was free and young and fit enough was abroad, so I volunteered for overseas service. Within a few weeks I found myself with seven other women doctors – and several thousand others – on a troop ship on the Clyde going, I felt certain, to North Africa. During the first few days it seemed that we went west half way to America to avoid German submarines, but on hearing the anti-submarine depth charges I was so seasick I did not care. However, to my consternation, we did not seem to be making for the coast of North Africa. In a loud voice I asked, 'Aren't we going to Algiers?'

A sergeant heard me and said, 'Don't you know where you're going, ma'am?'

I said, 'No – do you?'

'Yes,' he said, 'We're going to India.' Then he related a recent encounter with his CO:

'Hello, Smith,' said he, 'You OK?'

'Yes, Sir,' said the sergeant, 'But please can you tell me where we're going?'

'Sorry, Smith,' came the reply, 'can't do that because of security but when we get to Bombay I'll let you know.'

At about five o'clock one afternoon, the emergency bell clanged out and I rushed for my tin helmet to get to my action station which was in the poop or stern end of the ship. As I was running up a ladder a naval officer stopped me and told me to get back.

'Can't,' said I, 'I'm the Medical Officer for the poop.'

'My God!' said he, 'What is the army coming to!'

We were being attacked by a German plane. The anti-aircraft men above me, who had been in the London Blitz, were cracking jokes as they fired away. I looked at the raft and wondered how I would get on it. Suddenly, a great bang, and flames leapt up from the other side of the stern. The plane had been shot down by the gunners on the bridge and had struck the ship as it went down in flames.

We heard afterwards that two ships in our convoy were sunk. The one behind us carried Queen Alexandra nurses. They had to take to the boats and later joined with us when we docked at Alexandria. From there we went by rail across the Nile delta. We were encamped near the Great Bitter Lakes. Our camp was called the Bird Cage and surrounded with barbed wire – but whether to keep the inmates in or others out, we were never certain. We worked in tents and at the field hospital. Sulphonomides had been discovered – but there were no antibiotics. Dysentery was rampant. One of my last hospital notes read 'This man has dysentery. I have only cough medicine left. Please admit.'

After several visits to the brightly-lit, exotic city of Cairo, we had the final call to move on and were taken to the waiting ship which we nicknamed the Ash Can – the *Ascanius*. What followed was more like a cruise than a voyage on a warship – such was the relief to be away from enemy action. It was very hot and we were even allowed sunbathing outfits and saw flying fish, dolphins, and once a whale spouting.

I was posted to Colaba Military Hospital, Bombay. This was on a rocky promontory and had swollen in wartime, due to the war in Burma, to a thousand-bedded hospital. I lived in a hotel with another medical woman and went by ambulance to the hospital every day. I was on duty for the whole hospital one night a week. My first job in Bombay was as doctor in charge of the smallpox isolation hospital. The youngest patient was a baby boy who recovered. I must have been immune as I never 'took' though I vaccinated myself every week.

Social life for us girls was very full as we were somewhat at a premium. Tennis, swimming, dancing, the cinemas and the races making a kaleidoscope of colourful events. After a year I became engaged to another doctor and within a few months we were married. I remember someone asking us how long the engagement had been. When I replied 'Three months,' he said, 'That's about the limit in the tropics.'

When I finally came home in a troop ship in March 1946, how cold it seemed. We were greeted by the mayor of Southampton, the town band, and the quay packed with relatives. But nothing happened, no gangways went down. Then the yellow flag was hoisted: we had an infectious disease on board. A smallpox case was suspected and the medics had to revaccinate everybody, such were the army regulations. After three days we re-entered the harbour, this time with no mayor, no band, no relatives – but we did not care, there were the trains to take us home.

Belsen

~

Emily Bond

In the midst of our festivities following the declaration of peace, we were told that the whole unit of 29th BGH was going to Belsen, one of the concentration camps in Germany. We knew very little of the conditions we would find when we got there and the suffering we witnessed took us by surprise. Belsen originally had been intended as a transit camp, but during the last months of the war, as the German position weakened, thousands of Jews were moved there from other concentration camps to die.

My first glimpse of Belsen was of its enormous iron entrance gates with boards on them stating the number of people held and the number that had died up to that time. Ominous barbed wire fencing surrounded the camp. Near to the entrance hundreds of people were walking or crawling aimlessly. They were partly clothed, with heads shaven, some covered only by a grey blanket, hung over one shoulder.

British troops had liberated the camp a few weeks earlier, but still hundreds of people were dying, their psychological scars as unnerving as their physical ones. Our tents were erected a short distance outside the wire barriers. We learnt that typhus and cholera were rife: the spread of disease worsened because of the filthy conditions, with the camps infested by lice and rats. There were no latrines and people were lying in their own excreta, sometimes inches deep. We were all sprayed daily with DDT.

Our first duties involved feeding the survivors with suitable food. It would have been easy to worsen their condition by giving them food which was too rich. At first they were allowed only nutritious fluids and vitamins, gradually working up to solid food. Often, when giving out meals, it was very difficult to allow patients only the amount of food they were medically supposed to have. They used to plead for more with a haunted look in their eyes saying that before we came they had been starved. At night some of the patients broke into the food store. One morning, attending to a dying patient in her bed, I found many tins of food neatly packed around her. How could patients believe that now there was plenty of food for all and that they would continue to get regular meals in the future? Loaves of bread disappeared during a journey of a couple of yards when being brought from the cookhouse to the wards. Once I noticed clouds of smoke coming from a site where old wooden cupboards had been thrown out. Going to investigate I found people with billy cans boiling up garbage, collected from the rubbish bins around.

As a senior Sister I was in charge of an area known as Square Eleven, which housed a thousand people, hundreds of them patients. I often felt inadequate in my capacity as a nurse to even try to counteract in any way the atrocities they had suffered. Some of the young girls on the ward had been so starved that initially they were mistaken for old women. At first, hundreds of patients died each day, including a great many from my ward. We used to write down the number of dead on a blackboard outside. It was at least heartening to notice that, as the weeks progressed, fewer and fewer died each day. As some patients were recovering they decided to leave in search of their homes and were desperate to see loved ones again. We never knew whether they reached their destinations. One case I remember in particular was a beautiful young woman who was in a ward for patients with psychological problems. Extremely intelligent, she spoke nine languages, and had been severely battered, both mentally and physically by the Germans. She was desperately malnourished and had lost all her hair. She was so thin that one day she got out of the ward through narrow beams on the window. She was never seen again.

Also under my supervision in Square Eleven was a ward full of patients suffering from Cancrum Oris – extensive ulceration of the mucous lining of the cheeks due to lack of mastication and malnutrition. The patients developed holes in their cheeks, and the tongue could be seen moving as they spoke. Even though I had learnt of this condition during nurse training, this was the first time I had encountered it. Such was the lack of control over the mouth area that feeding was made very difficult. After each feed we also had to wash the mouth, cleanse the surrounding ulcerated areas, and spray them with penicillin, which proved extremely effective.

Some German women from a nearby village offered to come to assist us. But such was the distrust felt by the patients that if these women offered them medicine, or even a drink, it was immediately thrown to the ground or into their faces.

One of our patients, with at least three lots of numbers on her arm, had repeatedly been offered soap by the Nazis and given opportunities to be taken to a bath but had refused and thus avoided the gas chamber. Another young woman had all her teeth knocked out by her captors and now was wearing a set of teeth made out of peat.

The women were now interested in their appearance and we used to give them some of our own make-up to use. As the days passed it was evident that many patients were making rapid progress. It seemed to me that the women reacted to treatment quicker than the men on the whole.

The army had made up some wooden bed frames. The beds were paliasses filled with straw, with brightly coloured check material as covers. A sign that patients were recovering came one day when we discovered that bed covers had been removed. It did not take us long to find out that patients were busy sewing dresses. We decided to take the women to the army clothing store on the camp which we nicknamed, 'Harrods', to find suitable clothes for them. Going on duty one morning I saw a parade of women walking along in the sunshine in their new dresses. It was a wonderful feeling to contrast this to the scene when I first arrived at the camp only a few weeks earlier. We all agreed that the brightly coloured spectacle reminded us somewhat of Brighton on a summer's day!

With so many contagious diseases, certain areas of the camp had to be marked for limited access. In one such area were patients suffering from typhus. In front of their quarters was a large sign which plainly said 'Typhus –

Keep Out'.

It was often sheer luck whether a person survived the horror of the camp or not. One patient explained how two hundred people were kept in one Nissen hut. Once a day the door opened and food was thrown in. The nearest to the door ate all the food, while the people at the back were dying of starvation and too weak to move forward.

A climax to the horror we witnessed came for me one evening when I visited the house that Kramer, named the Beast of Belsen, and his wife, had lived in. Here I saw a lampshade which had reputedly been made out of tattooed human skin. The attractiveness of the lampshade sickened me beyond belief.

The only sound medical care which had been administered in the camp before our arrival was in a hospital for the use of the SS troops themselves. This we took over as one of our hospital bases, naming it the Glyn Hughes Hospital, after our Brigadier Hughes, Director of Medical Services.

Amidst all the negative experiences encountered at Belsen there were moments of excitement and celebration to remember. Such was the day when Mary Churchill, ATS Commandant, the daughter of Winston Churchill, came to visit the camp. Patients and medical staff had gone to great efforts to make the area presentable. As there were no flowers, the patients found tree branches and decorated the ward with these. I remember well the retinue arriving at Square Eleven near the entrance to one of my wards. At first, the patients were too awed by the presence of this important lady to say anything. Then we heard the clear voice of a slightly-built Polish lady, sitting up in her bed, proudly asking Mary Churchill if she would thank her father on behalf of all the Polish people for all he had done for them. Standing perfectly still, with tears running down her cheeks, Mary Churchill said that the situation had so moved her that she could stand no more. Shortly afterwards she left the camp and, although there was disappointment that she had left so early, we knew that she would take our story back to Britain.

As the weeks progressed spirits were raised by recovery rates of many patients, and fatality rates falling dramatically from what was at first 500 people a day. Every morning a staff sergeant would come to receive the number of fatalities for the last twenty-four hours and a three-ton lorry would come around to take the dead away. The German prisoners resident with us were made to dig mass graves ready for the burial.

Belsen had been structured into three separate units – Camp 1, 2 and 3. There was soon no need for Camp 1 to be used and the major event of burning it down was planned. Psychologically speaking, this was an important ceremony for all of us. We watched the flames together, the scene of so much past horror being burnt away. It was a comforting feeling as all of us, friends of different nationalities, stood together hand in hand against Nazism. Now there was no need to use guns and violence, as the war had been won. That evening we spent hours singing and dancing around the bonfire which symbolized for us the death-knell of Nazi beliefs.

Armistice

~

Margaret Emlyn Jenkins

Kneeling
remembering
and praying.

Repenting
the hatred,
forgiving
the enmity.

Bridging
the chasms,
searching
for unity.

Healing
the wounds,
mending
the wholeness.

Curing
the cancer,
forgetting
the hate.

Learning
to love,
living
to share.

For peace
we kneel,
we remember
and we pray.

Other contributors whose work will be part of the archives

Stella M. Bater lived near an Italian prisoner-of-war camp in Montgomeryshire where she first experienced stirrings of the heart.

Kit Bolton's childhood was spent in the area of Cwmbrân. Black market goods were accepted as usual, as were the evacuees.

Valma Burge experienced the bombing of the Rhondda and was taught how to construct 'bloomers' of huge proportions.

Evelyn Collier spent the war as an evacuee mother in Llwyngwril together with most of her immediate family as well as a number of lodgers.

Maidwen Daniel signed her conscription form as a Conscientious Objector and refused to sing in factories where guns were being made, but she did travel to the continent and Asia to entertain the troops.

Anne M. Davies's poem recalls the crash of a German plane in a field near her village on Ynys Môn.

Joan Glyde Davies joined the ATS in 1940, was trained at Lancaster and was posted to the Western Command Headquarters in Chester.

Peggy England-Bloggs served in a mixed radar unit and was responsible for entertainment in her ATS group.

Dilys A. Evans left Cardiff to enlist in the forces, was trained in Yorkshire and posted to Penarth – at a barrage-balloon station.

Jean F. Flintan was a pupil at Dr Williams School in Dolgellau throughout the war years.

Patti Flynn (née Young) was only two when war was

declared. She loved her Mickey Mouse gas mask. Three of her brothers were killed in the war.

Angela Gabb was evacuated with her mother to Llwyngwril in Meirionydd. Her grandfather brought home from the beach all manner of salvage including an entire silk parachute which was turned into household goods.

Dorothy Gibbons (née Warman) from Canton joined the National Fire Service as a typist, but found her niche in the Fire Service Benevolent Fund Drama Society held at the Ex-Servicemen's Club in Womanby Street.

Miss A. Goodman survived the May Blitz on Liverpool and joined the Land Army to work on the Vaynol Estate in Bangor where she is still living.

Phyllis M. Griffiths also joined the Land Army. She was stationed at Llandybie as a member of the Timber Corps.

Doreen Harris's (née Davies) college sweetheart whisked her off to be married after Dunkirk. Penbrokeshire Education Committee then terminated her employment as a teacher. She became one of the first home economists for the Ministry of Food. Her husband was killed in action.

Margaret Hicks (née Walter) enlisted in the ATS. She married a soldier and they were both posted to the Ministry of Supply Experimental Station at Ynyslas, Aberystwyth.

Joan M. Hughes discovered, during the series of bombing raids on Cardiff, that her Mam was not her real mother and, later, that she would not be able to learn Welsh at school, both of which troubled her deeply. Joan requested that her essay be removed from this volume; the editors have reluctantly complied.

Barbara L. Jackson was five in 1939. Her memories of the war are linked to chocolate and other confectionaries which her father was able to bring to her from his and colleagues' rations.

Joan Jackson was a young woman at the time of the London Blitz. Besides endless knitting and sewing, she and her family started a music society to learn and study classical pieces.

Lisa James recorded the profound changes which occurred in her village in Gwynedd. The diet was in keeping with present-day healthy eating recommendations. Conscientious objectors, she said, could not have been cowards; they suffered much locally for their beliefs.

Ros Jenkins lived seven miles from Swansea. She was awoken by her parents to witness the bombing of that port city. Chocolate made a change from the 'Spanish Root' the children enjoyed then.

Mrs D. Elwern Jones begged to be evacuated to America but spent the war in Rhyl where her grammar school was host to two other schools. The British Restaurant at the town hall helped to extend her family's meagre rations.

Mrs Jack Jones's poem *The Sons of Britain* expressed her gratitude to those who had fought the war.

E. Lander spent a week's leave with her husband on Ynys Môn where she was delighted by a gift of home-grown onions.

Etta Lewis had to give up her dream of becoming a Queen Alexandra Army nurse for the sake of her mother and future husband. She became, instead, a Staff Nurse at Whitchurch Hospital and stayed on the ward during the bombing raids on Cardiff in 1942.

G. M. Melita McCarter, in her short novel, *Learning to Love*, described life at the University of Wales, Aberystwyth as well as her first years of teaching.

Lorna Merrigan was knocked into a tin bath full of hot water by the explosion of a landmine dropped on Penarth Docks.

Eileen Parry became a Red Cross Nurse in Cardiff. During one bombing raid on the city, she sheltered ten babies in carrycots while herself recovering from the birth of her first child.

Glenys Parry's village in Gwynedd was invaded by evacuees as well as Indian and American soldiers before D Day. The Americans couldn't believe that the village children spoke a different language.

Sybil Pearce shared her Rhondda school-days with evacuees from Edmonton. She described the devastation in the Valleys as well as the events leading up to D Day and VE Day: 'We all went Crazy!'

Barbara Phillips's Christmas train journey to Wales in 1944 was fraught with delays and overcrowding. ATS girls were thrown through windows into carriages by soldiers who followed on the cupped fingers of their comrades.

Ivonne Piper regretted her dislike for the evacuees from Bootle and sugar rationing was a fearful prospect. Ivonne requested that her essay be withdrawn from this volume; the editors have reluctantly complied.

Lorna Pope remembered the wartime internment of Italian immigrants living in Aberdare. She also witnessed the nightly rendezvous of 'Mrs Alabama' and her soldier friend from America.

Hilda Price lost her job at Sherman's Pools in Cardiff. Conscription of Women meant that she could not fulfill her wish to become a nurse and she was persecuted for her Communist party affiliations. Hilda requested that her essay be withdrawn from this volume; the editors have reluctantly complied.

Joy Purdy was about to be evacuated to Canada but had not been allocated a place. The ship was sunk and she was, instead, evacuated to Wales. She used snow and vinegar to rinse her hair.

Anne Reid (née David) escaped from Holland with the Vic Wells Ballet just as the German Army began its invasion. Later, she was a Land Army girl in Pentyrch and a plotter in the WAAF.

Carys Richards remembered the Ministry of Defence gun emplacements and pillboxes which served as toys for the Porthmadog children. The area was host to a multinational contingent.

M. J. Richards (née Arthur), a nurse at Cardiff Isolation Hospital, survived the bombing of Cardiff, a virtual prisoner of Park Hall Cinema.

Alma Rosser wrote a short story about the antics of the local police, a Peeping Tom and the cosmopolitan inhabitants of 'Bottle Hill' in Neath during the bombing raids over west Wales.

Mrs H. Saliba (née Goddard) received a commendation for her work at Curran's oil company from the Ministry Of Supply.

Muriel Smith remembered that workmen made short shrift of dismantling park and house railings and gates from scrap metal.

Mrs G. Stanley was a member of the Red Cross as well as a fire-watcher.

Megan Stark served as a Lieutenant in Queen Alexandra's Military Nursing Service stationed in Africa and then at Bwlch where she nursed soldiers evacuated from Dunkirk.

Majorie Steer had been looking forward to a school holiday in the Rhine Valley when war was declared. She then worked at the Royal Ordnance Factory in Llanishen.

Jean Thomas harnassed two Alsations to a sledge and set off in search of coal through the snowbound streets of Cardiff.

Veronica Webster was evacuated from Cardiff to Aberdare but returned home after three months. Her sister had a baby by an American soldier.

Gwyneth White kept a detailed diary of the war which she has recorded for the 'Penarth Past' group. Her voluntary service was in Llandough Hospital.

Sheila Mary Williams was a counter clerk at the Newport Post Office where she met her husband. She was paid £1.7s.6d. and was grateful for the two-hour mandatory overtime each week.

Blodwen Williams was conscripted to work in the Royal Ordnance Factory near Wrexham where she reeled cordite.

Madezda Wright was involved in the recruitment of a female Territorial Army group in Caernarfon. The ATS was posted for training to Didcot where the Commanding Officer made it obvious they were not wanted.

HONNO VOICES
– bringing the past to life

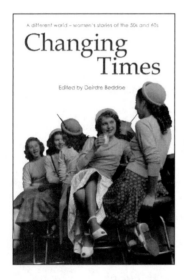

Changing Times

The 'New Look' and the 'Swinging Sixties' – from the hearth to the world of work

Edited by Deirdre Beddoe

"*Mornings were used to teach the basic three Rs and to progress us through our Janet and John readers. I only learned much later, in my thirties, how limited Janet's activities had been in comparison to her brother John's and how some scholars linked these textual role models to teenage girls' 'poverty of aspiration'.*"

Brenda moved to London and learned nursing in the traditional way, all hospital corners and 'nurses never run'. Heulwen determined to establish Welsh language schools and didn't stay at home with her own children. Let down by her married lover, Dot was treated appallingly by the dragons of the Moral Welfare department.

Like many other aspects of life, education in the 50s and 60s for most girls still meant segregation not just by gender but also by eleven-plus. Grammar school set you up for life, whilst secondary modern meant you were one of the 'workers'. Many women still lost their jobs on marriage and certainly if they became 'unmarried mothers'. But the 50s and 60s also brought rock-n-roll, rising hemlines and the first signs of female emancipation since the vote. With the pill came freedom from the threat of unwanted pregnancy. And though the 'swinging sixties' passed most of rural Wales by, they did bring electricity and the Dansette and the music of the Beatles...

ISBN: 978-1-906784-10-2   £11.99

HONNO VOICES
– bringing the past to life

Stories of everyday heroism between the wars

Struggle
or Starve

Edited by Carol White & Sian Rhiannon Williams

Struggle or Starve

Stories of everyday heroism
between the wars

Edited by
Carole White &
Sian Rhiannon Williams

---

*The past is different country, and there
were far fewer options open for women
then… Olive was never meek; she was
dauntless. She took the cards that life
dealt out to her – on the whole it was a
pretty lousy hand – and played it by the
rules and made the very best of it.*

Olive left school to run the household for her alcoholic mother – making sure that there was food on the table and that she extracted the housekeeping from her father at the mine gates before it hit the bookie's hand. And Olive was typical of the indomitable women whose voices come alive in these pages…

Others took in laundry, had broods of children only to lose their lives before their children were raised. In order to keep food on her mother's table Ivy James scoured the spoil tips of the local colliery for small lumps of coal to sell – this back-breaking task was paid so poorly that Ivy took on night work as a cleaner and chucker out at nearby hotels. Hard physical and demeaning work for anyone, never mind a woman. Each of their stories brings an insight into their struggle for dignity, recognition and wider opportunities.

'A delightful book…moving, poignant, funny and a very good historical record'.
Emeritus Professor Deirdre Beddoe, University of Glamorgan

ISBN: 978-1906784-09-6   £9.99

Further reading from Honno

Autobiography

Strange Days Indeed

This is a unique collection of autobiographical writings about motherhood penned by women from Wales. Funny, shocking and tender, it covers the whole spectrum of what it means to be a mother – from getting pregnant to the empty-nest syndrome.

"The empowerment, fear, doubt, sheer joy, and jolting ride that motherhood can be." www.girlistic.com

ISBN: 978-1-870206-83-9   £7.99

Even the Rain is Different (Anthology)

A compelling collection spanning 150 years of Welsh women's experiences abroad. Welsh women sleep in trees in Corsica, escape Stalinist purges in Moscow and curse head-leaping queue jumpers in China.

"compelling content...fascinating." Deirdre Beddoe

ISBN: 978-1-870206-63-1   £7.99

Fiction

The War Before Mine, by Caroline Ross

A brief wartime romance leaves Rosie heartbroken and pregnant, not knowing if Philip – on a suicide mission designed to stop the Nazi invasion – is alive or dead.

"More than a war story, more than a love story... A slice of living history." Philip Gross.

ISBN: 978-1870206-97-6   £6.99

Back Home, by Bethan Darwin

Ellie is brokenhearted and so decamps home. Tea and sympathy from grandad Trevor help, as does the distracting and hunky Gabriel, then a visitor turns the whole family's world upside down...

"A modern woman's romantic confession, alongside a cleverly unfolding story of long-buried family secrets." Abigail Bosanko

ISBN: 978-1906784-03-4   £6.99

Honno Classics

Dew on the Grass, by Eiluned Lewis
Set in the Welsh borders, this enchanting autobiographical novel vividly
evokes the essence of childhood and a vanished way of life through the eyes
of nine-year-old Lucy.

"Its pristine freshness and simplicity of language
gives it... a perennial appeal." Cambrensis

ISBN: 978-1-870206-80-8   £8.99

Betsy Cadwaladyr: A Balaclava Nurse –
An Autobiography of Elizabeth Davis
A republication of the fascinating story of the nineteenth century Welsh
woman Elizabeth Davis. Her time as a hospital nurse in Balaclava in the
Crimea, where she served under Florence Nightingale, is a central part of her
life story.

ISBN: 978-1-870206-91-4   £8.99

Stranger Within The Gates:
A collection of short stories, by Bertha Thomas
First published in 1912, this is a collection of witty, sharply observed short
stories. Bertha Thomas lightly but deftly sketches her characters with a
sharp eye for humorous and satirical detail. Her stories are by turns Gothic,
romantic, humorous, fantastic, satirical but always engagingly written.

ISBN: 978-1-870206-94-5   £8.99

All Honno titles can be ordered online at
www.honno.co.uk or by sending a cheque
to Honno. Free p&p to all UK addresses.

ABOUT HONNO

Honno Welsh Women's Press was set up in 1986 by a group of women who felt strongly that women in Wales needed wider opportunities to see their writing in print and to become involved in the publishing process. Our aim is to develop the writing talents of women in Wales, give them new and exciting opportunities to see their work published and often to give them their first 'break' as a writer.

Honno is registered as a community co-operative. Any profit that Honno makes is invested in the publishing programme. Women from Wales and around the world have expressed their support for Honno by buying shares. Supporters liability is limited to the amount invested and each supporter has a vote at the Annual General Meeting.

To buy shares or to receive further information about forthcoming publications, please write to Honno at the address below, or visit our website: www.honno.co.uk.

Honno
Unit 14, Creative Units
Aberystwyth Arts Centre
Penglais Campus
Aberystwyth
Ceredigion
SY23 3GL

All Honno titles can be ordered online at
www.honno.co.uk
or by sending a cheque to Honno.
Free p&p to all UK addresses.